Praise for *Driving*

"This book provides a window into a[...] ination forced Blacks into.... This well-written account will appeal to readers interested in civil rights, Black history, and travel literature."
—*Library Journal* (starred review)

"Illuminating... Hall pays moving tribute to the ingenuity and resourcefulness of Black Americans who hit the road, despite the dangers. This historical travelogue inspires and educates."
—*Publishers Weekly*

"Revisiting a vital resistance and survival tool for Black Americans... A hard-charging resurrection of Black lives in Jim Crow America."
—*Kirkus Reviews*

"Compelling... a book that brings history to life, while also reminding us that history is not so far in the past."
—*Book Riot*

"Required Reading: 10 Black Authors to Get INTO in January 2023."
—*Ebony*

"A historical examination of a sublime act of Black resistance... *Driving the Green Book* paints a painful picture of one aspect of the oppression Blacks endured during Jim Crow, while also illustrating the power of the human spirit to subvert an unconscionable system and still experience joy."
—*The Atlanta Journal-Constitution*

"Alvin Hall's *Driving the Green Book* is a tour-de-force blending exhaustive research, exquisite writing, and emotionally resonant visuals. The book is also a testament to Black resilience during the Jim Crow era, the strategic thinking that helped Black families not only endure but to prevail over tyrannical anti-Black laws, and the ingenuity that held Black communities together from east to west, north to south. This is a must read."

—Bakari Sellers, *New York Times* bestselling author of *My Vanishing Country*

"Alvin Hall's thrilling, deeply researched, and illuminating exploration of the world of the *Green Book*—revealing, enraging, and inspiring in equal measure—is a journey all Americans must take. Nothing tells us more about the country we have been, the country we remain in so many ways, and the country we should aspire to be."

—Ric Burns, filmmaker

"This smart, lively, and timely book is a testament to friendship and self-discovery and a reminder that the road to racial progress has been marked by dead ends and wrong turns. And yet there are so many beautiful and brilliant stories in these pages of family joy, courage, defiance, and triumph over the many racist indignities along the North/South highways of Jim Crow America, I couldn't put the book down. *Driving the Green Book* is a terrific place to start your own journey to understanding the nation's recent past and to chart a course for a better future."

—Khalil Gibran Muhammad, former director of the Schomburg Center for Research in Black Culture

"Readers who love to travel will want to tuck this in their carry-on or console. If there's a bit of quiet activism inside you, *Driving the Green Book* will fuel it."

—Terri Schlichenmeyer, The Bookworm Sez, syndicated column

DRIVING
THE
GREEN
BOOK

A ROAD TRIP THROUGH
THE LIVING HISTORY OF
BLACK RESISTANCE

ALVIN HALL
WITH KARL WEBER

AMISTAD

An Imprint of HarperCollinsPublishers

The credits on pages 275–77 constitute a
continuation of this copyright page.

DRIVING THE GREEN BOOK. Copyright © 2023 by Alvin Hall. All
rights reserved. Printed in the United States of America. No part
of this book may be used or reproduced in any manner whatsoever
without written permission except in the case of brief quotations
embodied in critical articles and reviews. For information, address
HarperCollins Publishers, 195 Broadway, New York, NY 10007.

HarperCollins books may be purchased for educational, business,
or sales promotional use. For information, please email the
Special Markets Department at SPsales@harpercollins.com.

FIRST HARPERCOLLINS PAPERBACK PUBLISHED IN 2024

Designed by Nancy Singer

Library of Congress Cataloging-in-Publication Data is available upon
request.

ISBN 978-0-06-327197-5

23 24 25 26 27 LBC 5 4 3 2 1

To the generous people who, over the course of my *Green Book* journeys, shared their experiences, memories, and truth to make all of us wiser, stronger, and kinder.

and

To J. Stephen Sheppard, my lawyer, agent, and friend, who never wavered in his passionate support of every phase of my *Green Book* journeys—the road trips, the podcast, and this book.

CONTENTS

THAT BLACK PEOPLE HAVE HAD TO CREATE MECHANISMS FOR SURVIVAL IS AN INDICTMENT OF AMERICA. BUT IT IS ALSO A TESTAMENT TO PEOPLE OF COLOR THAT WE HAVE FOUND WAYS TO COPE AND SURVIVE AND NAVIGATE THIS INCREDIBLY UNFAIR AND COMPLEX WORLD. *THE GREEN BOOK* AND A LOT OF OTHER THINGS LIKE IT WERE THE TOOLS THAT PEOPLE USED TO NAVIGATE.

—BRYAN STEVENSON, LAWYER AND FOUNDER OF THE EQUAL JUSTICE INITIATIVE

THINGS LIKE *THE GREEN BOOK* TELL US,
"THERE'S SOMEBODY IN MY CORNER,
SOMEBODY WHO WANTS TO MAKE SURE I
SAFELY GET TO MY DESTINATION." I THINK
THAT'S A METAPHOR FOR LIFE. WE WANT TO
HELP PEOPLE SAFELY THROUGH LIFE.

—T. MARIE KING,
COMMUNITY ORGANIZER,
FACILITATOR, AND TRAINER IN
BIRMINGHAM, ALABAMA

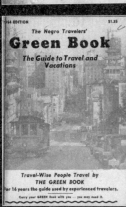

INTRODUCTION

You would think that my journey with *The Negro Motorist Green Book* would have begun in an automobile. In fact, it began in a plane. The year was 2015. I was flying to London and, as I often do, had brought along a stack of magazines to pass the time. One article about road trips around the US referred in passing to *The Negro Motorist Green Book*. As far as I remember, it probably mentioned that the travel guide had been used by Black travelers during segregation, but I don't recall the word "segregation" itself being used.

My interest was immediately piqued. I had never heard of the publication. That's not surprising considering that I grew up in the 1950s and 1960s "dirt poor," living on land my family owns in the rural Florida Panhandle. The phrase "dirt poor" means we possessed only that parcel of land that we lived on, growing and raising most of what we ate. Most Black people in the area lived along sandy, unpaved roads that wove through scrub pine forests with a few live oak trees draped with hanging moss.

A selection of *The Green Book* covers
from 1939 to 1961, during its three-decade
publication history.

Lots of raccoons, opossum, squirrels, snakes, birds, and insects lived in the underbrush. The landscape was not verdant. It always looked slightly dry. But it was always humid because the area was near the Gulf of Mexico.

We did not own a car. We could not afford one. We never traveled for vacations or other leisure activities. We only traveled to visit relatives, usually being driven by a family friend who owned a car, to places we could reach between sunrise and sunset. No one I knew drove overnight. So, my family would have had no need for *The Negro Motorist Green Book*. Nonetheless, the publication's name and the article's brief description captured my imagination. I resolved to find out more.

Back in New York after my work in London, I began my search by going to the Schomburg Center for Research in Black Culture. Located in Harlem and part of the New York Public Library, the Schomburg, as it is widely known, is America's premier archive for African American history. It contains a remarkable and growing trove of documents and artifacts about crucial, often little-known or overlooked histories, facts, and stories about Black Americans and their lives. Important for my purpose, and unlike any other archive I know, its collection of the publication I was looking for is almost complete; it lacks only one of the editions of *The Green Book*, which was published annually (except when publication was temporarily suspended during World War II) from 1936 to 1967.

There, while I sat in a conference room in the rare books section, associate chief librarian Maira Liriano brought me copies that I could hold in my hands and examine at leisure. (This is no longer possible; the paper they were printed on has become too fragile.) What I saw and read were listings of largely Black-owned enterprises—businesses that welcomed Black travelers in city after city and town after town across the US. I was amazed. Tallahassee, Florida, the nearest large city to where I grew up, was one of the first places I checked. Much to my surprise, I saw a listing for a lodging that I had never heard of, the Abner-Virginia in Ferguson, Missouri. Organized by Jeremy Grange, its purpose was to produce the thirty-eight-minute radio documentary. He and I conceived of the program as traveling not just through space but through time as well—my lifetime: from where I grew up in the Jim Crow South, where laws severely limited the rights of Black people as well as the social interaction between Black and white people, to the momentous contemporary events at that time in Ferguson. Jeremy, photographer Jonathan Calm, and I followed part of what is called the United States Civil Rights Trail, which links those cities, primarily in the South, in which African American activists and supporters from all ethnic, religious, and racial backgrounds marched, protested, and endured personal danger, sometimes death, during the 1950s and 1960s, to fight for the right to vote, for racial equality, for social reform, and for fair legal treatment in all parts of life in the United States. We stopped in Birmingham and Selma, Alabama; Jackson, Mississippi; Memphis, Tennessee; and finally, Ferguson, Missouri. We visited the locations of once-fancy and well-known hotels, tourist homes, restaurants, eateries, movie houses, and nightclubs that had been listed in *The Green Book*. We sought out and talked to people who generously recounted their stories of driving in the United States during the time when this guide and others like it were not just conveniences but lifesaving travel necessities. Our documentary, simply titled *The Green Book*, aired on BBC Radio 4 in November 2016.

The second road trip—twelve days in June 2019—started in Detroit, Michigan, and ended in New Orleans, Louisiana. Its purpose was to create my ten-episode podcast series, *Driving the Green Book*, and was largely organized by field producer Oluwakemi (Kemi) Aladesuyi. This trip was inspired in part by an exhibition at the Museum of Modern Art in New York City in 2015 called *One-Way Ticket: Jacob Lawrence's Migration Series and Other Visions of the Great Movement North*. Lawrence's ambitious, deeply affecting series consists of sixty tempera-on-panel paintings. Collectively, they vividly capture the shared hardships and disappointments African Americans experienced during the Great Migration, the period between 1910 and 1970 when more than six million Black people left the rural South and moved north and west for better opportunities. Terrorism sparked that transit—especially the drowning, burning, and lynching of Black men, women, and even families in the South. But the travelers also headed north in pursuit of better lives in new, growing industries, such as automobile manufacturing. The Great Migration remains the largest demographic shift in US history.

The introduction to the *One-Way Ticket* exhibition featured a fascinating infographic showing how significantly the African American population had increased in seven northern cities: Chicago, Cleveland, Detroit, New York, Philadelphia, Pittsburgh, and Saint Louis. The largest increase in those seven cities was in Detroit, whose African American population increased from 1.2 percent in 1910 to 43.7 percent in 1970. The auto industry served as a magnet for residents from Georgia, Alabama, Mississippi, Tennessee, the Florida Panhandle, and Louisiana. But despite their settling in Detroit, they left a part of their hearts back home. Many of these people would want and need to return to the South to visit relatives. And their relatives in the South would travel up North to visit them to see their new lives. This is why publications like *The Green Book* were crucial at that moment in history. Black travelers needed to know where it was safe to stop for even the most essential services, such as buying gasoline.

So associate producer Janée Woods Weber and I, accompanied by field producer Kemi Aladesuyi, took a more than two-thousand-mile road trip from Detroit to New Orleans, with side trips to cities and towns along the way that would have been destinations for many travelers from the Motor City. Our goal on this trip, as it had been with the first, was to find people along the route who had used or heard of *The Green Book* and who patronized or knew of the locations, establishments, and businesses listed in the travel guide. We wanted a direct link to that history.

THE RELEASE OF THE MOVIE *Green Book* in September 2018 unexpectedly increased my motivation and strengthened my resolve. I attended a screening of it in New York that was followed by a moderated talk with the director, producers, and principal actors. The moderator asked each a simple question: Had you heard of *The Green Book* before doing the movie? All said no. I was surprised, although I probably should not have been.

Although the movie is called *Green Book*, it decidedly is not about the travel guide. In fact, the publication is shown or referenced only three or four times. Viewers are left thinking that it is like a secret guide used by Black people. I knew that no one involved in the movie had investigated the accommodations available to an entertainer like pianist Don Shirley in the early 1960s when I saw the types of places in which he stayed in several scenes. Those choices played to stereotypes of where Shirley, Duke Ellington, Count Basie, Ella Fitzgerald, and Sarah Vaughan would have stayed.

In conversations, I have become aware that people equate the actual *Green Book* with a few scenes in the movie of blatant racism during Shirley's concert tour that is the central plot device for the story. These scenes hint lightly at why *The Green Book* was described as an essential publication. Moviegoers get no sense of the breadth of businesses in the state-by-state, city-by-city listings in the guide. The movie's story arc lets the viewer feel good about knowing the name "Green Book" but prompts little motivation to further explore and understand the history that necessitated the guide. That afterglow of the feel-good buddy movie is what people want to remember.

Months later, during the second road trip, I interviewed Evelyn E. Nettles, associate vice president for academic affairs at Tennessee State

University, whose relatives had migrated from Mississippi to Nashville. When I mentioned the movie, she said, "I had not heard of *The Green Book* until I saw the movie, and I'm an educated Black woman." Her statement echoed my own thoughts when I had first read about the travel guide on that flight to London. So, the movie, having used the travel guide's name as its title and having included disturbing scenes during the tour through the South, did have a benefit. It made more people aware of, and some even curious about, the historic publication and the period in the United States that made it a travel necessity. It's clear from conversations I've had that more people recognize the name of the publication founded by Victor Hugo Green solely because of the movie.

In this book, I share with you my journey with *The Green Book*. In truth, I feel I should use the plural—journeys—because in each chapter the people I met offer the stories of their lived experiences as African Americans in different states, cities, and towns when the travel guide was being published. I want you to learn from their journeys too—what they have seen, heard, felt, and sensed during the many incidents of what can be graciously described as rich experiences. These witnesses knew good times and brutal times.

During these journeys I have been educated by elders and contemporaries about so much US history that I didn't know. These people I visited are those who lived it, and whose experiences historians largely have left uninvestigated. I heard about the many Black streets and neighborhoods (often called Little Harlems) that provided safe harbors and places of pride and joy for travelers passing through, as well as for local residents. I learned the names of Black visionaries with access to capital in various cities, who created legendary businesses—the Gotham Hotel in Detroit; the Manse Hotel in Cincinnati; the Booker T Motel in Humboldt, Tennessee (also famous for its barbecue); the Ben Moore Hotel in Montgomery, Alabama—and activists whose courageous work challenged and defied the restrictions and stereotypes of that time. Person after person recounted stories—about traveling on highways, driving along hometown streets—that were frightening, sad, noble, defiant, and funny. I still marvel at how Black people lived through such difficult, mean-spirited times and maintained their hope and positivity.

There are also other journeys less obviously contained in this book—personal ones. I was born in the early 1950s in the segregated, rural South. Janée Woods Weber, who traveled with me and is biracial, was born in the late 1970s in a largely white suburb in Massachusetts. And Kemi Aladesuyi, another companion on the journey, who is a first-generation Nigerian American immigrant, was born in the 1990s in the United Kingdom and lived for a few years in Nigeria before moving to Illinois where she grew up. As Janée astutely observed: "Alvin, Kemi, and I are of different generations and were raised in different parts of the country by families that were quite different from one another. So even though we share some mutual ideas and understanding about American Black culture, our approaches to the road trip and how we contextualized what we discovered through the interviews were impacted by our varying life experiences."

This was true intellectually and emotionally. Often our discussions in the car started with a question, not directed at anyone, just spoken aloud. We'd put a subject into the air for us to think about and comment on. Such as:

- Is it possible for us today to feel what Black people, especially a Black family with children, felt traveling during segregation?
- What would be your worry if we had a flat tire or car trouble on a two-lane road in the 1940s, 1950s, or 1960s?
- Imagine what a sense of relief you would have if not one of the things you worried about occurred during your entire trip.

- Do the fears created by the incidents caused by "driving while Black" ever go away? How long do the cumulative traumas last?
- What are you learning about yourself?
- How did the personal story we just heard during our interview affect you? What did the story make you feel about America?

I share more of these questions in this book.

Other times, we'd ask one another questions as if we were interviewing each other. We all grew as the miles, the stories, the events, and the insights accumulated.

There were times in our adventure when I experienced the truth in Baldwin's quotation that you cannot know "what you find [on the journey] will do to you." Sometimes a person's story and their telling of it unexpectedly connected deeply with my own history growing up in the rural, segregated South and worshipping in a Baptist church. The person's voice, accent, and cadence were like hearing a spiritual or the humming of a gospel song I had known since the time I could *feel* music. I struggled to maintain my professional demeanor during many of the conversations. I simply had no emotional barrier against or filter for what that person was saying or how they were saying it. Their words washed through every fiber of my being. Amazingly, virtually every person, without my asking, connected their past experiences to current events. They just did it seamlessly. I understood and, most important, received the wisdom and insights these generous people were passing along to me about driving as well as living while Black in America then—and now. I will be as generous in sharing with you, the reader of this book, as the people I talked with were generous with me. I know they want me to pass on their wisdom.

Alvin Hall, New York City, 2023

Victor H. Green

Alma D. Green

Edith Greene

Dorothy Asch

Evelyn Woolfolk

Novera Dashiell

THE GREEN BOOK INVENTOR

A MAN OF A MILLION JOURNEYS

It is amazing to me that somebody took the time to research the information in *The Green Book*. It points to the resolve of Black people and their willingness to be strategic. That's something I want younger organizers to think about—that we have got to be more strategic in gathering and disseminating information. *The Green Book* is clearly an example of working smarter, not harder.

> — Danny Ransom, retired, lifelong resident of Birmingham, Alabama, who has always loved travel, maps, and geography

Inside page of the 1961 edition of *The Green Book* portraying its staff, including Victor Green and his wife, Alma.

I began my adventure with *The Green Book* completely open to what this intriguing travel guide might teach me about history, humanity, and myself. It is not part of my personality to speculate about things in advance. So I didn't think about who had created *The Green Book* before I went to the Schomburg Center for Research in Black Culture—the world's largest repository of books and other materials related to African American culture—to hold the actual guidebook in my hands. The reason I try to avoid creating narratives beforehand is because I've seen that emotional impulse inadvertently become self-fulfilling. I try to learn about people from the ways they present themselves.

Therefore, I would learn about *The Green Book*'s creators, Victor and Alma Green, when I began studying the guide's many editions as well as the other publications and books that their guide would lead me to.

Before I started the research, I knew *The Negro Motorist Green Book* was a travel guide. I also knew that it was published before some of the major improvements in printing methods. This made me wonder whether *The Green Book* would have pictures. If I had any expectations before holding the guide in my hand, they would have been based on my experiences of other commercial travel guides of the time. These typically highlighted key historical events, places of interest, and businesses (hotels, restaurants, clubs) that catered to tourists and travelers.

But when I first held one of the early editions of *The Green Book* at the Schomburg, I was surprised by how small and thin it was. Then I remembered that it was designed to fit into a car's glove compartment so it would be readily accessible during a trip. It was also an annual publication that would be replaced with a new edition each year. When I flipped through the pages looking at the state-by-state listings, the numbers of places varied dramatically in the few cities and towns listed in each state. Understandably, there were more places catering to Black travelers in key metropolitan areas that were the destinations of African Americans who migrated north, in cities that were part of the route that Black entertainers followed (called the Chitlin' Circuit), and in cities where major historically Black colleges and universities (HBCUs) were located. In smaller towns, the businesses were typically tourist houses and small restaurants, usually run by a local woman.

As I thought about the increase in the number of pages and listings in *The Green Book* as well as ads, some with pictures, in subsequent editions, I realized that the publication could be seen as an indicator of economic growth within Black communities and a self-created, expanding sense of freedom, although still segregated, promised by the American Dream. Then I thought of the guide's creator. This innovator was born in the very same city where I sat exploring his guide's pages.

Victor Hugo Green came into this world in New York City on November 9, 1892. By the age of twenty-one, in 1913, he was a letter carrier for the US Postal Service, working in Bergen County, New Jersey, not far from the town of Hackensack where he had grown up. He clearly had an entrepreneurial instinct that led him to find creative ways of supplementing his modest income from the post office. For example, by 1933, he was acting as the manager to a musician, Robert Duke, the brother of his wife, Alma.

We don't know much about Victor Green as a person. Little was written about him during his lifetime. However, based on what was written—as well as all that he achieved—he must have been charming and impressive. Known as "a man of tremendous drive and energy," he was described in the twentieth anniversary edition of *The Green Book* (1956) as "tall, well-built, always impeccably groomed, with an easy affable manner." In addition to his keen sense of the market, Green was clearly gifted with managerial talent and what today is called "emotional intelligence."

Alma S. Duke, who became Victor's wife, was born in Richmond, Virginia, in 1889. She moved to New York City in the midst of the Great Migration. She and Victor obtained a marriage license in Brooklyn on September 17, 1917. The couple then moved to Harlem, which was swiftly becoming a national center of Black art and culture. They lived in an apartment at 580 St. Nicholas Avenue, an area known as Sugar Hill because of the "sweet life" enjoyed by the people who lived there.

We don't know exactly how and when Victor Green came up with the idea of creating a guide for Black travelers. But he must have been inspired by his own experiences on the road with Alma, as well as hearing of the experiences of friends and acquaintances both in New York and when traveling. As Northern Blacks with roots in the South, Victor and Alma likely trekked "back home" to Virginia to visit her relatives and probably to other places below the Mason-Dixon Line to be with family and friends. Along the drive, they would have experienced the peculiar frustrations, indignities, and dangers that were part of Jim Crow America and segregation.

Victor's stint as manager for his musician brother-in-law would have involved booking appearances and making travel arrangements. Perhaps the stories that Alma's brother shared about his experiences on the road simultaneously disheartened and motivated Victor. It's interesting that he came up with the idea of *The Green Book* around 1932, began managing his brother-in-law in 1933, and published the first *Green Book* in 1936. It shows that he himself was dealing with the inconveniences, fears, and troubles of traveling while Black in segregated America.

A GUIDE TO SURVIVE

That first annual edition of what was then called *The Negro Motorist Green Book* was priced at 25 cents and, while named after its editor and publisher, also sported a green cover. (No known copies of the 1936 *Green Book* are in existence; the oldest edition at the Schomburg is the 1937 edition. It's a mere sixteen pages long and includes entries from only New York City and its environs.)

Green published the book in partnership with a friend, George I. Smith, who remained part of the operation for its first two years. William H. Green, Victor's brother, then joined the staff and served as an editor until 1945. For the first several years of its existence, *The Green Book* was printed by Gibraltar Printing and Publishing Company, located at 800 Sixth Avenue in New York and owned by Samuel Jacob Glener.

The first words in the 1937 edition—complete with questionable punctuation and spelling—are these:

PREPARDNESS

An old but true adage "An Ounce of Prevention is worth more than a Pound of Cure."

These words open an article offering advice on getting a car in proper shape for a road trip, with tips on tuning up and lubricating the engine, checking the brakes and tires, and other practical measures. But the general theme of preparing for a trip to avoid mishaps and dangers undoubtedly applied to more than the mechanics of an automobile. It was the whole purpose of *The Green Book*, whose Black readers had to do so much more than their white counterparts when making plans to travel.

For a more extended description of the origins and purpose of *The Green Book*, here is what Victor Green himself explained in the introduction to the 1949 edition:

> With the introduction of this travel guide in 1936, it has been our idea to give the Negro traveler information that will keep him from running into difficulties, embarrassments and to make his trips more enjoyable.
>
> The Jewish press has long published information about places that are restricted and there are numerous publications that give the gentile whites all kinds of information. But during these long years of discrimination, before 1936 other guides have been published for the Negro, some are still published, but the majority have gone out of business for various reasons.
>
> In 1936 the Green Book was only a local publication for Metropolitan New York, the response for copies was so great it was turned into a national issue in 1937 to cover the United States. This guide while lacking in many respects was accepted by thousands of travelers. Through the courtesy of the United States Travel Bureau of which Mr. Chas. A. R. McDowell was the collaborator on Negro Affairs, more valuable information was secured. With the two working together, this guide contained the best ideas for the Negro traveler. Year after year it grew until 1941. "PM" one of New York's great white newspapers found out about it. Wrote an article about the guide and praised it highly: "At the present time the guide contains 80 pages and lists numerous business places, including whites which cater to the Negro trade."
>
> There are thousands of first class business places that we don't know about and can't list, which would be glad to serve the traveler, but it is hard to secure listings of these places since we can't secure

enough agents to send us the information. Each year before we go to press the new information is included in the new edition. When you are traveling please mention the Green Book, in order that they might know how you found their place of business, as they can see that you are strangers. If they haven't heard about this guide, ask them to get in touch with us so that we might list their place.

If this guide has proved useful to you on your trips, let us know. If not, tell us also as we appreciate your criticisms and ideas in the improvement of this guide from which you benefit.

There will be a day sometime in the near future when this guide will not have to be published. That is when we as a race will have equal opportunities and privileges in the United States. It will be a great day for us to suspend this publication for then we can go wherever we please, and without embarrassment. But until that time comes we shall continue to publish this information for your convenience each year.

Those words reverberate with the warmth and caring Green intended for his readers. To me, this is the heart of the story of *The Green Book*. Green's poignant words show the guidebook's necessity, the sense of deep community from which it emanated, and the grace, strength, and vision of its creator.

He felt that necessity in the biggest northeastern city, the home of the Statue of Liberty, which was created long before *The Green Book* to recall the country's pledge to freedom. In fact, it might seem surprising to some that a Black man in New York City wrote and published *The Green Book* and first focused on safe havens in that area rather than in the Deep South, the region associated with the worst depredations of racism. I felt something different, paging through the guide in that archive in New York; seeing the locations listed in *The Green Book* for my city, New

York City, where I live, was not a surprise. Few of the safe businesses were below the 125th Street area. Nor was it a surprise when I looked at listings in the greater metropolitan area—Long Island, Connecticut, and New Jersey. Instead, it was a confirmation. The first wave of migrants from the South may have thought that New York and other cities in the North were going to be lands of milk and honey, but settling into their new hometowns, they encountered all the "unspoken" restrictions on their full right to housing, job opportunities, and overall freedom. It was the same racism and many of the same segregation practices as in the South, but more subtle. These new arrivals had to figure out the system. These people—even those who got well-paying jobs—did not keep their negative experiences and resulting insights secret. They shared what had happened to them within their families, communities, churches, and social organizations. I know this because of what my relatives and their friends, especially our cousin Joe Williams, who had fought in World War II and spent a very brief period in New York City, told me.

Joe said that the attitudes of white people in the North, as far as he could tell, were not really different from those in the South, except that in the North they didn't always say anything out loud. Instead, their attitudes showed in the way they acted toward you or ignored you. He warned me to be watchful, to pay attention.

Then I participated in the last wave of the Great Migration in the 1970s. When I say I "participated," I am specifically referring to when I left home and went to college in the North. I didn't know about the Great Migration at the time I made my journey north on an Eastern Airlines flight. I learned I was part of the statistics after the fact. There was nothing to see when I got there but a bucolic New England college campus.

But Victor and Alma's desire to create *The Green Book* came decades earlier and probably came out of that sense my cousin Joe had of wanting to share. The subtle segregation and racism in New York ironically did not make the city less attractive, less glamorous, or less inspiring. The urban limitations the migrants had to deal with offered far more opportunities than had cotton fields and farmlands, whether they were in the South or the North.

A RESTRICTED NEW YORK CITY

No part of the United States was entirely friendly to Black people in the era of Jim Crow. During this period, which lasted for more than a hundred years, from the abolition of slavery in 1865 to the passing of the landmark federal desegregation and antidiscrimination laws of the mid- to late 1960s, the inequitable treatment of African Americans across the country was slow to change. Discrimination and exclusion were sometimes less overt and obvious in the North, but they were almost equally pervasive and demeaning, even threatening.

Between 1920 and 1930, Harlem was changing from a mainly white area to a majority Black community—another consequence of the Great Migration. In 1920, the population of central Harlem was about 32 percent Black; by 1930, it was 70 percent Black. But it took time for Blacks to find a welcome. Doll Thomas, who spent years working at Harlem's legendary Apollo Theater, has described segregation in the 1920s:

> There were no blacks on 125th Street. It was all Irish . . . The theater that's now the Apollo, you entered from 126th Street up the back stairs. The Alhambra [another theater in Harlem] just wouldn't sell [Black people] an orchestra seat. They were either sold out or they'd flatly refuse. Also, on 125th Street, Frank's Lunchroom— you couldn't get served in there. Across the street was Childs.

You couldn't get served in there. Right down the street was Fabian's Seafood Shop. Couldn't get served in there. All the bars here and everything else was the same way.[1]

My friend the late John Heyman was a film producer who was born in Leipzig, Germany, lived in London, and eventually settled in New York City. One of his early jobs in the US was as a press agent, and among his first clients in the 1950s were four exceptional African American stars: Pearl Bailey, Dorothy Dandridge, Lena Horne, and Eartha Kitt. Working on behalf of these now-legendary singers and actors revealed to John the depths of American racial prejudice. When Lena Horne and Pearl Bailey played the Empire Room at the Waldorf Astoria Hotel, they had to enter the stage through the kitchen because in those days the hotel did not allow Black people, even stars, to enter through its main doors. They were also not permitted to stay there. So the Black entertainers who performed at the Waldorf often stayed at the Hotel Theresa at Seventh Avenue and 125th Street, then known as "the Waldorf of Harlem." (It's now an office building.) Many Black stars also maintained apartments in northern Manhattan for their visits. The idea that New York was an open, welcoming community for people of every race was not true, even for people as famous as those four women.

Given the areas of New York City where Black people could obtain housing at that time, which was primarily Harlem, businesses open to Blacks clustered in those areas. The listings in *The Green Book* reflect this de facto segregation. The guide also listed a range of businesses in the suburbs and rural communities adjacent to New York City. In the 1937 edition, "dining, dancing, and rendezvous" along with "Full Course Chicken Dinner" could be found at Donhaven's Restaurant in Westchester County's Pleasantville, New York—a town described as "45 minutes from Harlem" and already famous as the address of *Reader's*

A shoeshine business in Harlem in 1939.

Digest magazine. Heckscher State Park on Long Island promised that "camping could be had for 50 cents a day or two dollars a week." Some of the local establishments catered to customers nostalgic for the foods they'd grown up with: Week's Restaurant in New Rochelle described itself as "Where Old Friends Meet for Southern Hospitality," and the Southern Restaurant in White Plains promised "A Delight in Every Bite."

In addition to whatever travel information Green included that was based on his own travel experiences and recommendations from friends, Green's fellow letter carriers helped him out. Green was a member of the National Association of Letter Carriers (NALC), the union for postal workers founded in 1889. (Not all African American letter carriers were permitted to join this organization. Union locals had varying policies, and some, such as the Baltimore local, excluded Black workers into the 1960s. Black letter carriers turned away by NALC usually joined the National Association of Postal Employees, a Nashville-based union founded in 1913 explicitly to represent Black workers.)[2]

Calling on NALC's commitment to "public service," Green asked his fellow Black union members to recommend or look out for businesses that should be included in *The Green Book*. Accordingly, these letter carriers noted likely enterprises along their routes and in their communities and sent information about them to Green. Over time, as *The Green Book* became better known, readers began sending in recommendations for listings as well. Many owners of restaurants, motels, automobile shops, and other businesses provided information about themselves. Eventually, Green built a highly effective network of agents, salespeople, and scouts around the country to gather the information, listings, and advertisements that would fill the guide's pages.

As I sat that first day in the Schomburg on 135th Street in the center of Harlem, my journey had not yet begun, but my thoughts of what *The Green Book* represented had started to extend farther than that one desk. I thought of all the documents in the center's archive that are proof that in cities as big as New York, Chicago, Philadelphia, and Detroit, there was always the possibility that Black people could create different, new, and enriching paths around the restrictions to find their own success and enjoyment and to keep each other safe, to hold their dignity sacred.

I left the Schomburg to begin our *Green Book* road trip hearing an adage my relatives had often repeated inflected in more nuanced and layered ways: *Making a way out of no way.* On our road trip using *The Green Book*, we would find out how communities and individuals along our route "made a way."

— 2 —

THE AMERICAN HIGHWAY

OPEN ROAD, OPEN MIND

The road is so mythologized and romanticized in American culture. The whole idea of being able to go west and find opportunity, and find adventure, and explore . . .

— Allyson Hobbs, associate professor of US history and director of African and African American Studies, Stanford University

B efore I began planning the road trip from Detroit to New Orleans, I gave talks about *The Green Book* at a few museums and educational

A couple waving goodbye in the suburbs in the late 1960s.

institutions. During the question-and-answer period of each presentation, some of the comments and the ways the inquiries were framed made me more keenly aware that age, race, birthplace, and other factors strongly influenced how people perceived and responded to learning about the travel guide as well as the period of US history that made it necessary. An older white person, for example, would as a point of comparison and without any sense of irony equate Black travel stories with times that their teenage white son or grandson, usually driving his first car, was stopped by the police and given a warning "for doing things teenagers do." Younger people would share reflections about the travel habits and on-the-road advice their parents or grandparents gave them that always seemed quirky or from another era. And recent immigrants, always noting that they were not born in the US, would make carefully worded comparisons to apartheid or other suppressive practices in other countries. The comment that I heard often from the younger generation, and always said with a sense of total disbelief, remains, "You mean you couldn't just stop and buy gas anywhere, that stations wouldn't serve you or let you buy gas?" The experience confirmed an idea, an approach that I felt was essential to the road trip. I wanted to experience this *Green Book* journey with Black people who were likely to have reactions, perspectives, and thoughts that were different from mine about the places we visited, the people we met, the personal stories we heard, the breadth of experiences unique to the road trip.

Janée's name was on my initial list. We have been friends who are "family" for a long time—decades, in fact. Janée was an attorney before getting passionately involved in social justice. I always enjoyed how she talked about her experiences compassionately helping groups and individuals, but also with a clear-eyed understanding of the underlying issues and possible solutions. I liked the fact that Janée was of another generation, more than twenty years younger than me. When I called her to ask whether she would be interested in doing the road trip with me, she said yes immediately. We talked about her being biracial and growing up in an essentially all-white town in Massachusetts. In school, she had learned the "textbook" version of Black history—slavery, civil rights, Martin Luther King Jr., and the names of some Black "firsts." Her childhood and adolescence were influenced by her firsthand experiences with racism in its many blatant and subtle manifestations. I had often heard Janée speak of her and others' experiences using contemporary language, framing the events in terms that reflect where US culture is today. I found these conversations affecting and enlightening. I knew she would bring insights about the past into the present, making them more relatable for younger listeners. However, I did wonder whether she would be emotionally overwhelmed by the stories she heard. Having grown up in the South I knew how penetrating these stories could be. And I worried how she would be perceived, by southerners in particular.

Kemi Aladesuyi rounded out the team for the road trip. I met Kemi through Macmillan Podcasts. The managers were interviewing field producers who would research, locate, and organize the interviews as well as record along the road trip. Kemi's résumé stood out for me because her background added another perspective that interested me: that of recent Black immigrants from Africa who often, like young Janée, have only textbook knowledge of the African American experience in the US. I realized this when I began having regular phone conversations with a group of Africans who recently had graduated from Bowdoin College. I was, as a Black American, sometimes surprised at things that "we all know" but that they did not know, primarily because they had not grown up in this society with its distinct racial issues. Although Kemi's primary role was to record the interviews and only occasionally to participate in them, I expected to learn from her how to talk about *The Green Book*, framing its story and the recollections of the interviewees in ways that would move and educate a wider array of Black people, not only African Americans.

Once we had all signed on to the project, it took quite a few months to organize the route and find all the interviewees. Eventually, Kemi and I flew together and met Janée at the Detroit airport to start the twelve-day drive. This was not our trio's first meeting. We had gone together to the Schomburg Center in New York to have a conversation with Maira Liriano, the associate chief librarian at the New York Public Library who takes care of the *Green Book* collection. Now we were actually on the road. I did not anticipate anything about what our on-the-road conversation would be. But I did let myself be hopeful.

THE AMERICAN HIGHWAY: FREEDOM FOR SOME

The open road—what could be a more compelling, vivid symbol of America? This was one of the ideas that Janée and I discussed before and during that 2,021-mile journey from Detroit to New Orleans. We talked about the places and locations we would visit. We checked forecasts to see what weather we could expect during our trip. We fantasized about the delicious local foods—scrumptious barbecue, mouthwatering pan-fried chicken, or luscious cornbread—we hoped to discover and devour in each city or town. These little food fantasies focused on the southern cities in particular.

But what we talked about most was hearing firsthand what Black people have to say, in their own words, about living through and surviving the period of American history when the open road was full of blockades and barriers. We talked about making sure that we listened to each person and that our questions came organically out of what that person was saying—not from a list we had prepared in advance. Having been raised in the South and having traveled as a young adult, I imagined hearing the various regional southern accents. They can differ more than most people know. I wondered how each would sound to Janée, who had grown up in Massachusetts and knew little about these variations. And I wondered how the interviewees would hear her accent in return. The conversations were our chance to listen to and feel these truths, unfiltered and direct, from the Black perspective.

However, the one thing we never talked about—not once—was a quiet concern about being three Black people driving a nice SUV through the southern US. We were probably fearful that simply saying the words "What if we get stopped?" would increase the likelihood of it happening. Although in June 2019 that felt a bit irrational, our concern connected us to historic and ongoing Black experiences in the US that many Americans have never had to think about.

Back at the time *The Green Book* first appeared in the late 1930s, the automobile had seemed a likely safe haven for Black travelers—or at least safer. In a bus or on a train, a Black person ran the risks and humiliations of the laws and strictures around the use of public transportation due to segregation. That's why a car road trip was particularly important: travelers needed more protection en route to their destinations—whether that was going home to Birmingham, Alabama; to visit Uncle Jerome in New York City; or to gather with Alma Green's relatives in Richmond, Virginia.

Even in 2019, we felt the simmer of concerns about "driving while Black"; but imagine, back in the 1930s when *The Green Book* appeared, all the way up through the 1960s, planning a road trip to visit a relative or a family friend and, in the back of your mind, having to worry about the possibility of an encounter that could be intentionally demeaning or deliberately threatening, or that could turn unexpectedly violent, even deadly. African Americans knew then that simply driving—being behind the wheel of a car—was viewed in many parts of the United States as an affront to social restrictions based on white supremacy. In many towns, cities, and states, *any* white person—not just white law enforcement officials—could stop and challenge a Black person's right, as an American, to be on the road; the right to be in a particular neighborhood; the right to own a nice car; and the right to simply enjoy the roadways of the United States. These facts of American history shadowed every phase of our road trip.

And it all felt so deeply ironic.

From the earliest years of our nation's history, the idea of freedom to travel has been bound up in people's vision of the country. It's no accident that one of the most famous works of the first great American poet, Walt Whitman, is titled "Song of the Open Road." Published in 1856, it begins with the lines:

> *Afoot and light-hearted I take to the open road,*
> *Healthy, free, the world before me,*
> *The long brown path before me leading wherever I choose.*

Whitman's "Song" is just one of a long series of classic American writings that use the open road as an image of freedom, exploration, discovery, and personal growth. Works from Mark Twain's *Huckleberry Finn* and *Life on the Mississippi* to twentieth-century masterpieces like John Steinbeck's *Travels with Charley*, Jack Kerouac's *On the Road*, and William Least Heat-Moon's *Blue Highways* fall into this tradition, as do acclaimed movies like *Easy Rider* and *Thelma and Louise*. Whether traveling by raft, car, Greyhound bus, or customized Harley-Davidson motorbikes, the protagonists of all these tales are eager to explore the American landscape, in the process learning not just about our country and its people but about themselves. Steinbeck summed up the theme this way: "Every American hungers to move."

And for Whitman, as for millions of other Americans, the dream of the open road wasn't just about the freedom to wander and explore. It was also about equality and acceptance—a place where people of every sort would be welcomed and respected. Surely Whitman knew that this wasn't literally true in the America of his day, just as it isn't in the America of the twenty-first century. The myth of the open road as a symbol of American liberty is just that—a beautiful myth that may be true for some, but not for all. And Americans of color are among those for whom the roads have always held at least as much peril as promise.

Our own quiet concern was reflected in the innocuous but solidly performing SUV we chose to rent for the trip. The decision connected us to historic issues regarding the importance of the automobile in the lives of Black Americans, particularly related to socioeconomic growth and personal safety, and it connected us to those very first pages of *The Green Book* regarding preparation.

THE CAR MEANT YOU HAD ARRIVED

The advent of the automobile and its gradual evolution from luxury plaything to a ubiquitous source of mobility for people of almost every class and color transformed the first half of the twentieth century for all Americans. The coming of the car more specifically impacted the lives of African Americans, and yet this is less widely recognized.

That's why Janée and I chose to start our road trip in Detroit, the home of the US automobile industry. Our first interview was with Jamon Jordan, a former social studies teacher and now founder and guide of the Detroit-based Black Scroll Network History and Tours. Jordan arranged to meet us in a flat, nondescript section of the city where there were mostly one- and two-story, flat-roof, brick or cinderblock buildings containing multiple small businesses. Among the many automobile parts and repair shops we passed driving to the location in central Detroit, we also saw convenience stores, lunch-time snack shops, and a few vacant lots that looked like places where flea markets were held on weekends or perhaps periodically throughout the week. The area was not residential. It was not threatening or unsightly, but it was hardly pristine or interesting. And it was pouring rain. We could have been in any small business area in any medium-size city or town in the United States. We decided that starting in this location was probably a benefit, like starting from a blank slate. From here, Jordan guided our drive through the city, first to an area known as Black Bottom, and opened our eyes to the communities, locations, businesses, and people in Detroit history that would give it distinction related to *The Green Book*. In his early forties, Jordan is immersed in local Black history—including the impact of the auto industry on the lives of Black Americans who migrated to Detroit.

He explained that cars gave Blacks more security and more control of their time—when they could leave home to go to work, when they could go shopping, when they could go out at night. He put it like this:

One of the important things about having a car is that it allows you access—to be able to go from place to place and not be inconvenienced, or in some cases, threatened by what can happen to you in segregated areas. You can drive right through a town that you know you're not welcome in. You can drive right past a hotel that will not serve you. You can't do that when you're at the mercy of public transportation.

For this reason, having a car meant something very important for African Americans. It meant you'd arrived. It meant you now had the freedom of movement to be able to go from one place to another and to visit family.

As Jordan's comments suggest, car ownership was an economic and a social achievement. Not only had you worked and saved to be able to buy a nice car, but you *owned* it. In exchange, when behind the wheel, you knew your car gave you a real and metaphorical "sweet ride," offering relief from many of society's everyday strictures and annoyances.

The car also granted another form of freedom. The automobile industry directly impacted the financial conditions of African Americans. An article in the 1938 edition of *The Green Book* (the third edition to be published) told some of the story. In "The Automobile and What It Has Done for the Negro," Benjamin J. Thomas, the owner of a driving school, began by summarizing the explosive growth of the auto industry from 1890 to 1937. He went on to say:

The automobile has been a special blessing to the Negro, for the Negro is getting better wages and doing more business in the automobile industry than any other industry in the world. Take for instance 25 years ago, the average young colored man was either doing porter work, bell hopping, running an elevator or waiting on table, and the average wage at that time was $5.00 per week. That same young man as soon as he learned to operate an automobile, instead of paying him $5.00 per week, he would begin at not less than $15.00 per week, and as he progressed and became a mechanic his wages would be [raised] to $25.00 per week until today, men that are good mechanics and can master the trade, both as a chauffeur and mechanic, are being paid anyway from $25.00 to $50.00 per week, therefore, taking men out of the servant class and placing them in the mechanical class.

Thomas also discussed the jobs created for Black workers as taxi and bus drivers, and as employees in auto repair shops and manufacturing plants. "And taking it as a whole," Thomas concluded, "the Negro has made, and is making more money in the automobile industry than any other industry in the world. And the future looks bright, as the automobile business has just begun."

Jamon Jordan confirmed that Thomas's rosy predictions about the benefits Black Americans would derive from the auto industry largely came true. "The auto business was at the heart of the Paradise Valley era," Jordan said, referring to the economic boom enjoyed by Black business owners in Detroit from the 1920s through the 1950s. During this period, tens of thousands of African Americans, many of them migrants from the rural South, moved to Detroit to take advantage of job opportunities in the exploding auto industry. Paradise Valley was the business and entertainment district of the so-called Black Bottom area of Detroit, where most of the city's Black residents lived. More than three hundred Black-owned businesses thrived in Paradise Valley, including nightclubs, hotels, bowling alleys, theaters, and miniature golf courses. Stars like Pearl Bailey, Ella Fitzgerald, Duke Ellington, Louis Armstrong, and Dizzy Gillespie performed for audiences that included both whites and Blacks (until racial riots in 1943 caused many whites to avoid the area). In economic terms, the heyday of the US auto industry was a boom time for Black Americans in and around Detroit.

I think of how emotionally significant the achievement of owning a car must have been to the newly arrived people. They had worked, saved, and bought a vehicle of their own choice, freeing themselves from the humiliations experienced on public transportation. The good times of this period in places like Paradise Valley reflected the release of creativity that people feel when they're finally able to steer their own lives, at least in part.

No wonder Black columnist George Schuyler advised readers in the *Pittsburgh Courier* in 1930, "all Negroes who can do so [should] purchase an automobile as soon as possible in order to be free of discomfort, discrimination, segregation and insult."[1] Another Black writer wrote in a 1933 magazine article that in a car, "it's mighty good to be the skipper for a change, and pilot our craft whither and where we will. We feel like Vikings. What if our craft is blunt of nose and limited of power and our sea is macadamized; it's good for the spirit to just give the old railroad Jim Crow the laugh."[2]

MAPPING A SAFE PATH

The car gave millions of Black Americans the possibility of exploring the wide-open spaces of our country just as many white Americans had always done. Unfortunately, it didn't eliminate the difficulties and dangers. Powerful forces in American society, including the federal, state, and local governments, were not quite ready to allow Black people to participate in the freedom of the open road, and simply owning a car was not enough to free Black Americans from the discrimination and abuse that white people inflicted upon them. An article in the NAACP magazine *The Crisis* put it this way in 1947: "Would a Negro like to pursue a little happiness at a theater, a beach, pool, hotel, restaurant, on a train, plane, or ship, a golf course, summer, or winter resort? Would he like to stop overnight at a tourist camp while he motors about his native land 'Seeing America First'? Well, just let him try!"[3] George Schuyler cited a survey estimating that Black travelers were welcomed "in not more than 6 per cent of the nation's better hotels and motels."[4]

This unsettling, well-known reality did not keep African Americans from venturing onto the roadways. Instead, they developed strategies and behaviors to cope with the reality. *The Green Book* and other similar travel guides emerged from that realization but African Americans shared among themselves the true stories of trouble occurring on the road as cautionary

A Black driver asleep under his truck at a service station in Washington, DC, in 1940. Given the limitations on accommodations for Black travelers, it could present the best option.

tales. And yet, they still had fun. *We* had fun. We unburdened ourselves, at least temporarily, by sharing good times and laughter. The capacity to see humor, often ironic humor, in painful situations provided a needed release, especially when the frustration and fear became too much. Paulette Roby, a foot soldier in the civil rights movement in Birmingham, Alabama, shared childhood stories of her trips north that show the importance of humor: "I remember times that my mom was stopped [by police] when I was a little girl. We traveled to Chicago one time. The policeman asked my mom: 'How's the cotton down South?' My mom responded flatly, 'The same way it was when you left it.' We all snickered, quietly of course."

The stories people shared made Janée and me shake our heads in amazement or disgust, feel like we had taken a punch in the gut, made us laugh out loud, and left us silent. We heard stories of families always leaving in the early morning when it was safer because fewer people, including police, were on the road, and the family would then drive continuously. Eva Baham, assistant professor of history at Dillard University in New Orleans, recalled her family's travel patterns:

I came of age in the 1960s. I remember that everybody who took long trips was leaving at three o'clock in the morning to make those trips during the daytime. Today, there is a joke between my husband and me about a situation he thought was real funny. My mother needed to come visit me. She came two hundred miles from southwest Louisiana, here to southeast Louisiana. So I called her and asked her, "What time are you going to get here and what time are you leaving so I could start worrying about you?" She said she was coming with her cousin who was an elderly woman. She told her cousin that they were going to pull out real late, that they may not leave until 7:30 in the morning. Well, my husband thought it was so funny. He asked me "If 7:30 is late, what is early?" And I said to him that any time we traveled, or people were traveling to come see us from other places in the country, the magic hour was three in the morning.

Baham commented that while there are many stories about trouble while driving Black in America, there are probably more word-of-mouth stories or cautionary tales about trying to avoid trouble, trying to diminish the likelihood of being stopped by the police or some random white person. Parents told children how to behave in such situations. One tactic a Black man might use was to wear a chauffeur's cap or keep it in view to suggest that the nice car he was driving belonged to his white employer. As Baham points out, "As African Americans, as is common knowledge, we have to live with the ideas of how to prevent problematic encounters."

Some of these patterns persist even today. If you're Black, you probably would not be surprised by the stories we heard. In particular, you might see some of the avoidance strategies in the way your own relatives travel today. But if you're white, you may be shocked. In much of the United States until the late 1960s and even beyond, segregation and racist laws (called Black Codes), policies, and practices persisted, forcing African Americans into corners and areas of the nation that most White Americans rarely visited. This was during the time when a significant percentage of America's white population was buying houses in the suburbs, subsidized by US government housing policies. Many were living the American Dream lifestyle exemplified on television shows like *The Adventures of Ozzie and Harriet*. Because of their often deliberate racial isolation, most white people gave little or no thought to how African American lives and living conditions differed from their own. As the old adage says: out of sight, out of mind. If white people did think about Black people, they often bought into the pervasive negative narrative and stereotypes proffered by politicians, elected officials, news organizations, and members of their own families.

This simple reality of how humans perceive and experience the world helps to explain why it's problematic to set much store by the experiences, observations, and opinions of white Americans as to whether or not racial prejudice against Blacks is a serious problem in the United States. Open-minded and honest as they may be, white people simply have few, if any, opportunities to observe racism firsthand and therefore have no way to judge its reality.

To do that, you have to ask Black people. And the things you hear will leave no room for doubt.

The boyhood memories of Hezekiah Jackson, now in his early sixties, a minister and a member of the Civil Rights Activist Committee in Birmingham, Alabama, are typical. As a young adult, he was on the frontlines of the movement: marching, protesting, speaking, and writing. His vivid boyhood memories are part of what motivates him to continue to fight for equality. He recalled traveling north to visit with relatives after a death in the family and experiencing a frightening encounter with racism while his father was carrying out what seemed to be a routine chore:

My father was like most Black men. He was very proud. But mother would give you a drill: that if we are stopped or if some white people say anything to us, you are not to talk. And we'd say, "Okay, we're not to talk." And then she said, "And you are not to look at them."

We had an aunt who lived in Detroit, and she died. So, we planned a trip to pay our respects to her. It would also be a chance to see our cousins, who we wouldn't normally see. I was about ten at that time.

I can recall when we got into Detroit, my aunt had worked as a domestic, and her husband, he didn't have a car and they had to ask Daddy if [he] would go by and pick up Aunt Beatie's last pay. So that took us into the white area.

When we got to this very, very nice neighborhood, I thought it was something like on television. I said, "Who in the world lives here?" I can recall Daddy said we were not to get out of the car and the man was going to meet him at the door, and Mother said, "Well, don't tarry."

Before he could get out of the car, I recall seeing these two white [police] officers and then they said something to Daddy like, "You lost, boy?" And my brother, he almost lost it, 'cause he was like, "That white man just called Daddy a boy!" We had so much respect for our Daddy, and Daddy didn't allow nobody to disrespect him, it was almost, like, traumatizing to us.

And Daddy was looking at the ground, 'cause we was looking right at him through the car window and he said, "No sir, I'm not lost. I'm here to pick up a package."

And the other one said, "You ain't here to steal," and then "N———, you ain't stole this good-looking car? What you do for a living? You work for some rich white folk? They loan you this car?"

I can hear all that in my mind. And Mother kept putting her finger up to her lips to indicate to us that we weren't to make a sound, not a sound. And I said to myself: *She had trained herself so well.* It's no telling how many times she had to do that.

Jackson's father did finally collect Aunt Beatie's final pay:

So the white man said, "I'm going up here, boy, and if I find out you lying, I'm taking everybody in this car to jail."

And we were saying, "To jail!? What we did?"

So he went up to the door, knocked on the door, and whatever he said to the person that came to the door, they gave the police officer the envelope. And then he told Daddy to get back in the car, and he dropped it into Daddy's lap.

It was very traumatizing. Then we wanted to know what had happened. Daddy wouldn't say a word. Mother said, "No, we can talk about something else. We'll talk about the Sunday school lesson." She just changed the subject.

So, we couldn't get the gravity of what had happened, why it had happened, what we were supposed to have done? We were like, "What did we do? I mean, what did Daddy do? He didn't do anything. I mean, we don't get it."

Not only was the open road not a welcoming place for Black people, but neither were suburban neighborhood streets. This was true in white suburban communities and small towns across the US. However, what strikes me most about this encounter is the collateral damage to the Jackson children, especially Hezekiah's older brother. I continue to wonder how the disbelief and anger generated by the disrespect and condescension the police officer showed his strong father shaped his distrust and disdain of such authority as an adult. Black parents tried, as best they could, to shield their children from such encounters.

WHEN A DREAM CAR BECOMES A NIGHTMARE

Simple innocuous acts, like Jackson's father going to pick up a relative's pay at her employer's home, could expose an African American to degradation, resentment, hatred, and danger. For African Americans, owning a nice car could also be a trigger.

For millions of middle-class Americans, buying a first car is an exciting rite of passage. Lots of people, especially young ones just starting out in life, save money by buying used cars or basic vehicles with few options or accessories. But those who can afford new cars with powerful engines, roomy interiors, stylish designs, and state-of-the-art options are often proud to do so—and many love being seen by friends and neighbors tooling around town in their fancy wheels.

Owning your own car has become a traditional piece of the American Dream. But owning a "nice car"—meaning any car a notch or two above the most basic—has always been a mixed blessing for a Black person in America. The late activist and educator Gwen Patton of Montgomery, Alabama, recalled an incident from her childhood that happened when a highway patrolman noticed her family's new car:

> My father was driving a nice new shiny car from Detroit back down South when we passed a patrolman going in the opposite direction on the two-lane road. Daddy had slowed down and was

deliberately not looking directly at the patrol car as it approached and continued by us. After it passed us, my father kept repeating, "I have a bad feeling about this" while also checking the rearview mirror. Daddy knew that a Black man behind [the wheel of] a new car was a common reason to be stopped and harassed. And as Daddy feared, the patrol car started to turn around to come our way. My father did not wait to see what was going to happen. He stepped on the gas to get as far ahead of the patrolman as he could. Our car had a powerful engine, probably a V8. As he went around a curve and was way out of sight of the police car, my father remembered there was a Black church just off the road ahead. He slowed down quickly, pulled off the road carefully so dust wouldn't be raised, and then drove quickly on the grass to get behind the church. We sat in the car behind the church, as my father watched the patrol car go up and down the road several times. It was frightening. When the sun finally set, my father pulled out carefully onto the road and we continued our trip, making sure not to bring any attention to ourselves. That part of the drive was frightening too.

Part of the problem is the widespread assumption among white people, especially law enforcement officials, that a large percentage of Black people are poor—or should be. And that assumption feeds the belief that buying an expensive vehicle is a wasteful, impractical extravagance that helps to explain why Black people remain mired in poverty.

I recall an Irish American friend who grew up in Newark, New Jersey, who said to me casually during a conversation that his entire family believed—and often said—that Black people "just didn't know better" about housing, about jobs, "about anything." Another white friend, this one from New England, told me that his father told him and his siblings repeatedly any time he saw a Black person in a car better than his that "Black people are lazy, don't work hard enough, and waste their money on big, new cars."

It isn't only white people who believed (and sometimes still believe) such things. The mother of my friend Karl Weber, who was of Japanese ancestry, often made similar remarks about the supposedly wasteful tendency of Black people to squander money on fancy cars—while at the same time she spoke proudly about her friendships with Black colleagues from the public school where she worked in Brooklyn, New York.

These assumptions and stereotypes were especially pervasive during the time *The Green Book* was published. They were fueled in some measure by simple ignorance on the part of white people who either didn't know many Black people or were unable to fully understand the lives and circumstances of the Black people they did know. Sadly, these beliefs were also embraced by many white people for less excusable reasons. Believing that Black people are foolish and wasteful in their behavior provides a socioeconomic explanation for poverty in the African American community that eliminates the role of racism and discrimination. If Black people bring poverty upon themselves and therefore "deserve" to be poor, there's no need for white people to accept any responsibility for the legacy of racism—a comforting rationalization.

The reality of life for African Americans could not have been more different. Living in a society that erected barriers to success and achievement specifically aimed at them forced Black Americans to be *more* creative, resourceful, and ingenious in managing their lives. It was simply a matter of necessity.

Buying comfortable, powerful cars that white people considered "fancy" and even "wasteful" was a survival tactic for many Black people. Two main factors help to explain the strategy. First, for generations, laws, covenants, and widespread customs prevented most Black Americans from buying decent houses in well-maintained, desirable neighborhoods. Unlike their white counterparts, Blacks were too often denied the opportunity to invest their savings in valuable real estate, specifically home ownership—the key asset for long-term wealth-building in the United States. The barriers to home ownership helped to perpetuate poverty in many African American communities. However, denying Black people access to home buying also had a little-recognized side effect: many instead put the money they saved into the next-largest consumer purchase available to Americans—a car. For many African Americans, investing in a vehicle—a symbol of achievement and freedom—that would serve them and their families well for many years simply made good sense.

The second factor behind the popularity of large, "fancy" cars among some Black Americans was racial discrimination in hotels and motels. In countless communities across the country, it was impossible for Black travelers to find lodging that would accommodate them. As a result, millions of Black families driving across country to visit family or friends may have had to sleep in their cars in roadside rest sites while another person in the car stayed awake watching for possible trouble. Also, if you were traveling with children they could play and nap easily on the long bench seat in back. No wonder many Blacks developed a philosophy that they passed on to their children: "When you buy a car, get the most comfortable and powerful one you can afford. You never know when you may have to sleep in it or when you may need the horsepower to get away from a problem."

When you consider these perspectives among Black people, the popularity of big cars like the Cadillac Eldorado, the Lincoln Continental, the Chrysler New Yorker, the Pontiac Bonneville, and the Buick Electra 225 becomes an example of practical, clever adaptation to challenges most white people never had to face. The same kind of thinking could be seen among everyone from ordinary working-class folks to prominent civil rights leaders. Historian Gretchen Sorin observes, "NAACP Field Secretary Medgar Evers selected the large, imposing Oldsmobile Rocket 88 for his excursions—not only for its power to avoid ambush and getting pushed off the road but also because his 6-foot-4 frame could stretch out on its wide seats to sleep, if necessary. (He certainly was not welcome at most hotels.)"[5]

But even a nice *parked* car could instigate racist backlash. Vernetta Sheppard-Pinson, now in her eighties and living in Detroit, recalled an incident as she and her family drove back to visit her parents in Little Rock, Arkansas, in the mid-1950s:

Let me tell you something really funny that happened. We'd bought a 1955 green Chevy. It had whitewall tires and the white slash on the back. It was beautiful. We got down to Little Rock and we stopped at the light. And when we stopped, this old white lady came up to the car, and she looked, and she said, "Them's n———s." She had tobacco in her mouth and she spit on the tires and she said, "N———s, get outta here!"

It was because it was a new car, and because we were Black, and because she was just prejudiced. She didn't know any better. So, I chalked it up to that woman's ignorance. And when you have the Lord in your life, you learn how to look over ignorance.

What would you have done in that situation, given the era, the place, and the circumstances? Understandably, Sheppard-Pinson and her family felt they had no choice. Rather than expressing their anger at the white woman's insulting and nasty behavior, they just moved on, relying on their Christian faith as a path to forgiveness and grace.

This too was a reality of Black American life. When confronted with hateful acts, Blacks understood that refusing to react or retaliate was necessary to keep themselves and their families safe. But it took an incredible amount of self-control, discipline, and restraint.

Black people with nice cars even had to be careful in their own cities. Hezekiah Jackson told us how his father and his father's friends developed pragmatic ways of avoiding the dangers of the white gaze:

Back then the car was for special occasions. My daddy rode with other fellows to work. And like most men of his time, Daddy didn't believe in his wife having a job. So Daddy worked two jobs. He rode with his friends, and they rode in raggedy trucks. They were afraid to drive their good cars around the white people on the job. We didn't have garages too much in the Black neighborhood back then. So white people started selling car covers, and you hid the car behind the house. 'Cause if the white people saw you had a good car, it was going to be a problem.

Jackson's story opened my eyes about something among my own relatives that I quietly had thought was "stupid" or "ignorant" when I was growing up. I could not figure out why they often parked their new cars behind the house, or on the side of the house where it could not be seen clearly from the road. I reasoned that they did this so they could keep a close eye on their new pride and joy from their bedrooms. I also noticed that many kept their "ol' piece of car" or "junker" in the driveway and continued to go to work in it every day. I figured they did this because their new cars were likely to get dirty or have the finish damaged at their job sites. Since hearing Jackson's story, I now understand and have enormous respect for all they were protecting: their livelihood, their accomplishment, their pride, and their safety.

HIGHWAYS OF DEATH

The damage done by racism on highways and local streets went deeper than just inconvenience, embarrassment, or even harassment. Many hospitals would not accept Black patients. That meant African Americans injured in car crashes might have to be driven scores or even hundreds of miles to find the nearest medical facility that would care for them. Unfriendly police departments and ambulance corps were known to take far longer to arrive to help injured Black drivers and often behaved as if their needs were less real or serious than those of white victims. Such delays could easily prove fatal. In an article in *National Geographic* magazine, Erin Blakemore describes a situation that was all too common:

George White was critically injured. But when surgeons in his Atlanta hospital found out he had black ancestry, they kicked him out mid-examination, shipping him across the street to a black hospital despite the pouring rain. He died in the overcrowded, underfunded hospital days later. The year was 1931, and like hundreds of thousands of other black people in the segregated South, White was a victim of Jim Crow segregation laws.[6]

For many years, the story of the death of blues singer Bessie Smith was often told as another example of negligent medical care during Jim Crow. Smith was gravely injured when the Packard she was in ran into a truck in Mississippi. She supposedly bled to death from her partially severed arm as the white doctor at the scene attended to the white couple who had been in a light accident nearby. Although the story is now thought to be apocryphal, the underlying assumptions about Smith not receiving life-saving medical treatment properly reflect real-life, on-the-road medical emergencies shared by word-of-mouth stories among African American communities.

Consider too the ways in which Black drivers had to behave differently because of their color. A driver worn out from too many hours on the road is well advised to visit a restaurant or a roadside cafe for a rest stop. This option wasn't widely available to Black drivers. In some states and counties, even pulling over onto the shoulder of the road for a quick snooze could invite an assault from a highway patrol officer, a self-appointed local "enforcer," or a person just looking to harass someone. As a result, many road trips for Black drivers involved multihour stretches behind the wheel, increasing the risk of an accident.

This risk was not just theoretical. It was real and led to an untold number of avoidable deaths. Here's an example, as recounted in a story from the *Albuquerque Tribune* for August 16, 1955:

An official of the National Assn. for the Advancement of Colored People has charged that Albuquerque motels and others in New Mexico along U.S. 66 are not opened to Negroes.

He said it was "not surprising" that six Negroes met death in a traffic accident at Clines Corners last week.

"They could not have found a welcome at any of the courts on Route 66 from the Texas border to Albuquerque," said Edward L. Boyd, special assistant to the legal redress committee of the Albuquerque branch of the NAACP.

The accident, a collision between a truck and a car, took six lives. The truck driver told police he believed the driver of the car fell asleep at the wheel. State Police Chief Joe Roach said the accident apparently was caused by "speed and fatigue."[7]

African Americans often favored larger automobiles because they provided a greater margin of safety in a collision—whether accidental or instigated.

This, then, was the paradox of the open road for Black Americans. The coming of the automobile played a crucial role in expanding the zone of freedoms they could enjoy. Yet at the same time, the bigotry and discrimination sanctioned by law, custom, and social attitudes ensured that those freedoms would remain severely limited.

These factors and many more made Detroit a fitting place for Janée and me to begin our road trip. As we have seen, the US automobile industry had opened up new opportunities for African Americans through the jobs it created and the possibility of mobility it provided—though both were limited by the continuing realities of segregation and Jim Crow. Detroit was also one of the cities transformed by the Great Migration of the twentieth century, which brought millions of African Americans from the rural South to the cities of the North. That made the city both a destination and a starting point. It was the northern city to which countless Black citizens traveled from the South, like Hezekiah Jackson's family, to visit relatives and friends who had made the long journey north for better opportunities. Detroit was at the same time the city from which recently arrived African Americans traveled back to the South to visit family and friends who had chosen to stay and to participate in all kinds of local gatherings, such as graduations, weddings, ordinations, funerals, and reunions.

The complexities and challenges faced by those people who moved to Detroit were much on our minds, especially after all we had learned from the local residents we talked with about the city's history, particularly related to housing and job opportunities. We could imagine how the busy, buzzy city felt so promising upon arrival. But the reality of daily life, with its struggles and restrictions, undoubtedly dampened that optimism. Still, the future those migrants experienced was probably better than the lives of those people left in the South. Victor Green had created his *Green Book* for people like those travelers.

VISITING HOME

RETURN FROM THE GREAT MIGRATION

During the Great Migration, there was a sense of crossing over to where you thought you were going to be better off. We felt that, once we got across the Ohio River, out of the South, things were going to open up. But it felt like not that much had changed.

> — Kenneth Clay, cultural and arts leader, author, and entertainment producer in Louisville, Kentucky

---

Young boys in Chicago celebrate Easter Sunday in 1941. Their families were among the millions of Black Americans who left the South for what they hoped would be better lives in northern cities.

As Janée and I drove south to Columbus and Cincinnati in Ohio, then on to Louisville in Kentucky, and Nashville and Memphis in Tennessee, we talked first about what it must have been like for the people who moved north during the Great Migration, letting go of the burdensome feeling of entrapment that came with poverty and the threat of terror while also feeling a growing sense of optimism, tempered with a little caution, about the future. This made me think of something one of my relatives used to say to me: sometimes all you have is yourself and your belief in yourself.

I tried to imagine what those independent, courageous people saw on the way back south when they visited their former homes. Janée and I wanted our route—which included stops for interviews in eleven cities—to follow the two-lane, secondary roads that travelers would have taken during the years *The Green Book* was being published, before the interstate highway system was built. This would have taken us through many small towns along the way. But budget and time limitations necessitated that Janée, Kemi, and I make the trip as efficiently as possible by using the interstate highways. Most of our twelve-day drive was on four-lane roads that alternated between forested areas or flat farmlands that looked pretty much the same from one state to the next. The service marts where we sometimes stopped to buy gas or snacks also looked similar. Occasionally a sizable patch of wildflowers would be blooming in the grassy area that divided the two sets of lanes. Each time I saw those flowers, I recalled the 1960s "Beautification Project" of Lady Bird Johnson, then First Lady of the US, to "beautify" America by planting wildflowers along its roadways. Seeing them surprised us and made us smile a little each time.

Janée preferred using Google Maps to set our route from one location to the next. I preferred a paper map and had brought along a large spiral-bound US atlas, which made Janée laugh because she thought it was old-fashioned. I liked planning the trip this way because I had an overall picture, like a view from a drone, of where we were going. And I wanted to see what towns and attractions were short detours from our route, especially well-known places like Muscle Shoals, Alabama (home of a legendary recording studio), and Kosciusko, Mississippi (where Oprah Winfrey was born). I was also interested in the towns listed in James W. Loewen's revelatory 2005 book *Sundown Towns: A Hidden Dimension of American Racism*. These were towns in which, by local law or practice, African Americans were prohibited from being within the town limits after sunset. Black people might be able to work in such a community, but they had to be out of town by the time the sun went down. If they were not, they could be harassed, arrested, beaten, tarred and feathered, or even killed. There was often no official or legally stated punishment, but it was understood that Blacks would have no recourse to whatever happened to them.

Sundown towns were never mentioned in *The Green Book*. Travelers and locals knew about them by word of mouth, usually from a story about a Black person who made the mistake of being within that town's limits after sunset. In 2016, Robert Moman, a man in his late seventies whom I interviewed at his dining room table in his home near Tougaloo College in Jackson, Mississippi, recalled a boyhood story from trips his family took in the 1950s: "My daddy told us when we were driving up through north Mississippi there was a little town called Duck Hill; he always said in Duck Hill, they [white people] tarred and feathered a Black man." As Moman talked about this, shaking his head as he imagined the act of terror, his cousin, who was sitting in a chair next to us at the table, suddenly recalled a long-suppressed memory from her childhood: a Black man being dragged to death through the streets of Tougaloo to warn African Americans in the town of the consequences of challenging or breaking the Jim Crow laws at that time in any town, sundown or not. We all went silent, trying to cope with the sickening feeling in our guts and hearts.

African Americans often lived quite near these towns. However, many Black people never went to them because they knew what could happen, as Jerome Gray, in his eighties and a voting rights activist since the 1960s, confirmed:

There were two [sundown towns] in Monroe County [Alabama] about twenty miles from my hometown. One was called Excel and the other was called Frisco City. Then the saying was: Negroes—they used the N-word back then—were not supposed to be caught in those towns after sundown. And we didn't go to those places. In fact, I can't recall having gone to Excel or Frisco City during my growing-up years, even though they were just twenty miles from where I lived.

Even on our journey, we stuck to our schedule of traveling during the daylight as much as we could, always getting an early start.

Between Detroit and Columbus, Google Maps took us off the interstate and onto some two-lane, secondary roads in Ohio. It was a sunny day. We drove through farmland, the landscape flat in all directions. The views prompted Janée and me to imagine what it would have been like, in the 1940s or 1950s, or even the early 1960s, driving on these roads, with narrow shoulders and few trees offering shade or shelter. We talked about what it must have felt like to be in a car without air conditioning on a cloudless, hot, humid day. All of the windows would have been rolled down to catch any cooling breeze, but the air from the

road would have been uncomfortably warm as well as tiring and sopo-
rific. This brought up a strong visual memory that I had not thought
about in decades.

When my great-uncle Son (that was his nickname) drove us from
south of Tallahassee, Florida, to visit my mother's uncle Louis, in Lake
City, Florida, in the summer, my mother or grandmother would often
have a washcloth in a small container of ice on the floor next to the
front seat. When Uncle Son started to look tired or drowsy, she would
tell him to wipe his face with the ice-cold cloth and then rest it on his
forehead. It always seemed to rejuvenate him. Then I remembered that
during our interview with eighty-year-old Vernetta Sheppard-Pinson in
Detroit, she shared a similar story about applying cold washcloths to her
husband's head to help keep him awake and alert during their nonstop
nighttime family drive from Detroit to Little Rock, Arkansas.

Janée and I also only briefly talked about what it must have been like
for Black people to have a breakdown that they could not fix themselves.
A flat tire would make them vulnerable until they could repair it and
get on their way. However, engine trouble was certainly more worrying.
They would be vulnerable for much longer, and therefore the possibility
of all types of bad encounters increased. Among Janée, Kemi, and me,
talking about such incidents and dangers felt too much like tempting
fate, even when we were driving a fully insured, recent-model car, in good
condition. Our conversation would end. And then we would each sit
quietly with or without our private anxieties, watching the road go by.

As we approached every city, the roadways became six lanes, usually
going through parts of the cities where light industrial businesses operated. It was never scenic. It was what we had to get through to find the
location where we would interview the local residents.

We talked too about how the travelers probably thought of themselves on the journey "back down South." How would you want to

present yourself to family members, to the community you had left? This question was not theoretical to me; it was deeply autobiographical.

MOVING DURING THE GREAT MIGRATION

When I began doing research about *The Green Book*, I was surprised, as I said earlier, to discover that my leaving the Florida Panhandle to attend Yale Summer High School in 1969 and to matriculate at Bowdoin College in Brunswick, Maine, in 1970 made me part of the last wave of the Great Migration (1910–1970). The first time I returned home to the small rural community where I grew up, I worried about how I would come across, how I would be perceived. Some people wanted me to "show off" what I had "learned up North," while others wanted to be reassured that the young man they had known since his birth and had helped raise was still recognizable to them.

As I learned more about the Great Migration, an enormous, often-neglected event in US history, I gained a new perspective on and insights about my own family's history in the rural South as well as the restrictions that whites, southerners in particular, imposed to reclaim their racial dominance over Black Americans.

Before 1910, every one of the decennial censuses taken in the United States showed that more than 90 percent of Black Americans lived in the South. Of those, only about 20 percent lived in cities. Though slavery had been technically abolished in 1865, the life circumstances of many Blacks remained largely the same. This was true of my family, but I didn't know it growing up.

By the end of World War I, the northern states had experienced several decades of industrial development. Steel mills, car factories, meatpacking plants, and other industries had exploded. And then World War II caused labor shortages as young, mostly white men were sent abroad to fight. (Remember, the armed forces were segregated until 1948; Black men who served were usually assigned menial jobs.) These two facts encouraged northern industries to look to the South as a source of cheap workers. They sent labor agents to the southern states, promising a bright future to Black workers who would agree to travel north and sometimes even handing out passes for the train trip. African Americans began abandoning the farms, first in a trickle, then in a series of migratory waves.

During the teens and the 1920s, an estimated 1.3 million southern Black people made the move north. The Great Depression of the 1930s decimated job opportunities across the United States and slowed the stream of workers from the South. But the movement resumed with the advent of World War II and continued into the 1960s, accelerated not just by industrial work in the North, but also by the growing industrialization of agriculture, which was eliminating farmwork for Blacks in the South.

By 1970, the percentage of African Americans living in the South had fallen from more than 90 percent to around 50 percent. What's more, American Blacks had joined the national shift from being overwhelmingly rural to overwhelmingly urban; by the 1970 census, some three-fourths of African Americans lived in cities.[1]

The cities of the North were also transformed. In 1910, just 1.2 percent of the population of Detroit was African American—about 6,600 people. In 1970, at the end of the Great Migration, the number had increased to 43.7 percent—more than 660,000 people. St. Louis reflected a similar change. In 1910, 6.4 percent of that city's population was African American, and by 1970, the percentage was 40.9 percent.[2]

Baltimore, Cleveland, Chicago, Cincinnati, Philadelphia, Newark, and New York experienced similar shifts, and some western cities, like Los Angeles, San Francisco, Oakland, and Denver, showed smaller but still significant Black influxes.

The workers who migrated didn't find the utopia they may have imagined. Even with their skills, knowledge, and drive, Black factory workers were often paid less than the European immigrants with whom they competed and were generally excluded from management positions. In Detroit, as we drove through areas where the then recent Black migrants would have lived, Detroit historian and tour guide Jamon Jordan explained:

Henry Ford [in the 1920s and 1930s] partnered with five Black institutions in the city of Detroit to help recruit African Americans to take some of those jobs [at the Ford factory], which [even] with all of the faults of Henry Ford, places him as a progressive in comparison to the other factory owners who were not hiring African Americans at all or only hiring African Americans as strike breakers. So, Henry Ford, who once practiced the same things, has now moved much further in hiring African Americans than any of the other factory owners and now begins paying them an equal wage to the white workers, which is $5 a day—which would be about $85 today. This is double what most factories are paying in the city of Detroit at that time.

So now you have African Americans coming from Mississippi, Louisiana, Alabama, North Carolina, South Carolina, and Georgia, who were [previously] working as tenant farmers and sharecroppers and in some form of low-skilled labor and not really making that much money or in perpetual debt as a sharecropper on a plantation. They're now coming to the city of Detroit [and] making a living wage, more money than they ever would have made as sharecroppers in Mississippi.

Still, Ford and the other automakers of Detroit continued to apply racially discriminatory policies. Kefentse Chike, a professor of African American studies and a community activist in Detroit, told Janée and me that most Black workers were automatically assigned the worst jobs in the auto factories—for example, in the foundry where iron and steel castings were produced and where the work was notoriously hot, dirty, and dangerous. Chike gave us a fuller picture of the lives of Black workers:

They also oftentimes were in the most deplorable communities. There was also a pecking order. Before there was a mass influx of African Americans, there were Polish people, people from the Middle East, and these people were considered on the lower rung in society. And as Black people came here, because some of those people could easily fit into the white construct, they moved up, so to speak, and Black people assumed that position on the lower rung.

Furthermore, Chike pointed out, some Black workers found that the famous $5-per-day salary did not apply to them. Instead, these workers found themselves receiving paychecks of just around $3.50 per day from Ford. When they complained, they were told that, if they demonstrated themselves to be of "upright moral character," they could arrange a special account at their neighborhood church, through which the additional pay *might* be received.

Despite these harsh realities, most Blacks who made the journey north considered themselves better off than they had been. Many now had steady jobs with a regular paycheck and a living wage. They could accumulate savings. They could begin enjoying the benefits of their increased socioeconomic status, one of which was the economic freedom to be entrepreneurial, as Jordan made clear:

So, what did Black people do with that money? They did two things. First, they became customers of businesses they never would have been able to be customers of before. Many of these businesses, of course, are African American–owned businesses in [the] Paradise Valley [district of Detroit]. The second thing is they're using the money that they have now, their disposable income, to start businesses. So, yes, they may work at an auto factory on the assembly line, but they are starting their own businesses. What they really are, they're blacksmiths, seam-stresses, cobblers, cooks, or they have some other skill. And now they have the money to finance this other business that they can be a part of.

Many of the people starting their own businesses in cities and towns across the US were Black women. Jordan's words prompted me to recall women in the rural area where I grew up who had the skills and entre-preneurial drive that he described. They wanted to make better lives and achieve financial independence for themselves and their families. My cousin Dot Harris straightened and curled women's hair in a back room of her home. Quite a few women were expert seamstresses who made special-event dresses for both white and Black women. Others set up businesses washing, ironing, repairing, and delivering laundry for white families. Once they got up North they diligently saved their money and then used the skills to become self-employed. Multidisciplinary artist Derrick Adams "grew up in a family with a lot of women who were very strong. They always kept things under control. They were always handling everything. For example, they allowed the man to be the face or figurehead of the church, but the women really ran it. They decided what type of events were going on in the church. They even decided what the pastor wore, because most of them were making what he was wearing anyway."

In reality, Black women were often the economic backbone and social heart of their communities. *The Green Book* listings are perhaps the first place the many roles of Black women entrepreneurs were gathered, acknowledged, and made broadly known.

In Detroit, despite the many restrictive covenants and limited access to capital, a few African Americans bought their own homes—often in the area known as Black Bottom. They also started businesses that catered to their everyday needs so they could enjoy good lives. Many cities across the United States witnessed this same phenomenon after World War II. Importantly, segregation kept most white people unaware of this transformation and the progress that Black people were enjoying. Recalling the world of his childhood in Birmingham, Alabama, Hezekiah Jackson's words echoed the experiences of many Black people in communities across the country, including my own when I was growing up: "Everything in our world was okay with us because we very seldom saw anybody who wasn't Black. And we traveled in a small circle, like a five-mile radius. We went to school there. We shopped there. We lived there. Most of our friends were there."

Black people were, in effect, creating their own neighborhoods and their own economy where they could be in community with other creative, entrepreneurial, ambitious, skillful, and intelligent Black people. Equally important, they were creating spaces free of the commonplace, pervasive, demeaning treatment that Jim Crow and segregation imposed on every aspect of their daily lives, whether on public transportation, in shops, in medical facilities, or on the streets. In relative terms, they were taking the first steps toward becoming part of the American middle class and participants in the American Dream, even though they were not totally racially or socially integrated into their adopted cities. The economic, social, and cultural impact of these shifts was enormous for Black people, and for the United States as a whole.

A Black family just arrived in Chicago from the South in 1922 during the Great Migration.

NO PROMISED LAND IN THE NORTH

But not everyone celebrated this growing economic health in the Black community. The Great Migration produced a backlash in many northern cities, towns, and regions. As whites and Blacks competed for industrial jobs and affordable housing, racial conflicts erupted. As early as 1919, rioting, fomented by white workers angry over the perception that their jobs were being "stolen" by lower-paid Blacks, took place in cities from Washington, DC, to Omaha, Nebraska.

Another part of the backlash was an increasing pattern of racial segregation in northern cities. Demographic data show that even as millions of Black Americans moved from the South to the North, some counties, cities, and towns in northern states witnessed a sharp *decline* in the number of African American residents.

Sociologist James Loewen presents some exemplary numbers. Consider what happened in New England states like Maine, New Hampshire, and Vermont. In 1890, Maine had fourteen counties with at least eighteen African American residents. By 1930, the number had fallen to five. In 1890, Hancock County had fifty-six Black citizens; by 1930, only three. New Hampshire and Vermont had no all-white counties in 1890; by 1930, each state had several.[3]

What was happening in these communities? As Blacks, especially those from the South, became a noticeable presence in the North for the first time, some whites organized to push them out and exclude them from their towns and cities. One result was the creation of those sundown towns. They must have been at the front of Victor Green's mind when he created *The Green Book*, and they came to my mind on the road ahead.

On the day we started our trip south, we left Detroit early to avoid the morning rush. Our destination was Columbus, Ohio, the second city on our way to New Orleans. We would stay there long enough to interview one person, Mary Ellen Tyus, before continuing to Cincinnati. The beautiful day was perfect for driving. We all felt optimistic. Our conversation was focused on preparing for our first interview so that the necessary background information was fresh in our minds. Janée, who loves to drive, was happy to take the wheel. While she and I never explicitly discussed who would drive, Janée drove most of the two-thousand-plus miles we traveled, specifically because we both were aware that a Black man driving a nice car can invite unwanted scrutiny and interference. Janée never told me during the trip that she, in fact, checked the tires each day to make sure they were in good condition, and she carefully monitored the gas tank level so we wouldn't get stranded accidentally in a place where we might not be welcome. She also checked the lights to help prevent our being pulled over by a police officer for having broken lights.

Sometimes, using my big spiral-bound paper atlas, I would point out the names of the historic sundown towns along our route. None of us ever wanted to stop in those towns.

Because of the restrictive Black Codes created in virtually every southern state and reinforced by Jim Crow laws enacted after Reconstruction, many people who have heard of sundown towns automatically assume that most of them were located in the South. That's quite wrong. Sundown towns existed throughout the United States, and there were actually more in the North than in the South. By the end of the 1960s, as many as ten thousand towns across the country were effectively off limits to Blacks. These included such large suburbs as Glendale, California (population 60,000 at the time); Levittown, New York (82,000); and Warren, Michigan (180,000). More than half the incorporated communities in Illinois were sundown towns.[4] Oak Park, just west of Chicago and the home of a longtime white friend of mine, was one such place.

During one of my stays at his late parents' house, which he still lived in at the time, I mentioned this history to him. He said he had no knowledge of it, although he grew up there when Oak Park was all white and openly hostile to Black people. What fascinated me more was his deep, subconscious resistance to this historical truth. I would send him articles or recommend books about the racial history of Oak Park or Chicago, but he rarely mentioned them during subsequent phone conversations. I suspect he didn't read them. The beautiful idyllic Oak Park in which he grew up was important to him. He wanted and needed to maintain a narrative in which the nastiness of its racism remained unseen.

The residents of many of these towns boldly advertised the fact that they were sundown towns, ready to enforce their whites-only-after-dark rule by any means necessary. The unofficial nickname of Anna, Illinois, which had violently expelled its African American population in 1909, was "Ain't No N———s Allowed."[5] The nickname was also an acronym for the town's name. The slogan of Greenville, Texas, was "The Blackest Land, the Whitest People." The town proudly displayed this slogan on a banner stretched across Main Street as well as painted on the local water tower.

A white female friend who grew up in the Midwest in the 1950s once commented to me that there were no Black people in the Indiana town where her grandmother lived, other than domestic workers who left every day. After I started doing research about the towns we would visit or drive through on the road trip to record the *Driving the Green Book* podcast series, I told her about sundown towns, especially in Indiana, Illinois, Michigan, and Ohio. I wonder if she ever researched whether her grandmother had lived in a sundown town. I did. But rather than tell her what I uncovered, I decided to wait to see if she said anything about the subject again. As happened with my friend from Oak Park, silence was the least uncomfortable and easiest path to take.

How did sundown towns become such a widespread phenomenon in the North? A major part of the explanation is the rise of virulently racist groups. The 1920s was a major period of rebirth and growth for the Ku Klux Klan, not just in the South but also in the North. Some fifteen thousand Klan members attended a state convention in Maine in 1923. An estimated ten thousand people attended a Klan rally near Montpelier, Vermont, in 1925. That same year, the *Washington Post* estimated Klan membership in New England at more than half a million. Others estimated membership in New Jersey at the same time at more than sixty thousand.[6] The Klan, primarily groups of white protestant Christians who donned white robes and conical hoods, threatened and terrorized Blacks in particular. James Loewen points out in his book *Sundown Towns: A Hidden Dimension of American Racism* that the Klan members didn't reserve their hatred for Blacks alone; they reviled and threatened Jews and Catholics as well as any ethnic group they viewed as only marginally white—Italians, Greeks, and Eastern Europeans. But they reserved their most intense hatred and most egregious acts of violence for Blacks.

Such domestic hate groups often operated with impunity because of indifference or support—tacit or explicit—from local governments, police departments, elected officials, and citizens. Using intimidation, brutality, arson, and even murder, whites sent an unmistakable message: no Black people are welcome here, so get out as quickly as possible. One town after another in the North became virtually all white during the 1920s. And as new suburbs were built after World War II, they implemented the same rules, becoming sundown suburbs.

Although the racially motivated laws may not be on the books today, the practice still exists in many places. A 2021 article, "Sundown Towns Are Still a Problem for Black Drivers," by Ade Onibada, a BuzzFeed News reporter, recounts the story of then thirty-year-old hiker Marco

Williams's stop in 2020 at a small service station in Kentucky and being warned by the cashier, "You best not be around here after dark. This is a sundown town."

As we traveled the country gathering research materials, Janée and I met many individuals who experienced that geographic segregation firsthand, often in the form of limits on where they were allowed to rent or buy an apartment or house. Usually, one street formed the main artery of the Black business district, with hotels, motels, restaurants, clubs, movie theaters, and retail shops exclusively on that street or on surrounding streets. Black people often lived nearby on streets parallel or perpendicular to that main thoroughfare. We would be visiting many of these neighborhoods on our journey ahead.

4

JIM CROW LAWS

SLAVERY BY ANOTHER NAME

If you don't know your past, how can you plan your future?

— Joyce Coleman, amateur historian and longtime resident of Cincinnati, Ohio

For many African Americans who had migrated to Detroit, driving to the South was an annual summer ritual. They went back to remain connected to relatives who had stayed in the South, to participate in family gatherings, and to experience the specific joys of their small, often rural communities. For many young Black Americans who had been born in the North, trips to the South with their families were their

---

A Black man going into the colored entrance of the Crescent movie theater in Belzoni, Mississippi, 1939.

first exposure to the full weight of the racist practices and policies known as Jim Crow.

The Green Book does not include references to things to do or see in the South. Victor Green knew the sort of travel his readers would be engaging in. Black people traveling didn't typically stop in towns along the way. They would drive continually, only stopping to buy gas where they *could* (not every service station accepted Black travelers) and to go into "the bushes" for a comfort break. They would only care about the city that was their destination. In the case of my friend Carl Williams, who grew up in Detroit and who now lives in Washington, DC, *The Green Book* listed no locations at his family's yearly travel destination. They stayed with relatives. Carl told me about his family's annual trips, when they would stop first in Memphis, Tennessee, and then go on to Itta Bena in Leflore County, Mississippi. As Janée and I began our road trip, Carl's annual trip was definitely on my mind.

When Carl's family first started making this ten-hour trip in the late 1950s, there were only two-lane roads the entire way. His parents would pack the car with food his mother had cooked specifically for the trip, and the family would leave between three and four a.m., so that they would arrive in Memphis by early evening at the latest. They wanted to drive straight through and avoid stopping unless it was an absolute necessity. His father's preferred route in those days was through northern Indiana, down the length of Illinois, through the western edge of Kentucky, and finally into Tennessee. Later, when the Interstate Highway System was built, the trip became shorter, going from Michigan through Ohio and Kentucky and finally Tennessee and Mississippi. This was similar to the route Janée and I took.

As he drove south, Carl's father would tell his children about how to behave in each state to comply with its local Jim Crow laws and practices. Carl remembers the conversation being full of specifics, all clearly based on his dad's experiences growing up in the Deep South before migrating to Detroit. The children were to keep their heads down any time they were in the presence of white people. They were not to look at white people, and definitely not in the eyes. They were not to speak to white people unless a white person spoke to them first. They had to say "Yes, sir" and "No, sir," "Yes, ma'am" and "No, ma'am" to every white person, regardless of their age. They had to get used to hearing their father being referred to as "boy" by seemingly any and every white adult and child. There were even places where Black people could not walk on the same sidewalk as a white person. If they saw a white person walking their way, they had to step off the sidewalk and let the white person pass before continuing. All of this was on top of obeying the "Whites" or "Colored" signs posted at the entrances to businesses, on water fountains, and in sections of public facilities like buses. When they crossed the Kentucky state line, young Carl was aware of how the restrictions began to tighten. The farther south they drove, the more limiting and repressive the rules became.

Carl's father knew it was wise to have this conversation with his children because they had grown up in Detroit. They were unfamiliar with the unwritten, often capricious, area-specific restrictions in the southern states and the possibly life-threatening reactions to violating them. This is one of the reasons it is impossible to fully understand the importance and meaning of *The Green Book* without grasping the true nature of the America that made it necessary.

Later in our journey, as Janée, Kemi, and I drove into Birmingham, Alabama, one of the legendary cities in the history of the civil rights movement, we saw not only the physical artifacts of segregation but heard from witnesses who had endured it. We reached the Historic 4th Avenue Business District with the last remaining part of the once-vibrant central business and cultural corridor of African American life during segregation and Jim Crow: approximately two blocks of mostly one-story brick buildings. One of the buildings now functions as a community cultural center, where we met with a group of people in their sixties and seventies who had been local foot soldiers during the civil rights movement and who remain politically active today: Hezekiah Jackson, Paulette Roby, and Tony Ramsey.

Jackson, now a minister, vividly remembered his family using *The Green Book*:

My father and my grandfather swore by *The Green Book*. My mother had a brother who left Alabama when he was very young and moved to New York. He did like a lot of Black people did during the fifties and sixties: they left the South because they were fleeing segregation, oppression, the whole nine yards. . . . Every year after Christmas Day, my mother would bundle all of us up and we would hit the road for New York to see our uncle Jerome. Daddy would always say, "*The Green Book* is good because we are always going to have to run from the white folk." So, Daddy had his *Green Book* and his little pocket Bible. We kids didn't understand until years later that it was because of segregation and because of fear that *The Green Book* existed.

During the era of Jim Crow, millions of people in the United States, either actively or passively, not only indulged in bigoted and discriminatory behaviors and attitudes, they remained silent when they saw them happening. Politicians and community leaders wrote anti-Black policies into the laws and enforced them with sometimes severe penalties by local, state, and national government agencies wielding the full power of American society, up to and including the death penalty.

The name "Jim Crow" was the colloquial term for a group of

primarily southern, segregationist, anti-Black laws and practices, although segregation practices were found across the US. The name came from a fictional character created by a white minstrel singer named Thomas Dartmouth "Daddy" Rice in the 1830s. Caricaturing a stupid, clumsy enslaved man, Rice would wear blackface makeup and sing a song with the refrain, "Weel about and turn about and do jis so, eb'ry time I weel about I jump Jim Crow." The popularity of Rice's act in the United States and Britain led to "Jim Crow" becoming a popular derisive term for Black people, and then the name of the system by which, for generations, African Americans were controlled and denied participation in the freedoms written into the US Constitution.

Under Jim Crow, Black Codes harshly restricted what people of color could do. In much of the country, Black people were prevented from voting, serving on juries, running for office, or defending their rights in court. They worked under systems of labor like sharecropping that were designed to keep them in poverty. Sharecropping was a farming practice in which someone, usually a white person, owned the land, while a tenant farmer, usually a Black person or family, worked the land for a share of the crop. During the planting and growing season, the tenant farmer would pay for seeds, tools, food, and rent using a charge account with the landlord farmer. Once the crop was harvested and sold, the tenant farmer would receive a small percentage of the sale price, minus the expenses accrued in the charge account. Some tenant farmers made a small profit or broke even. However, many did not make enough to pay off the charge account in full and therefore remained in debt to the landlord farmer year after year. When a sharecropper or any other Black person managed to amass a bit of money or property, unscrupulous white people supported by government officials would often seize it.

When Black communities became successful and financially independent through hard work and entrepreneurial zeal, gangs of resentful whites violently attacked and destroyed them. The attacks were usually explained away by unfounded, racist rumors about a crime supposedly committed by a Black person. Perhaps the most notorious example was the 1921 Tulsa Massacre. (For many years, the event was deliberately and misleadingly referred to in the media, especially print media, as the Tulsa Race Riot.) On June 1, 1921, rampaging white mobs—many of them armed and deputized by the Tulsa police—destroyed thirty-five blocks of businesses and homes in the prosperous Greenwood District, then widely known as the "Negro Wall Street," after a black shoeshiner named Dick Rowland was accused of assaulting a young white woman named Sarah Page. Hundreds of Black people were killed, ten thousand were left homeless, and the property damage—for which no compensation has ever been paid—amounted to more than $30 million in today's money.

The Tulsa Massacre was not an isolated event. There were many similar attacks, generally ignored or hidden by the local press and government. Few people today talk about the Red Summer, the name given by James Weldon Johnson to the 1919 wave of anti-Black terrorism (lynchings, draggings, drownings, shootings, and beatings) and riots that occurred in more than thirty-six cities across the US—including New York, Philadelphia, Baltimore, Knoxville, Montgomery, Chicago, New Orleans, Omaha, and Washington, DC. Many times, the incidents were not spoken of even by the Black people who survived the terror— the trauma and fear of a recurrence were too great. Other events have come to light, including massacres in Wilmington, North Carolina, in 1898; in Elaine, Arkansas, in 1919; and in Rosewood, Florida, in 1923.

In addition to these unpredictable but periodic waves of terrorism, Black people were victimized daily by homegrown, racist-motivated violence from individual white people and groups. Research by the Equal Justice Initiative in Montgomery, Alabama, estimates that, between

1877 and 1950, more than four thousand Black men, women, and children suffered "racial terror lynchings" in twelve southern states—more than the number of Americans who have been killed by Islamist terrorists, including on 9/11.[1] Janée and I walked in silence through the National Memorial for Peace and Justice in Montgomery (also known as the national lynching memorial). Reading the signs giving the reason a person or family was hanged or killed left us dumbstruck by how trivial the reasons frequently were, such as for chastising a young white boy for disrespect. The victim in that case was a Black woman.

Of course, the victims were many more than those who were actually killed. The purpose of racial terrorism was to instill fear in Black people throughout the community, warning them of the consequences should they offend social customs by daring to excel in business, challenge the authority of any white person, exercise the right to vote, or simply demand respect. The use of terrorism across the United States to enforce racial hierarchy is one of the most consistent and horrific aspects of America's Jim Crow era.

But the rules of Jim Crow went much further, as the Black Codes of Birmingham, Alabama, show. The central, ongoing exhibit at the Smithsonian Museum of African American History and Culture in Washington, DC, reproduces a selection of the racial rules imposed by various sections of Birmingham's General Code. The laws were passed from 1944 to 1951 and amended periodically to make them even more restrictive. Section 369 forbade the serving of food to white and "colored" customers in the same restaurant unless the two groups were "effectually separated by a *solid* partition extending from the floor upward to a distance of seven feet or higher." Section 859 prohibited mingling of Black and white people in any "room, hall, theatre, picture house, auditorium, yard, court, ballpark, public park, or other indoor or outdoor place"; and other sections extended the same rules to streetcars, jitneys, buses, and taxicabs. No possible opportunity for white and Black citizens to encounter one another was too trivial for the laws of Birmingham to forbid. Section 597 even made it a crime for Blacks and whites to play cards, dominoes, or checkers together.

Victor Green was definitely a diplomat when he compiled his guide. *The Green Book* did not refer to specific racist practices in the South or the North. In fact, the word "racism" doesn't appear in the guides at all. Sundown towns were never mentioned—not once. The language in the publication is filled with gentle euphemisms that would not offend white people. Green was aware that more explicit references would limit access to information from the government (for example, the article in the guide on train travel) and from corporations like Exxon. Within the Black community, many things were discussed one-on-one or in groups, but a great deal could not be put in print until years later.

I know this because I grew up in the world of segregation and Jim Crow. Over the years, I developed almost a second sense about the sometimes subtle signs of racist hostility. Janée, on the other hand, who is mixed race and a generation younger than me, was one of the few people of color in the Massachusetts town where she grew up. Her experiences certainly informed and motivated her social activism. As we discussed the subject, we decided that it was best not to look for trouble (something my parents said to me many times), but to be mindful of the situations in which we found ourselves, whether they were aggressive or passive-aggressive.

When I mentioned my concerns to a white neighbor before the trip, she said, with some pride, that her daughter didn't know anything about this aspect of US history "except what she had been taught in school." When I spoke to her daughter, now a young adult, she seemed to have a vague impression that the racial injustices of this period in American history had arisen more or less spontaneously as a natural outgrowth of racist attitudes and beliefs on the part of "a few white people back then."

OPPRESSION FROM THE TOP DOWN

The fact is that American schools do a bad job of teaching what every objective historian knows—that Black Codes and Jim Crow were deliberate and conscious creations of white leaders, in both the South and North and even in the White House. Woodrow Wilson, president from 1913 to 1921, was an avid segregationist and supported white supremacy. The goal of Jim Crow and segregation was to prevent Black people from experiencing the freedoms, privileges, and potential access to intellectual, political, and financial success and power that white people enjoy. Also, laws like those in Birmingham's General Code were designed to make sure no interracial friendships or romances arose. They kept the hierarchy of slavery in place, recast as master and servant, boss and employee.

Anti-Black codes arose as part of a backlash to the period of Reconstruction following the Civil War—a brief era that represents the only time in US history when national leaders made a concerted effort to introduce true racial equality into our political, social, and economic systems. Reconstruction formally started in 1865 with the military defeat of the Confederacy and the passage of the Thirteenth Amendment to the Constitution, which abolished slavery. It was extended by further actions on the part of the federal government, all driven by the Republican Party of Abraham Lincoln. (The Democratic Party, at that time, was largely sympathetic to the South and to the interests of former slaveholders.)

What's striking to me is how relatively quickly legislation followed, and how detailed it was. Considering how difficult it is to get any kind of law and act passed in Congress now, it took great vision and will to enact these comprehensive reforms. Congress passed two other import-ant amendments to the Constitution in the next years. The Fourteenth Amendment (1868) guaranteed the rights of citizenship to every per-son born in the United States—including former slaves. The Fifteenth Amendment (1870) protected the right to vote against discrimination on the basis of "race, color, or previous condition of servitude." That same amendment established a mechanism to enforce the law: the Freedmen's Bureau (1865–1872), intended to protect the legal rights of formerly enslaved people, to negotiate labor contracts for them, and to help them set up schools and churches. Equally important, the Enforcement Acts (1870–1871) were passed to protect Black citizens' rights to vote, serve on juries, and hold public offices. Congress put muscle behind the promises of these acts and amendments. The Reconstruction Act of 1867 divided the South into five military districts, and federal troops were deployed to enforce the legal protections for civil rights that the Republican Congress had passed.

The Civil Rights Act of 1875 marked the last major legal bulwark of Reconstruction. Passed by Congress in March of that year, the law affirmed the "equality of all men before the law" and made it a crime to practice racial discrimination in public places and facilities such as restaurants and public transportation. All lawsuits arising under the Civil Rights Act were to be tried in federal courts, rather than at the state level. Shockingly, the Supreme Court declared this Act unconstitutional in 1883. The US Congress did not pass another civil rights bill until 1957—almost seventy-five years later—even as anti-Black restrictions and discrimination became more harsh and violent across the United States.

Reading and writing about this history and all of the promise of equality it contained in the mid-nineteenth century makes the current twenty-first century state-level voter suppression and disenfranchisement efforts by right-wing Republicans seem not just atavistic but filled with the same mendacity and evil. Janée and I asked ourselves, Why are Black people in America still fighting these battles? Why was there so much resistance to the John R. Lewis Voting Rights Advancement Act of 2021? Do the politicians and citizens who support these suppression efforts want to take America back to a time of segregation, Jim Crow, and *The Green Book*?

The worry and fear we feel about the social road ahead today must be similar to the fear people felt on the roadways of America when Victor Green's guide was being published. The difference today is that as people become aware of this history, realize how little has really changed, and see the same practices continue in new, sometimes subtler ways, there arise stronger feelings of hurt, frustration, and defiant anger. The pattern of the ongoing, deliberate betrayal of the rights of Black Americans, as well as other people of color, is undeniable. Back during the Reconstruction era, all these efforts to throw off the legacy of slavery and racism had significant impacts, especially in the South. Hundreds of thousands of formerly enslaved people enjoyed the right to vote and represented an actual majority of voters in states like Mississippi and South Carolina. African Americans were elected to state legislatures and to the US Congress from states across the former Confederacy, and, during the 1870s, two Black politicians—Hiram Rhodes Revels and Blanche Bruce—represented Mississippi in the US Senate.

But even during the heyday of Reconstruction, whites in the South mounted fierce efforts to fight back. Gangs of angry whites killed scores of Blacks, robbed hundreds more, and terrorized thousands in cities like Memphis and New Orleans in 1866 and Wilmington, North Carolina, in 1898. The Ku Klux Klan was born in 1865 in Pulaski, Tennessee, launching a wave of terror attacks across the South and leading to murders of assertive Black leaders and countless Republicans, including Arkansas congressman James M. Hinds, the first member of Congress to be assassinated while in office. Hinds was shot in the back and died on the eve of the 1868 presidential election. The Klansman who murdered him was never brought to trial.

The first Grand Wizard of the Klan was Nathan Bedford Forrest, who had risen from the rank of private to become a general in the Confederate Army. He became notorious when soldiers under his command killed some three hundred Black soldiers who had reportedly surrendered after the Battle of Fort Pillow in Tennessee. In the decades after his death in 1877, numerous monuments to Forrest were erected throughout the South, many as part of an explicit campaign to assert continuing support for the doctrine of white supremacy that Forrest embraced and implemented with violence.

Over time, the commitment of white leaders in the North to enforcing the principles of Reconstruction and protecting the rights of Blacks weakened. In 1874, the Democratic Party, which strongly opposed Reconstruction, regained control of the House of Representatives. And in 1876, a contested presidential election offered an opportunity for the Democrats to negotiate a bargain. There was no clear winner on election day. The results were too close. In Florida, Louisiana, and South Carolina, accusations of voter fraud, intimidation, and violence in certain districts resulted in votes being declared invalid and thrown out by the Republican-controlled officials who determined the election results. Rutherford B. Hayes, a Republican, was declared the winner. As part of the bargain to resolve the contested presidential election, Republicans agreed to withdraw US troops from the three southern states where troops still remained. Even Ulysses S. Grant, the Republican president who had previously been a staunch supporter of Reconstruction, was heard informing members of his cabinet that giving formerly enslaved people the right to vote had been a mistake: "It [the Fifteenth

Amendment] had done the Negro no good, and had been a hindrance to the South, and by no means a political advantage to the North."[2] Reconstruction was effectively dead.

Whites in the South moved swiftly to reassert their racial supremacy. In 1883, the US Supreme Court declared the 1875 Civil Rights Act unconstitutional, opening the door to racial discrimination in countless forms, including both legal restrictions on Black rights and informal social codes used by whites to oppress and exploit Black people. This ruling was followed by the 1896 *Plessy v. Ferguson* case, in which the Supreme Court ruled that "separate but equal" accommodations for Black and white people—for example, in public schools and in public facilities like hotels, restaurants, and transportation—were constitutional. These rulings, which would be the law of the land until the 1960s, paved the way for the construction of the Jim Crow system. A display at the Smithsonian Museum of African American History and Culture in Washington, DC, shows some of the Jim Crow laws, formally known as Black Codes, state by state.

All of this information makes it clear why traveling, especially state to state, was highly risky for Black people. It also explains why the creation of publications like *The Green Book* was essential and inevitable. The safe harbors in its listings, first shared by word of mouth, were also places away from the suspicious, accusatory, racist white gaze.

One powerful element of Jim Crow was the use of criminal justice laws and systems to regulate and strictly limit the freedoms that Black Americans could enjoy. For example, in 1901, Virginia wrote a new constitution that changed the state's criminal justice system. It now classified many crimes committed mostly by poor people, such as "petit larceny," as felonies. It also made a provision that ex-felons would lose the right to vote forever. Furthermore, the suffrage article in the new constitution imposed a poll tax (from which white Civil War veterans

LOUISIANA

Every negro is required to be in the regular service of some white person, or former owner, who shall be held responsible for the conduct of said negro. But said employer or former owner may permit said negro to hire his own time by special permission in writing, which permission shall not extend over seven days at any one time.

MISSISSIPPI

If any freedman, free negro, or mulatto, convicted of any of the misdemeanors provided against in this act, shall fail or refuse for the space of five days, after conviction, to pay the fine and costs imposed, such person shall be hired out by the sheriff or other officer, at public outcry, to any white person who will pay said fine and all costs, and take said convict for the shortest time.

SOUTH CAROLINA

No person of color shall migrate into and reside in this state, unless, within twenty days after arrival within the same, he shall enter into a bond with two freeholders as sureties.

FLORIDA

When a person of color working on a farm or plantation deliberately disobeys orders, is impudent or disrespectful to his employer, refuses to do the work assigned, or leaves the premises, he can be arrested.

NORTH CAROLINA

No person of color can testify against a white person in court, unless the white person agrees to it.

TEXAS

Only white men can serve on juries, hold office, and vote in any state, county, or municipal election.

TENNESSEE

No colored persons have the right to vote, hold office or sit on juries in this state.

were exempt under what became known as the "grandfather clause"), created a literacy requirement (which local officials could enforce as they saw fit), and "required voters to answer any questions posed to them by an election official."[3]

Carter Glass was a delegate to the Virginia Constitutional Convention (1901–1902) and later became an important US senator, best known as one of the sponsors of the Glass-Steagall Act of 1933 (also known as the Banking Act of 1933). This act governed financial markets for decades, separating commercial banks from investment banks. It also established the Federal Deposit Insurance Corporation (FDIC), which insures customers' bank deposits up to set amounts. Glass was one of the leaders most actively involved in the transformation of the Virginia criminal code into a tool for controlling Black people. In a 1901 speech at the state's Constitutional Convention, Glass said: "Discrimination! Why that is precisely what we propose, that is exactly what this convention is for." He described its goal quite explicitly:

This plan will eliminate the darkey as a political factor in this state in less than five years, so that in no single county . . . will there be the least concern felt for the complete supremacy of the white race in the affairs of government. . . . The article of suffrage . . . does not necessarily deprive a single white man of the ballot, but will inevitably cut from the existing electorate four-fifths of the Negro voters.

The speech was met with an enthusiastic ovation from the white delegates to the convention. And Glass's prediction was quite accurate. Soon after the passage of the new constitution, the number of black voters in Virginia fell from around 147,000 to 22,000—an 85 percent drop.[4]

Virginia wasn't the only state with laws like this. One of the first states to pass a similar set of laws was New York. Today, laws in both North and South still prevent more than five million ex-felons from voting. Today, many states are enacting voter suppression laws that are a jaw-dropping echo of the past. These current laws, variations on old ones used during segregation that few people remember, are aimed not just at ex-felons but often at law-abiding citizens, especially people of color.

The draconian and illogical criminal codes passed in many states didn't merely prevent Black people from voting—though this was, of course, a crucial part of their value, since depriving Blacks of political power by denying them the ballot would help to make their oppression all but permanent. They also created a criminal justice system that could be used as a tool for controlling almost every aspect of the lives of Black people: whether and how they worked, where they lived, their ability to own property and accumulate money, their access to education, and much more.

Thus, laws were passed in several southern states that required Black people seeking work to present a "discharge paper" from their previous employer—in effect, preventing Blacks from choosing their own employers. Other states simply made it a crime for a Black person to change employers without permission. And Blacks who were outspoken, self-assertive, or otherwise offended the racist social code of the South could be arrested at any time on vague charges like "vagrancy," a newly invented offense tailor-made for arbitrary application by local government leaders and the sheriffs who served them.

Being stopped by police while driving made Black travelers subject to whatever "vagrancy" law the sheriff might choose to cite or make up in that moment. Diplomatically countering the accusation with the truth could be seen as "disrespect and vagrancy." Arbitrary stops could lead to fines for Black travelers, as well as jail time. Turning Black people into "criminals" was the cornerstone of the southern Black Codes that author Douglas A. Blackmon says practically reinstated "slavery by another name"—the title of his 2008 Pulitzer Prize–winning book.

In all these ways, Jim Crow was the American equivalent of South African apartheid and of the racial laws passed in Germany under the Nazi regime of the 1930s. And these similarities are not merely coincidental. Historians have uncovered growing evidence showing that racist parties around the world, including in Nazi Germany, were inspired and guided by the example of American Jim Crow.[5]

And while the scaffolding of laws, regulations, and unwritten social codes that constituted Jim Crow is no longer in effect, it's easy to see its legacy today—not just in the felon disenfranchisement laws but also in the capricious use of criminal justice power to terrorize and keep African American citizens "in their place." Every time a Black person in a car is arbitrarily pulled over by a police officer for minor infractions such as a broken taillight or an unfastened seat belt—or for no good reason at all; every time a Black person driving in a mainly white community is stopped and questioned by local law enforcement officers; and, most tragically, every time a Black person is killed by a racist or panicky officer during a supposedly routine traffic stop, we are seeing reenacted the legacy of the Jim Crow era and the long centuries of enslavement that laid its foundation. For instance, in 2016, Philando Castile was fatally shot by a police officer who fired seven rounds at close range after stopping Castile for having a broken taillight.

Remember this history when people who doubt the continuing impact of racism ask why civil rights advocates "keep dredging up this ancient history." The fact is that "ancient history" keeps coming back to bite us. That's because it is, in fact, recent history. For me and many Black people born in the US before 1970, we lived it. Many of the practices, events, and encounters detailed here occurred during our lifetimes; they happened to us. And as the phone and email records in the Ahmaud Arbery murder trial in 2021–2022 in Brunswick, Georgia, showed, the beliefs and attitudes that created and sustained Jim Crow remain brutally, remorselessly, and unapologetically alive in many individuals and communities in the United States today.

In 2018, I gave a presentation about *The Green Book* and afterward received an email from a man named William Fonvielle, who had been in the audience. Mr. Fonvielle directed me to the story of his grandfather, William Frank Fonvielle, as recounted by the historian Glenda Elizabeth Gilmore.[6]

In 1893 Fonvielle took a road trip through the South "to report back to his classmates [at Livingstone College in North Carolina] on racial progress and oppression." The Jim Crow regime was new, and by the time Fonvielle got to Spartanburg, South Carolina, his "new education in white supremacy began." When he saw signs that read "This room is for colored people" and "This room is for white people," he wrote that "the whole thing burst upon me at once, and [he] interpreted it to mean: The Negroes *must* stay in here and *not* in the other room, and the 'superior' civilization goes where it pleases."

In Atlanta, which Fonvielle found "chained down with prejudice," he encountered for the first time street cars where Blacks had to ride in the back. Later, he had to travel on the "Jim Crow car" of a train, where Black passengers, who paid the same fare as whites, "sat amid smoke and coal dust, packed in with luggage" while whites sat "on cushioned seats."

Fonvielle believed the "ridiculous restrictions would be temporary," but Gilmore reports that "ten years later, by 1903, the conditions that Fonvielle had observed as curiosities would be institutionalized by law throughout the South, even in his own beloved North Carolina."

ACTS OF RESISTANCE, TOOLS FOR SURVIVAL

Victor Green created *The Green Book* in response to this deliberately repressive, dangerous period in US history. The guides were both acts of resistance and tools for survival. In the words of professor Eva Baham of Dillard University:

> *The Negro Motorist Green Book* is an act of resistance, taking the bull by the horns. This was not the only one; it was one of many, many acts of resistance. That's what's important about teaching and sharing information on *The Green Book*, because it is an act of resistance, and acts of resistance imply that these are people who did not take their condition lying down. In *The Green Book*, we can see what African Americans did for themselves.

The conversation that Carl Williams's father had with his children during their annual drives south starting in the late 1950s was a similar survival tool—in this case, imparted by word of mouth, generation to generation. I also remember similar talks. My mother and grandmother would tell my six siblings and me how to protect ourselves by avoiding situations that might incite physical violence. They told us firmly and repeatedly to ignore mean and nasty words that might be said to us. I don't ever recall my parents or grandmother using the word "racist." Instead, the sentence I remember hearing most in response to a degrading, mean, or racist situation is "You know how they are." Indeed, we did.

There is little doubt that the history of Jim Crow and its associated threats quietly casts shadows over the minds, emotions, and intuitions of many African Americans when we get in our cars to take a trip today. It's not just that Jim Crow concepts sometimes echo in the actions and words of white people in the places where Black people live and drive.

A Black man drinking at a "colored" public fountain in
a streetcar terminal in Oklahoma City in July 1939.

It's that the practices at the heart of white supremacy seem never to fully go away. Many—too many—of them have simply morphed into more subtle, insidious forms that are often unseen entirely or denied when they are seen.

After watching the 2020 PBS documentary *Driving While Black: Race, Space and Mobility in America*, which featured *The Negro Motorist Green Book*, a white friend wrote to me: "So much unusual information in [the documentary] that I didn't know (Victor Green's partnership with Esso being only one morsel) and, of course, the belated realization that my experience of the country—traveling by car as a boy with my parents and as a teenage hitchhiker—was so different than a large minority of the population because I was free of certain fears and indignities."

I think there were only a few times during my trip with Janée when we felt we did not have to be vigilant, that we had the degree of freedom that my white friend has always taken for granted.

When Janée and I arrived in Cincinnati, Ohio, we drove to the National Underground Railroad Freedom Center, a modern building that sits on the banks of the Ohio River, right across the state line from Kentucky. The center is in the North, but in full view from its plaza is the South. Crossing the Ohio River is the only way to get from one to the other. We were both flooded with thoughts about the people who traveled to freedom along the Underground Railroad and those who came north during the Great Migration. When we walked into the lobby, large portraits of legends in the fight against racial hatred and injustice, in the fight for equality, hung on the wall, including one of the late Elie Wiesel, Holocaust survivor, author, Nobel laureate, and political activist.

In a typical corporate-style conference room with no windows we met Joyce Coleman, now in her seventies, and her lifelong friend Carl Westmoreland, who is in his eighties. Both are longtime residents and activists in Cincinnati. Like many Black people who live in the North today, Coleman has southern roots and was part of the Great Migration. Cincinnati was an exception to the pattern of having a single dominant African American district in a city, which is why we chose to visit it. Instead, African American neighborhoods were scattered around Cincinnati. Coleman explained why:

In the South, we all had to live together. I was born in the South, so this I know. We all lived in one particular area; but once we got north of the Mason-Dixon Line, we kind of spread out a little bit, and we lived wherever we could. Many people came [north] to be domestic workers. Many came to be automobile workers. So, they worked in places where they could get employment, and they lived near those places.

Coleman went on to explain that Cincinnati also had areas where Black people were threatened:

In Cincinnati, there were places that were, as I'll call it, "rough," as Alabama. There was a section of Cincinnati called Norwood that had the General Motors plant. Norwood was a sundown town. You dared not let the sun go down and catch you in Norwood. Reading, Ohio, was a sundown town. And Sharonville, Ohio, was a sundown town. And yet they were only a mile and a half or two miles east of Lincoln Heights.

Lincoln Heights was incorporated in 1947 as the first self-governing Black-majority community in the North.[7] To this day, its population is overwhelmingly Black.

This reminded me of what Jamon Jordan had told us back in Detroit. He explained the sundown practice in that city, beginning as early as the 1920s, and how, as more Black migrants came to the city, more white areas made themselves de facto sundown neighborhoods.

In Detroit, the neighborhoods are segregated. You cannot live in certain areas. You cannot be in certain areas after dark. [In the past, these would have been] known as sundown neighborhoods. Detroit has sundown neighborhoods, and it's surrounded by sundown towns where Black people have to be out of there by sundown.

What were some sundown neighborhoods in Detroit? The Cass Corridor neighborhood was the most notorious sundown neighborhood in the 1920s and 1930s. African Americans in Black Bottom referred to the Cass Corridor as "Cass-tucky." As African Americans were coming from down South to get jobs at the factories, particularly at the Ford Plant, so were poor, working-class, southern whites coming to get those good jobs as well. The whites settled in a southwestern part of the city, on the west side of Woodward. That is the Cass Corridor neighborhood. African Americans knew to stay out of that area, particularly after dark. Another sundown neighborhood in Detroit was on the far east side—the area that's close to the borderline of Grosse Pointe, which was totally a sundown town.

Jordan pointed out that when Janée, Kemi, and I had driven into downtown Detroit from the airport, we had gone through an area that had been one of the city's many sundown neighborhoods. "Even when I was growing up in the 1950s," he told us, "it was a known fact that you didn't drive through Dearborn, not even in the daytime. There was always the possibility of getting harassed by the police—or something worse."

NOT NEXT DOOR TO ME: WHITE FRIGHT

Did most whites in the North actively participate in or passively support the backlash to the Great Migration? Unfortunately, the answer is yes. The evidence can be seen in an endless stream of small, symbolic acts and in sweeping, society-wide behaviors during and after the Great Migration. For one thing, there is the much-analyzed phenomenon of "white flight," in which white families abandoned once-thriving neighborhoods because of fears of incoming Black neighbors, a practice exacerbated by real estate brokers spreading misinformation and fear in the wake of desegregation.

From the 1930s through the 1960s, Black people, especially those recently arrived in the North, were largely excluded from renting in "nice," lower-cost neighborhoods or from getting home mortgages. Local banks and the Federal Housing Administration (FHA) drew red lines around Black neighborhoods, rating them D-level areas, thus making them ineligible for government-backed mortgage loans. As a result of this practice, called "redlining," most Black people couldn't buy homes, even when they had good jobs with steady paychecks. Predatory lenders often offered the only source of funds. For example, some Blacks had so-called sign-on-contract deals that charged them two or three times what the house was really worth. And since the lender kept the deed until the house was completely paid for, the family could be evicted if they missed a single payment, with no recourse to the equity that the property may have accumulated. This system made a number of white on-contract lenders wealthy. At the same time, it helped turn many Black neighborhoods into slums.[8]

Restrictive covenants in property deeds also represented a backlash to the increase in financial resources that the Great Migration brought to many Black people's lives. These clauses forbade selling, leasing, or renting real estate to Black people. In fact, they imposed legal barriers to allowing Black people to occupy any part of a residence in a white neighborhood, with just one exception—live-in servants working for white employers. Such covenants began to appear in deeds in the North in the early years of the twentieth century and were used until the 1960s.

Restrictive covenants were not some sort of aberration only used by an occasional bigot. They were much more the norm than the exception. In fact, from 1924 to 1950, the National Association of Real Estate Boards warned realtors that selling or renting to a Black person should be considered a violation in its published Code of Ethics: "A Realtor should never be instrumental in introducing into a neighborhood ... any race or nationality, or any individuals whose presence will clearly be detrimental to property values."[9]

The federal civil rights statutes of the 1960s outlawed restrictive covenants. But many other real estate practices, like racial steering by agents, persisted. These exclusionary practices still exist today—sometimes more subtly, but not always. In 2019, *Newsday* published the results of a three-year investigation on Long Island into discrimination by real estate agents. The opening paragraphs are reminiscent of articles about real estate in any city in the US during the Great Migration:

> The three-year probe strongly indicates that house hunting in one of the nation's most segregated suburbs poses substantial risks of discrimination, with black buyers chancing disadvantages almost half the time they enlist brokers.
>
> Additionally, the investigation reveals that Long Island's dominant residential brokering firms help solidify racial separations. They frequently directed white customers toward areas with the highest white representations.[10]

For a Black person, being prosperous, accomplished, and nationally famous was no shield against such racial discrimination in real estate. When the great Brooklyn Dodgers baseball star Jackie Robinson sought to buy a house in Connecticut with his wife, Rachel, they were able to find a property in Stamford only after prominent white people interceded on their behalf. To fight back against and overcome such limitations, African Americans banded together to support one another and to share the services they needed in creative ways—such as *The Negro Motorist Green Book* and similar publications.

5

GETTING DOWN TO BUSINESS

GROWING WITH THE BLACK CUSTOMER

This story must be told. It must not be forgotten.

— Denise Gilmore, director of
cultural preservation for the city
of Birmingham, Alabama

Victor Green was not the only person to recognize the business potential in a travel guide for Black Americans. In fact, his *Green Book* was part of a little-known, scattered industry of Black-oriented travel guides that arose in response to the growth of the African American middle class and its desire to see the United States, comfortable and

The exterior of the famous Dooky Chase restaurant, a long-running Black-owned business in New Orleans.

safe in their Fords, Chevrolets, Chryslers, Buicks, Oldsmobiles, and Cadillacs. In 1933, an article on the need for a source of reliable guidance for Black travelers was printed in *Opportunity: Journal of Negro Life*, an academic journal published by the National Urban League. The author, Alfred E. Smith, described the troubles Black travelers had in finding lodgings and then observed:

> Obviously, the answer [to the problem of where to stay] lies in an authentic list of hotels, rooming houses, private homes catering to the occasional traveller, tourist camps, and every type of lodging whatsoever, including those run by members of other races and open to Negroes; and the availability of such a list to our growing army of motor-travellers. Such a list would[,] if complete, be invaluable (and I can hear your fervent amens) for I am convinced that within the area of every fifty square miles of the more frequently travelled sections there are lodgings to be found at all times. If we just knew where they were, what a world of new confidence would be ours.[1]

The pages of *The Green Book* illustrate this point. Many towns and cities had a very limited number of listings. For some destinations, *The Green Book* offered only "tourist homes"—private residences where travelers of color could rent rooms—a more random equivalent of today's Airbnb service. In Mobile, Alabama, for example, Dr. James Franklin, a wealthy black physician, opened his home to local visitors from the obscure to the renowned. His guest book, now part of the collection at the History Museum of Mobile, includes pages signed by guests like opera star Marian Anderson, baseball legend Jackie Robinson, and NAACP officials Walter White and Roy Wilkins. None was welcome at any of the city's fine hotels.[2]

Before guides like *The Green Book* were available, African Americans learned about places to stay, eat, and fuel their cars from family, friends, and other people in their communities or along their travel route. Assembling this information in a reliable, nationwide source, available at local newsstands and bookstores in Black communities as well as by mail, provided travelers with a frustration-reducing, potentially life-saving resource.

Of the other early guidebook creators, there were two business associates who assembled a forty-eight-page booklet called *Hackley & Harrison's Hotel and Apartment Guide for Colored Travelers*, published in 1930–1931 and claiming coverage of three hundred cities in the US and Canada. The "Harrison" of the title was Sadie Harrison, secretary of the Negro Welfare Council, while the "Hackley" was a lawyer and journalist named Edwin Henry Hackley, who evidently provided financing for the project.[3] Most of the entries were private rooms for rent rather than true hotels; other travel services, such as restaurants and gas stations, were not listed. *Hackley & Harrison's* ceased publication after just two years. We have no way to know whether Victor Green ever saw or heard of it.

In the 1940s, musician William "Billy" Butler launched an annual publication geared to the needs of touring performers under the title *Travelguide*, endorsed and supported in its distribution efforts by the African Methodist Episcopal (AME) Church. Other guides for Black travelers, with titles like *Smith's Tourist Guide*, *The Bronze American*, and *Grayson's Travel and Business Guide*, were also published; however, copies can no longer be found even in specialized library collections. Their existence is confirmed by ads their proprietors placed in Black newspapers and magazines.

In 1941, the US government even published a short-lived guide for African American travelers. Following the model of the Depression-era

Works Progress Administration (WPA), which had produced travel guides to various regions of the United States, the Department of the Interior published a small guide titled *Negro Hotels and Guest Houses*.

In 1952, the Nationwide Hotel Association (NHA), a DC-based organization of Black owners and managers in the hospitality industry, published *Go, Guide to Pleasant Motoring* as their official directory. Andrew F. Jackson, an attorney specializing in public relations who was affiliated with the NHA, oversaw its creation. The collection at Harlem's Schomburg Center contains issues of it through 1965. Although *Go* wasn't explicitly geared toward Black readers, it advertised in *Ebony* magazine, promoting itself as a listing of businesses with "owners and/or managers who agreed to accept as guests all well-behaved persons regardless of race, creed or color." *Go* was distributed in the South by Amoco service stations. All these guides offered competition to Victor Green's publication. But *The Green Book* became the most popular of the Black travel guides and survived the longest.

In its early years, *The Green Book* was evidently not a big money-maker. In 1940, Green reported his annual income as $2,100, which is supposed to have been about average for a letter carrier in those days.[4] Thus, whatever extra money Green was making as a publisher was not enough to produce much of a boost to his taxable income. It's also notable that Green maintained his job with the post office until 1952, when he retired at age sixty after thirty-nine years of service. For all those years, he had to compile and publish *The Green Book* as a part-time, second job, making it an even more impressive feat.

As a publisher, Green was ambitious and had a long-term vision. He quickly began to expand the coverage of *The Green Book*, both geographically and in terms of categories, adding hotels, motels, restaurants, nightclubs, beauty salons, tailors, dry cleaners, and other facilities offering services to Black travelers. The book also covered a growing list of

US destinations, many of which Green personally visited to check the accuracy of his listings.

Green also explored many opportunities to promote and market the guide. Within a year of its launch, he managed to secure an endorsement from the US Travel Bureau, a then-new department of the National Park Service created as part of the Roosevelt Administration's efforts to encourage tourism. Official recognition of this kind gave *The Green Book* a degree of credibility most other travel guides lacked, and Green proudly trumpeted such endorsements whenever he could get them.

A "SECRET ROAD MAP" AND MUCH MORE

Victor Green was ambitious when it came to his vision for *The Green Book*'s role in people's lives. In his guide, he often quoted, as a kind of motto, a famous line from Mark Twain's 1869 travel memoir *The Innocents Abroad*: "Travel is fatal to prejudice, bigotry, and narrow-mindedness." Green generally omitted the latter half of Twain's sentence: "and many of our people need it sorely on these accounts." That was a characteristic tonal choice on Green's part. He generally opted for diplomatic language when alluding to the abuse and oppression imposed upon Black people by whites, as when he referred to the "inconveniences" Black travelers experienced.

But it was also characteristic of Green to appropriate a line from Twain, perhaps America's most iconic writer, to describe the importance of the freedom to travel. For Victor Green, the ability of Black Americans to move freely around the country was not just a matter of simple justice. It was also a weapon to be used in the battle against bigotry. If white and Black Americans could meet one another face to face in neutral territory—the campground, the beach resort, the national park—perhaps they would learn to understand and to respect one another more.

Today, *The Green Book* has become a symbol for an era when Black Americans lived in a world apart, forced to use their own ingenuity and social capital to live the kinds of rich, adventurous lives that most white Americans took for granted and assumed that few Black people, other than performers and professionals, lived. In the words of filmmaker Yoruba Richen, who created the Emmy-nominated documentary *The Green Book: Guide to Freedom*, it's a reflection of community, "a kind of parallel universe that was created by the book and this kind of secret road map that the Green Book outlined."[5]

As the audience for *The Green Book* grew, so did the size and breadth of the book's coverage. The 1938 edition expanded from sixteen to twenty-two pages and included listings from twenty-one states (all of them east of the Mississippi River) as well as the District of Columbia and had a special section on "summer resorts." New York continued to enjoy an outsize share of the attention. However, alongside a thorough list of hotels, restaurants, beauty parlors, barber shops, and gas stations in New York, the guide included a special two-page spread listing "Points of Interest in New York City," beginning with the Empire State Building (then the tallest in the world) and continuing with Ellis Island ("the first landing place of the immigrant"), "The Theatrical District of New York" (with special mention of "The colored show houses . . . located in Harlem"), Chinatown ("which has been the place of countless murders caused by the rivalry of the Leong and Hip Sung Tongs"), the seaside resort of Coney Island, and a long list of famous museums. This feature, designed for visitors to the city, would continue to appear in *The Green Book* for years to come. Other cities, such as Chicago, Louisville, and San Francisco, were also highlighted. Green clearly wanted his readers to see that traveling to different cities and resorts in the US was not just informative, but also an opportunity to have enjoyable new experiences.

The 1939 edition made another big leap forward. *The Green Book* now grew to forty-eight pages and included listings from forty-four states, with only Nevada, New Hampshire, North Dakota, and Utah excluded. The price remained unchanged at 25 cents. Utah joined the fold for the 1940 edition, though with just a single listing—the "New Hotel J.H." in Salt Lake City, which claimed to be "the newest and best hotel West of Chicago and East of Los Angeles" and offered rooms for 50 and 75 cents per day.

In 1941, the first international listing appeared—a single tourist home, that of a Mrs. Horace Morse, located at 3164 St. Antoine Street in Montreal, Canada, tucked in as the final entry on the last page of the book. Perhaps this lone foreign offering was intended to complement a special article included earlier in the book—a two-and-a-half-page account by Baxter F. Jackson titled "A Canadian Trip." In it, Baxter described hiring a "chauffeur-guide" to lead a tour of the city of Quebec. He went on to report:

> Everywhere the people were most courteous to us. If we asked a question and we were not understood (which was seldom), they would not leave us until they definitely found out what was wanted. On one occasion I was taken a block out of the way by a young man to a police officer who then directed me where I wanted to go. When offered a reward for his kindness he refused and thanked me for asking him and went about his way,—it seemed as if he was doing his civic duty.

(The police officer did accept the gift of an American cigarette, however.) Given the history of relations between police and African

Americans in the United States, the note of wonderment and pleasure in Baxter's account of being treated respectfully by an officer of the law is understandable.

After the 1941 edition, World War II interrupted publication of *The Green Book*. Travel restrictions due to gasoline rationing and wartime demands for other necessities caused severe reductions in tourism for the duration of the fighting.

But it returned in 1946, and in the late 1940s and 1950s it swung into its heyday. Annual editions of the guide, still published in April or May, swelled to eighty pages or more, the price rose to 75 cents, and a variety of new features began popping up in its pages. Sales during this period have been estimated at fifteen thousand copies or more per year. Victor and Alma Green assembled a talented, all-female staff at the company's office at 200 West 135th Street in New York City to help with the editorial, administrative, and operational tasks involved in assembling, producing, and distributing the travel guide. Victor managed all this while continuing to hold down his day job with the US Postal Service.

However, it wasn't always easy for Green and his editorial team to find suitable businesses in every part of the United States. Take the 1948 edition as an example. It includes listings for forty-five states, the District of Columbia, and, rather remarkably, the territory of Alaska (a single hotel, the Savoy in Fairbanks). Well-traveled locations received very thorough coverage. The guide included hundreds of listings in states like California, New Jersey, and New York; and even a less-populous state like Arkansas boasted 125 restaurants, hotels, gas stations, and other businesses. But for some parts of the country, the numbers were much more scanty. In Nebraska, just forty-six businesses were listed; in Idaho, only six; in Maine, four; and in Montana, one lone business—under the category of "Tourist Homes," a Mrs. M. Stitt offered her residence at 204 South Park Avenue in Helena for Black travelers.

The small numbers of listings in some states wasn't due to Green's lack of effort as an editor. In that same 1948 edition, under the headline "Replies from our correspondents," Green printed excerpts from letters he'd received from his agents scattered throughout the country, explaining the difficulty in identifying businesses for inclusion in the book. One agent, writing from Gordon, Nebraska, reported: "No Negro families here—likely could stay at Cabin camps. Do not know attitude of hotels. Yellow Cabins—Gordon, Neb., would take Negroes."

Another agent, based in Devil's Lake, North Dakota, wrote, perhaps somewhat disingenuously: "We don't have any Negro families living in our city or community and consequently would have no occasion to offer housing, etc., to the Negro. I believe if Negro travelers were to pass through Devil's Lake, they would be treated as well as anyone else. The situation has never presented itself to this community to my knowledge, and therefore I am at a loss as to what they would encounter in this vicinity."

A third, in Shelby, Montana, commented: "A pretty reasonable attitude exists here, but we have had so few colored people in this area that I would hesitate to say to what extent many more would be at liberty to come and go without running into difficulty."

And a fourth, also in North Dakota, asserted that "hotel operators, barbers, and others contacted . . . were all eager to provide whatever services were required by Negroes visiting Dickinson." However, this correspondent also observed that "several places of business, while they are glad to provide for Negro customers, do not care to advertise for Negro trade."

From notes like these, it seems safe to conclude that most business owners in these remote Western towns were not exactly eager to attract Black customers, though they did not appear to be aggressively hostile.

SPECIAL FEATURES IN *THE GREEN BOOK*

Over the years, the contents and style of *The Green Book* varied as the publisher experimented with new topics that caught his fancy. The 1947 edition, for example, reprinted an article from the *New York Times* about the importance of higher education for Black Americans and praised a fund-raising drive then being spearheaded by the United Negro College Fund. This was followed by a list of "Negro Schools and Colleges in the United States" that Black travelers were urged to visit. "Take time out to read [about] or to see these great homes of learning," *The Green Book* said, "where the young folks of today and tomorrow are having their characters moulded. Plan for the future of your children so that in time to come they will face life with a fine equipment."

Note that this was the era when the G.I. Bill was providing billions of dollars in funding to help soldiers returned from World War II pursue their dreams of a college degree. Unfortunately, a disproportionate share of this funding was channeled to whites only, leaving just a tiny share for Black veterans. But *The Green Book* used this period as an opportunity to express Green's characteristic optimism about the opportunities for life improvement made possible through individual effort, despite the obstacles thrown up by society.

The 1947 edition also included a list of "Leading Negro Publications of the United States," ranging from the *Weekly Review* (published in Birmingham, Alabama) to *Color* magazine (Charleston, West Virginia).

In many years, *The Green Book* featured articles touting the latest innovations being offered by auto manufacturers, evidently based mainly on information provided by the car companies themselves. The 1947 edition, for instance, had four pages about cars from General Motors, seven pages on Ford cars, and a two-page story titled "Facts on Future Automotive Design." The 1948 edition included stories about the cars being turned out by the Keller and Tucker automobile companies, while the 1950 edition featured Studebaker. The back cover of the 1950 *Green Book* also advertised customizable calendars from Victor H. Green & Company, useful for "keeping the name of your business ever before the eyes of those you want to reach." The "Sepia Art Pin-Up Calendar" shown in the illustration featured photos of comely African American models in (rather modest) bathing attire, suggesting the timeless strategy being employed for attracting those (male) customers' eyes.

Green and his editorial staff continued to look for ways to expand the guide's offerings. In the late 1940s and into the 1950s, postwar America began an economic boom. Returning soldiers were finishing school or college, getting married, and starting families. They were getting jobs, buying cars, and filling their houses or apartments with the new consumer appliances that were now available. While African Americans didn't participate in this economic explosion as fully as whites, they got a share of the benefits—which included a growing ability to enjoy vacation travel and provide educational experiences for their children. To meet this expanding demand, beginning in 1949, Green and his team produced and marketed a kind of spin-off guide, *The Green Book Vacation Guide*, dedicated to listings of mountain and seaside resorts in the eastern states of New York, Pennsylvania, and New England.

This wasn't the only entrepreneurial opportunity that publisher Green sought to exploit through the reach afforded by his annual travel guide. In 1947, he launched a travel agency business catering to Black travelers that was advertised in *The Green Book* annually until 1957. The services offered were a natural extension of the benefits provided by *The Green Book*, and advertising for the agency continued the same theme of "travel without worry" emphasized throughout the guide as a whole. The 1949 edition, for example, included a display ad that said, "Going to take a trip, attend some convention—make sure of your accommodations before you leave.

HOUSING CONDITIONS MAKE THIS NECESSARY . . . We have contacts with all Hotels, Tourist Homes and Vacation Resorts. Send us a list of the cities that you expect to pass through, the dates wanted, how many in your party, and have us make your reservations."

More than one Black traveler had experienced being turned away by a hotel desk clerk or manager who hadn't realized that the nice person whose reservation he'd taken by phone was actually a "Negro." Anyone who had lived through that infuriating situation would find the promise of a courteous welcome and a ready room very appealing.

Carl Westmoreland shared a story about his father's traveling to Minneapolis in the mid–1940s where the hotel had "no record" of his reservation:

When I was young, I watched my father negotiate [his travels]. He had a *Green Book*, but he was also a Mason; he had contacts and he always understood where he was going. Professionally, Dad was a CPA and a municipal official. He went for a municipal finance officers' meeting [in Minneapolis] where he had hotel reservations and everything. When he got to the hotel where the conference was being held, they said he wasn't registered. He was the only Black person there. Dad was about six-three, six-four. He knew he was in a situation that was potentially explosive. He was able to reach the then mayor of Minneapolis Hubert Humphrey. [He would later be elected to the US Senate and serve as vice president from 1965 to 1969.] Humphrey told the registration clerk, "He is my guest. I'll take him home if necessary. He will be in this program." A room at the hotel was found.

Westmoreland continued, telling us that he had an experience "almost just like my dad's" but a mere twenty years ago, in the early 2000s. He was checking in at the Hotel del Coronado in San Diego where he was attending and speaking at a conference given by the National Trust for Historic Preservation. His name was on the banner for the conference. When he walked up to the registration desk and introduced himself, the clerk said, "We are not hiring today." Westmoreland was a bit amazed, so he pointed to his name on the banner. The clerk, now a bit flustered, said "I can't find your reservation." Westmoreland had to call the trust's chair in order to get a room. Imagine how this experience in San Diego, so parallel to his dad's in Minneapolis, must have flabbergasted and infuriated him so many years later.

1940S: BILLBOARD JACKSON AND ESSO SERVICE STATIONS

Beginning in 1940, Esso service stations, owned by the Standard Oil Company of New Jersey, became the only national chain of gas stations that carried *The Green Book*. At the time, Esso was also one of the few national companies that franchised gas stations to African American owners. In fact, the 1953 edition of *The Green Book* included a list of "some of the nearly Two Hundred Esso Stations operated by Negro managers and owners."

Esso earned a reputation for greater racial openness in other ways. For example, the presence of Black employees throughout the company ranks shows that Esso was, for its time, a relatively enlightened corporation. By the early 1940s, 312 of the 830 Esso dealers in the United States were Black, and Blacks worked in jobs as distributors, pipeline workers, and chemists for Esso.[6] In addition, many Black drivers found that Esso stations were more likely to allow them and their families to use the restrooms than other gas station chains (although not all local

Esso owners followed this practice, nor did the parent company require them to do so).

Esso's relatively enlightened racial policy may have been due in part to the influence of Laura Spelman Rockefeller, the wife of Standard Oil's cofounder John D. Rockefeller. Her parents had been noted abolitionists in Cleveland, Ohio, and she transmitted a belief in racial equality to her husband, which the family maintained. Rockefeller and his wife donated to the Atlanta Baptist Female Seminary in the late 1800s, which was renamed Spelman Seminary (now Spelman College) after Laura Spelman

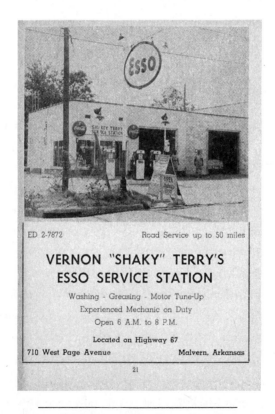

ED 2-7872   Road Service up to 50 miles

**VERNON "SHAKY" TERRY'S
ESSO SERVICE STATION**

Washing - Greasing - Motor Tune-Up
Experienced Mechanic on Duty
Open 6 A.M. to 8 P.M.

Located on Highway 67

710 West Page Avenue   Malvern, Arkansas

21

Interior page of the 1960 edition of *The Green Book*. Esso not only carried *The Green Book*, they encouraged Black ownership of their franchises.

Rockefeller. It remains one of America's most notable historically Black colleges. Furthermore, John D. Rockefeller II was essential in the founding in 1944 of the United Negro College Fund.

However, an even more powerful driving force behind Esso's racial policies was the efforts of James "Billboard" Jackson, a remarkable trailblazer in the world of Black American media and entertainment. Jackson's career included a stint, starting in 1920 in New York, as the first Black editor of the "Negro Department" of *Billboard*, the magazine of the entertainment business (hence his nickname). He used this position to promote Black singers, actors, and other performers during the Harlem Renaissance of the 1920s. In 1934, he was hired by Esso as its first African American marketing and public relations specialist, and he stayed with the firm for twenty-one years, promoting Black businesses around the country. He also became the first Black member of the American Marketing Association.

Jackson's importance in the Black business community was symbolized by the fact that Ellis Marsalis Sr. named his Esso station in New Orleans—Billboard Esso—after Billboard Jackson. It was advertised in several editions of *The Green Book*. Jackson had personally trained Marsalis in gas station management. The naming showed Marsalis's gratitude and acknowledged Jackson's widely known reputation for helping Black businesses. Marsalis went on to become a prominent businessman, political activist, and civil rights leader. His Marsalis Motel, a converted barn, attracted many famous visitors, from Ray Charles and Cab Calloway to Martin Luther King Jr. and Thurgood Marshall. Four of Marsalis's grandsons, who include Wynton Marsalis (trumpeter, composer, and recording artist) and Bradford Marsalis (saxophonist, bandleader, and composer), have gone on to become distinguished musical figures.

Today, Billboard Jackson's legacy is honored through the James "Billboard" Jackson Business Development Grants. They are awarded annually by Phi Beta Sigma, an historically Black fraternity founded at Howard University in 1914, and provide funds to support college and graduate students who are seeking to launch a business.

1950S: GOING INTERNATIONAL

As the decade of the 1950s unfolded, a burgeoning middle class enjoyed unprecedented purchasing power. In the quickly spreading suburbs, millions of families bought homes filled with newly affordable appliances—washers, dryers, refrigerators, freezers, record players, and television sets. People displayed their gleaming, chrome-accented cars in their driveways. And the spread of television facilitated an explosion in advertising. The 1950s was an era of advertising jingles, slogans, and brand names that were on everyone's lips—from Coke and Pepsi to Schlitz and Budweiser, Tide and Colgate to Westinghouse and GE.

The Green Book, however, reflected a distinctly African American attitude to this era: Black families worked twice or three times harder to carve out their share of the national prosperity, hampered by barriers and stumbling blocks that included discriminatory housing policies, inadequate educational systems, lack of access to proper health care, and widespread racial prejudice among employers. Still, there was optimism, in particular about achieving equality and total freedom as American citizens in the not-so-distant future.

As new modes of travel became popular, offering travelers more destinations, *The Green Book* kept African Americans informed. In 1949 international destinations in Bermuda and Mexico were added to the guide's coverage. Over the years, *The Green Book* listings expanded to include every state in the Unites States as well as Canada, Bermuda, the Caribbean, and parts of Europe.

In 1952, the official title of the guide was changed from *The Negro Motorist Green Book* to *The Negro Travelers' Green Book*. Perhaps in anticipation of this change, the guide began highlighting familiar and new modes of travel. The 1951 version of the guide was called the "Railroad Edition." Not only did it feature a sleek diesel-powered locomotive on the cover, but it opened with an illustrated six-page article touting the benefits of traveling by train: "Today, every train ticket includes unsurpassed comfort, safety, dependability and convenience.... Whether the trip be in a coach or a sleeping car, every effort has been made to assure a more pleasant journey." Incongruously, the photos accompanying the article depicted carefree travelers, all of them white, being attended by uniformed waiters and conductors, all Black. The Railroad Edition of *The Green Book* was evidently an experiment, and perhaps it fell flat, since it was never repeated. Certainly, the reality of railroad travel for an African American—relegated to the luggage-packed, smoke-filled uncomfortable "Jim Crow car" right behind the engine, as William Frank Fonvielle had reported two generations earlier—was totally different from that portrayed in the feature.

Similarly, the 1953 edition was dubbed the "Airline Edition," linking the book to the growing popularity and availability of air travel. It included articles about the history of major airlines and enthusiastically recommended flying as a new resource for Black travelers. But while air travel continued to be mentioned occasionally in later editions of *The Green Book*—and of course would have been the fastest, most modern way to travel to the newly featured international destinations in the Caribbean and in Europe—for the most part, the annual guides reverted to the traditional emphasis on auto travel as the most common way for Black Americans to go on vacation.

Sometime in the 1950s, Victor Green's active role as editor of the publication appears to have diminished. No one knows exactly why this happened, but some have speculated that health problems may have been involved. His wife, Alma, stepped into the editorial role, assuming the official title of editor for the 1959 edition. For the rest of *The Green Book*'s history, Alma edited, managed, and published the annual guide with the support of an all-female staff, including Novera C. Dashiell, the assistant editor who wrote many of the features in the book; Evelyn Woolfolk, who sold advertising space; and Dorothy Asch, a white woman who managed public relations. Thus, *The Green Book* became not just a racial standard bearer but also a landmark in the history of entrepreneurship among Black women.

The 1956 edition of *The Green Book* featured a twentieth-anniversary message by Dashiell that included this comment about Victor Green's approach to business:

> He regrets the shortsightedness of most of our businessmen to see the urgent need and value of advertising. "If Negro-owned business is good" he says, "it can be better with advertising." His philosophy is that we can create our OWN "name brands." We should have the patience to build. Build for ourselves and the future of our children. The Green Book is the symbol of one man's patience. Today, twenty years later, it is an established business.

On one level, this comment from Victor Green, as filtered through Dashiell's voice, is simply a publisher's lament over the difficulty of selling advertising space to Black business owners with scant funds to invest in marketing. But on a deeper level, it shows Green's wish to contribute to a rising tide of African American capitalism, in which more of the Black community's growing wealth would remain in Black hands, benefiting Black families and helping them build a better future.

Dashiell's 1956 anniversary message also included the observation,

"In looking ahead . . . a trip to the moon? Who knows? It may not be so improbable as it sounds. A New York scientist is already offering for sale pieces of real estate on the moon. When travel of this kind becomes available, you can be sure your Green Book will have the recommended listings!"

It's easy to catch the undercurrent of sadness beneath this playful remark. Dashiell assumed, perhaps without thinking about it very much, that if and when American adventurers landed on the moon, they would still be living in accordance with the discriminatory practices dictated by Jim Crow. (For the record, the twelve US astronauts who walked on the moon's surface between 1969 and 1972 were all white males. No African American traveled into space until Guion Bluford in August 1983.)

Another feature of the 1956 *Green Book* that reflects a bittersweet mood is the article about the Nationwide Hotel Association (NHA), the organization of Black hotel owners that published *Go, Guide to Pleasant Motoring*. The article in the *Green Book* quoted a speech made by the association's president, Dykes Brookins, beginning with the happy claim: "Today we are making rapid strides in the field of interracial relations. In almost every section of the country color barriers are being broken down." This might sound like unalloyed good news. But not necessarily for Black business owners. Brookins continued:

> Segregation created the need for the Negro businessman as we know him. Negroes in the past went into business to meet the needs of our people because other businessmen did not want our business. From the beginning we planned to serve only the Negro public; we had a monopoly. As a result the Negro Businessman is not prepared to enter the market serving all people. The NHA is aware of this problem and believes that the salvation of the Negro businessman and particularly in the hotel industry lies in raising

standards. I am convinced the Negro traveler would just as soon stop among his own if he could get—not comparable, but fair accommodations.

Brookins went on to describe plans for an annual Clean Up–Paint Up Month when NHA member hotels were urged to modernize and improve their properties. He concluded with a plea: "We want you to patronize those establishments who are members of the NHA, because in spite of all the problems and handicaps, standards are being raised, services are being improved, buildings are being modernized and well equipped motels are being built throughout the country where they are needed."

Brookins's speech presciently reflected some of the tough realities that changing legal and social norms brought. Of course, the breaking down of barriers that restricted the freedom of Black Americans was both urgently needed and desperately desired, a matter of simple fairness and humanity. But when those barriers were removed—or at least reduced in their power and impact, as began to happen when the civil rights movements of the 1950s and 1960s gained force—a new set of headaches was created for Black communities, by apparently reducing the need for the unique and separate networks of organizations and businesses that had been generated in response to segregation.

Once Jackie Robinson broke the color line in Major League Baseball in 1947, it was only a matter of time before the Negro Leagues would fold. (The Negro National League disbanded after 1948; the Negro American League, shrunken in status and audience, survived a while longer, then folded in the early 1960s.) It was a classic good news/bad news story. When Black baseball as an independent entity died, Black ballplayers were given spots on the rosters of almost every Major League team. But what about the Black team owners, managers, coaches, scouts, concessionaires, sports reporters, and countless others who had built livelihoods thanks to the existence of the Negro Leagues? The Major Leagues had no place for most of them.

Other independent, Black-focused businesses would soon face similar challenges as the products and services they offered gradually became available to all customers through mainstream white-owned businesses, seemingly making Black-owned equivalents superfluous. One of those businesses that would come to seem unnecessary was *The Green Book* itself.

1960S: PRIVILEGES

Victor Green always predicted that one day, *The Green Book* would no longer be necessary. As he put it, "There will be a day sometime in the near future when this guide will not have to be published. That is when we as a race will have equal opportunities and privileges in the United States."

This assertion was in the best American tradition—brave, optimistic, and perhaps a bit naive. How you define "the near future" is a bit subjective, of course. Remember that chattel slavery was a legal, economic, and cultural institution in the United States from 1619 to 1865, a matter of 246 years. In that context, a generation or so might not be regarded as a very long time. But for those individuals who had to put their dream of freedom and equality on hold, thirty years probably felt like much too long to wait. That's about how long it took from the publication of the first edition of *The Green Book* in 1936 until the passage of the Civil Rights Act of 1964, which for the first time mandated equality in the provision of public accommodations throughout the United States, regardless of race. Although the Civil Rights Act was a big step forward for the concept of equal rights under the law in the United States, it didn't eliminate the risks and inconveniences of traveling while Black—not by a long shot.

But before the United States could get to the point of passing and signing a federal law mandating equality and outlawing discrimination, a historic movement spearheaded by some of the country's most courageous leaders and involving hundreds of thousands of risk-taking activists, Black and white, would be necessary. And *The Green Book* reflected that movement while also playing a role in its success.

Victor H. Green died in 1960, but *The Green Book* survived for a time. In 1962, the business was purchased by Langley Waller, a Harlem businessman, and Melvin Tapley, a popular cartoonist for the *Amsterdam News*, New York City's leading African American newspaper. Green's widow, Alma, continued to serve as editor, while Tapley began contributing cartoons to the publication's pages—for example, creating a feature called "Green Book's History-Makers" that highlighted little-known African American heroes.

The Green Book's name changed over the years as its listings expanded and the markets covered changed. The 1963–1964 edition was called *The Traveler's Green Book: For Vacation Without Aggravation*. This edition included resorts and information about places in Mexico and the Caribbean. The 1963–1964 edition added European listings.

By the 1960s, the annual editions of *The Green Book* contained listings of more than three thousand establishments that welcomed Black travelers. Growing numbers of mainstream, white-owned hotels were included, reflecting the slow breakdown of the traditional restrictions imposed by Jim Crow and segregation. It has been estimated that the 1962 edition of *The Green Book* reached almost two million readers, though this might be an exaggeration since no business records have yet come to light.[7]

Some people whom Janée and I interviewed said they eventually began questioning their reliance on *The Green Book*—not only because more hotels, motels, restaurants, and other businesses were becoming open to Black customers, but also because the civil rights movement had championed and begun to spread a more assertive strategy for achieving equality. Rather than sticking with the safe path of patronizing the welcoming businesses featured in *The Green Book*, some Black Americans began to feel it was their duty to demand accommodation at whites-only businesses.

Some of these acts of self-assertion were personal, as Nelson Malden of the Malden Brothers Barbershop in Montgomery, Alabama, recounts when he and his wife went for an evening out at a formerly white-only venue:

Two or three nights later [after the Civil Rights Act of 1964 was passed], I went home and I said to my wife, "Let's go out to the Diplomat Inn and check out the Civil Rights Bill." She said, "Okay." So we get all dressed up and go to the Diplomat Inn, which was a restaurant, a cocktail lounge, and a hotel. So we went in the cocktail lounge and ordered a round of drinks. The [white] waitress was pretty nice. Five white boys came over [and sat at] the adjoining table. A little bit later, there was a live band playing. So one of the band members says, "Do we have anyone who wants to make a request?" And one of the white boys jumps up and says, "Play 'Dixie.'" And boy, the band cut loose on "Dixie." Soon it got a little bit rowdy and kind of loud. They [the five white guys] started calling people coons. We were the only Blacks in the cocktail lounge. So I told my wife, "I think we better leave," and she said, "I think so." So we got up to walk out and the band played "Bye Bye Blackbird."

Some of these acts of self-assertion were organized as part of the national civil rights movement itself. A well-known example are the sit-ins of the late 1950s and 1960s that targeted segregated restaurants: Black protestors, often students, would occupy seats at "White Only" lunch counters or diners and refuse to vacate them until forcibly ejected by local police.

Less famous were the so-called wade-ins, which aimed at pressuring public beaches to stop discriminating against African Americans. Inspired by a series of wade-ins begun at Lido Beach in Florida in 1955, Gilbert Mason Sr. led a group of protestors into the waters of the Gulf of Mexico at a public beach in Biloxi, Mississippi, in May 1959. Mason was arrested, but he returned repeatedly, gradually assembling a larger and larger group of supporters. In 1960 Mason's group of about one hundred men, women, and children were attacked with clubs, fists, chains, and even guns. The wade-ins eventually precipitated a lengthy court battle, which finally ended in 1968 when a court ruled that segregated public beaches were not permissible.

In other cases, Blacks began asserting their rights to public accommodations not as part of an organized strategy but through simple individual acts of defiance and rebellion. Jesse Turner Jr., retired president of Tri-State Bank of Memphis, told Janée and me about how he engaged in one such act as a teenaged traveler:

As teenagers in 1966, 1967, and 1968, we used to drive to visit our grandmother in West Point, Mississippi. And our parents trained us to get out of the car at a gas station and, before buying gas, ask the attendant, "Where's the restroom?" And if he said, "We don't have one," we'd say "Okay, we'll get our gas down the street." Because we knew the attendant didn't work there all day without a restroom. If they wouldn't let us use the restroom, we weren't going to spend our gas money there. So we'd head to the next gas station. And when we got there, they better not have two restrooms with "White" and "Colored" signs on them!

I asked Turner, "If they did have separate restrooms, what would you do then?"

He replied, "We'd probably just go to the white one. It's hard to grow up with parents like mine and not have a certain rebellious streak in you!"

Another of our interviewees, Kathryne Gardette of Cincinnati, spoke about how her uncle Walt had literally "stood up" for human rights by deliberately standing on the corner in sundown towns like nearby Norwood:

Many times he would go to the other side of the railroad track into Norwood or St. Bernard's, knowing that a policeman would come along and put him in handcuffs because Black people were not supposed to be in that location after dark. Uncle Walt was arrested many times and even put into prison. But he felt it was well worth it. Later, when he was an elder, if he saw a drug dealer, he would go up to them, very upset, and say, "I didn't stand on the street corner so you could sell drugs here. It was so you could be respected as a man as you walk through town after dark."

"Giving back in services has always been important in my family," Gardette said. "For my Uncle Walt, one of his ways of giving back was standing on the corner."

The passage of the 1964 Civil Rights Act, along with other early successes of the civil rights movement of the 1960s, was mirrored in the pages of *The Green Book*. A two-page article headed "Civil Rights:

Facts vs. Fiction" in the 1966–1967 International Edition included the quietly triumphant sentence, "The Civil Rights Act of 1964 is a new bill of rights for everyone, regardless of race, creed or color." The editors then acknowledged the powerful impact of organizations like the NAACP, the National Urban League, the Congress of Racial Equality (CORE), the Student Nonviolent Coordinating Committee (SNCC), the Southern Christian Leadership Conference (SCLC), and others dedicated to the battle for civil rights. "In fact," *The Green Book* noted, "the militancy of these civil right[s] groups exhibited in sit-ins, kneel-ins, freedom rides, other demonstration[s] and court battles has widened the areas of public accommodations accessible to all."

But people of color—including the publishers of *The Green Book*— were well aware that the mere passage of a law didn't mean that segregation and discrimination were things of the past. So they presented the then-current status of legal protections for Black Americans in a series of state-by-state listings. For example, the listing for California states, "Anti-jimcro law in recreational facilities. Violators are subject to civil suits for damages plus $250." (The fanciful alternative spelling of "Jim Crow" was used by some other publications of the era, not just *The Green Book*.) For many states, including Iowa, Kansas, Maine, and Nebraska, the guide noted that violators of antidiscrimination laws were "subject to criminal punishment (court proceedings)," which meant that practical steps to enforce the laws would depend on the commitment and aggressiveness of local prosecutors. In other states, protections for Black travelers were scanty. The entries for Montana and New Mexico simply read, "No specific sanctions," while the entry for Virginia noted, "Prohibition of advertisements discriminating because of religion," with no mention of color. For Alabama, Georgia, Mississippi, and sixteen other states, there were no entries at all.

In this way, the publishers of *The Green Book* quietly made the point that their publication was still relevant and necessary, even after the historic signing of the 1964 act by President Lyndon Johnson on July 2 of that year in the presence of Dr. Martin Luther King Jr.

The final edition of *The Green Book* was published in 1966–1967. Titled *The Travelers' Green Book: 1966–67 International Edition: For Vacation Without Aggravation*, its cover featured a cartoon drawing of a light-skinned woman skiing—a curious reflection of the way the world Victor Green had known was changing. Its pages were filled with the traditional listings of Black-owned establishments, many of them modest in size, that had always welcomed African American travelers. But those entries jostled others that revealed how the white business establishment had decided that the color they cared most about was green—and that the dollars Black customers had to spend were just as green as those their white clientele carried. So the New York hotel pages included not just the Hotel Theresa in Harlem but such mainstream midtown landmarks as the Algonquin, the Mayflower, the New York Hilton, the Plaza, and the Waldorf Astoria.

As the uniqueness of *The Green Book* faded, so did the demand for its guidance. There would never be a 1968 edition. Lonnie Bunch, historian and the fourteenth secretary of the Smithsonian Institution, told a *New York Times* reporter that many African American families today still have copies of *The Green Book*—not on their bookshelves or desks, but tucked away in boxes somewhere. "As segregation ended, people put such things away," he said. "They felt they didn't need them anymore. It [the end of segregation] brought a sense of psychological liberation."[8]

But did "psychological liberation" mean that, in Victor Green's words, "we as a race will have equal opportunities and privileges in the United States"? This has not proved to be true because passing a law or series of laws, as African Americans saw after Reconstruction and have seen again since 1964, is no guarantee that people's beliefs or behavior will change—the next day, the next year, or even sixty years later.

— 6 —

THE MAGIC HOUR

PACKING UP AND THE PROTECTIVE DANCE

These traveling habits are taught generationally out
of the need for safety.

— Dr. Noelle Trent, director of
education at the National Civil Rights
Museum, Memphis, Tennessee

Lonnie Bunch's phrase "psychological liberation" was in my thoughts and Janée's too from the start of our trip to the end. During the drive we discussed whether it were possible to liberate ourselves as African Americans from the history we had learned about segregation, the reason underlying *The Green Book*'s creation, and Jim Crow laws, especially as we drove deeper into the South. For people who had experienced the

---

Interior page of the 1949 vacation
edition of *The Green Book*.

restrictions and been subject to unnerving incidents during this time in US history, some effects would most certainly remain. For instance, throughout the trip, we talked about strictly obeying speed limits so that we would not attract any attention.

After leaving the Underground Railroad Freedom Center in Cincinnati, we crossed the Ohio River—often referred to as the Jordan River in spirituals about escaping to the North to be free—and we were in the South. During each interview, the individuals would say a phrase, recall an observation, or share a family story related to living Black in America then and now. For example, when we left Nashville, we talked and smiled about how Willie Nettles did not trust atlases because he felt that white people wrote them for white people and so there was nothing he could learn from them. When we left Birmingham for Montgomery, we talked about Hezekiah Jackson's father telling him that "we would always have to run from white people." And on the final day of our interview in New Orleans, Jan Miles, author of *The Post-Racial Negro Green Book*, which lists acts of racist incidences rather than lists of hotels and restaurants (see Chapter 11), when asked when she expected a decline in such incidents, especially on the road, said, "Not in my lifetime. If I had a child, probably not in that person's lifetime either."

We also considered the impact that a family's or community's negative experiences on their local streets or on the highways during the time of *The Green Book*'s publication would have had on how Black people prepared for a road trip when many of the country's institutions, businesses, and citizens were not "asking you to call" (to borrow the lyrics from "See the USA in Your Chevrolet," an old Chevrolet commercial jingle). You know in advance that you'll have limited access to basic services and comforts like clean bathrooms, restaurants, motels, and even a drink of water because of prevailing laws and social practices. But there's also the unknown—the potential for a seemingly harmless encounter, like stopping to buy gas, asking for directions, or looking at a white person "the wrong way," to become more than aggravating. It could become hostile, threatening, violent, or even fatal.

Mervin Aubespin, retired associate editor of the *Courier-Journal* in Louisville, Kentucky, described the psychological shadow this awareness cast over travelers:

> Sometimes the idea that it could happen and the knowledge that it has happened to others made you feel awful. You were so tired when you got to the end of your trip, if you are driving, from watching to see if the car that pulled behind you was a sheriff's car or somebody who was just going to irritate you. Or you're driving along the highway not bothering a soul and somebody passes by and waves that pistol. That's not good at all. So when you got to where you were going, you were tired and you needed rest. Then you had to think about going back through it [on the way back]. It was not nice.

This was true for African Americans driving south, north, west, and east in the United States throughout the time *The Green Book* was published—and for years, even decades, afterward.

Under conditions like these, planning a trip was a quietly pressure-filled exercise in three ways: what to do physically; what to do psychologically; and what to do to help others, especially children. If people were traveling with children—their own or a relative's—there was the added pressure of protecting their innocence from the puzzling, demeaning, threatening, even shocking behavior of some white human beings toward Black human beings who happened to be the child's beloved parents or relatives. Nonetheless, African Americans certainly hoped to experience enjoyment and have some fun too during a road trip, but more mental and emotional energy would be quietly focused on survival. Comments from people I interviewed for the BBC Radio 4 program *The Green Book* convey this:

- It was difficult.
- Most Black families traveled safe routes.
- And you were very cautious, cautious about where you stopped, when [you traveled], and how you presented yourself.
- You traveled during the day.
- You tried to get to where you were going before nightfall. Because the least little thing could trigger violence.

Along with some service stations not selling gasoline to Black motorists, sometimes station attendants would refuse to touch a Black person's car to either put gas in it or repair it. Most travelers therefore carried an extra container of gas to help make the trip without having to stop. Travelers knew such things from experiences that other travelers shared with them. Frequently, when African Americans were planning a trip, they would talk to someone who had recently completed the same route to get updated information. Word of mouth helped travelers stay up to date about no-go places.

Many of the people Janée and I talked with told us about service stations that accepted Black customers but would put gas in a Black person's car only after all the white people in line had been serviced first. This was frequently a practice at gas stations in the South that begrudgingly allowed Black travelers to buy fuel. This practice was a not-so-subtle reminder of the hierarchy of white supremacy: white people first, Black people last. In the worst case, several people told us indignantly, if a Black family became frustrated and tried to drive away, the station owner might pull out a gun and threaten to shoot the car or the people in it if they left before he told them they could. The family would be forced to sit and wait until the station owner was ready to provide them with service—often accompanied by some "accidental" damage to the finish of the automobile.

The risk of being intimidated and threatened just for trying to buy gas was nothing compared with the risk of trying to use a bathroom. Virtually every person we interviewed had a story—most horrifying, but a few that were funny. The Reverend Doctor Henry Steele, who is nearly eighty years old and the activist son of the civil rights campaigner C. K. Steele, recalled his experience at a southern service station in the 1960s:

I stopped in Butler, Georgia. I wanted to use the restroom while they were servicing the car. The [white] guy said they were out of order. There was a Black guy working under the hood and when the white guy turned his back, he said, "Nothing's wrong with those restrooms. They just don't want you all to use them."

So I went back to the [white] guy and said, "Are all of the restrooms out of order?" He said, "Yeah, they are." I said, "Would you show me?" Then this other [white] person who was getting his car serviced intervened, and walked up and slapped me in the face, saying "We don't like your kind around here." He had a son, about fourteen years old, who ran to the car, got a gun, and put it in my face. And I slapped him.

Reverend Steele acknowledges that he survived by pure luck what could easily have become a deadly confrontation.

When a service station had "Colored Only" bathrooms, they were typically repulsively filthy and pungent, so much so that stopping beside the road and "going in the woods or bushes" was often a better option, despite the snakes, ticks, spiders, and other creepy-crawly vermin. And that's exactly what many people, including my own family, did.

Families created strategies to reduce the need to stop, such as controlling the amount of water or soda that children drank. If a family had to stop, some would carry sheets to hold up or to tie to small trees so that women could have some privacy. This was preferable to using the outhouses often located a short walk from rest areas. These usually "stank to high heaven," to quote one of my great-uncles. Vernetta Sheppard-Pinson remembered the "open, dirt toilets" that were their only options at some rest areas for Black travelers: "There was like a hole in the ground. You would squat over them. And they smelled from here to heaven. I was afraid my kids were going to fall into that. We had to use what we could, but we survived." One of Sheppard-Pinson's sons remembered that his mother was honest and open with him and his brothers about why these deplorable conditions existed.

In other situations, some parents cleverly turned the experiences into teachable moments for their children. Jesse Turner Jr. recalled his family's trip to visit his grandparents in the Deep South. His father employed a strategy that incorporated an important lesson about how to use their hard-earned money:

My mother's parents lived in New Roads, Louisiana, down highway 61, which is still there. My father's parents lived in West Point, Mississippi, over near the Alabama line. So our trips were primarily going to them. One of the things I remember vividly, especially on the trip to New Roads, which took about eight or ten hours, was where would we stop for gas? Almost every place had colored or white restrooms. But my father found a service station in Vicksburg, which was about halfway, that didn't have separate restrooms, though the station was white-owned. There were Black folk who worked there. Because it had no "Colored" and "White" signs, anybody could use the same restrooms. So that's what we did.

For other trips, our folks would try to keep us [Turner and his two brothers] from drinking a lot of water or other liquids, so we wouldn't have to go [to the bathroom]. Their solution was to buy us little urinals. We would be in the back seat. The older cars had a hump in the middle which would sometimes get hot. Because we were small boys, we could worm around the hump and half stand or sit on the edge of the seat and use the urinals.

A hotel reserved for Black patrons on
Beale Street, Memphis, Tennessee, in 1939.

Such creativity, along with resilience, was at the heart of Turner's parents' strategies to cope with the aggravations and indignities of road travel. Like so many other parents, they modeled life lessons for their children.

The danger involved in the simple act of trying to buy gas helps to explain why Willie Nettles, the father of Evelyn Nettles, associate vice president of academic affairs at Tennessee State University in Nashville, was so excited to buy a Tesla electric vehicle shortly before his death. "It just gave him great joy not to go to a gas station," Evelyn Nettles recalled. "He really loved that car. There came a time when we had to tell him that he couldn't drive very far anymore. So, Daddy would drive his Tesla to the mailbox and drive it back." Willie Nettles remembered the past and created his own psychological liberation.

So before the basics of making sure the car was in good order and before putting the keys in the ignition, Black travelers had a longer and more complicated preparatory checklist—with additional psychological considerations—to think about and go through. This list was built from the knowledge of experiences and "the knowledge that it has happened to others" and therefore could also happen to them and their family.

SHOEBOXES OF FOOD

"That was some good eating." This sentiment was expressed by Joyce Coleman in Cincinnati as she recalled the food her mother cooked for the family to eat while they were driving to visit relatives or taking the train. Memories of preparing for a road trip are similar among countless Black families who traveled during Jim Crow and segregation as well as more recently. Many people tell stories of mothers, grandmothers, aunts, and sisters spending the day before a trip preparing the food—hard-boiled or deviled eggs, fried chicken, corn bread (made without milk), plain pound cake, and tea cakes made with cane syrup or molasses—all packed neatly in a container, most often a shoebox lined with tin foil (the colloquial name for aluminum foil) or wax paper. There were also ice-filled coolers stocked with jugs of water (often boiled beforehand), cola, fruit-flavored sodas, and local brands of soft drinks. Hezekiah Jackson remembered such preparations:

> My father was like a lot of men of that time. They relied heavily on their wives for planning and direction. So Mother charted our course based on talking with other people. My mother was like most ladies of that day; she didn't drive. But she would go all through [*The Green Book*] and designate where we were going, what we were going to do.
>
> And then she and my sisters, who are younger than me, would make the picnic baskets. The boiled eggs, the biscuits, the chicken—the chicken was number one—the plain cake, all those kinds of things. We were kids and we had a little habit. You didn't have to wear seat belts back then. We would be on the back seat [on our knees] and we would turn backwards, so that we could see the people and see the traffic. We would sing little songs. Mother would teach us little rhymes and things. One I can remember very well: "Row Daddy, row. Put it to the flo'."

There were so many questions to consider when planning a trip. Which towns, cities, rural areas, and in some cases entire states were safe to travel through? What stops, if any, would you want to make along the way? Who would you contact if you experienced a problem? The purpose of planning was to figure out how to take care of basic necessities during the trip and avoid problems.

Kefentse Chike, a community activist, African cultural musician, and professor of African American studies in Detroit, pointed out that the shoebox lunch was also taken along on other modes of transportation: "When you got so far down South, [the shoebox lunch] is what you resorted to. Even if you weren't going by car, you did this on the bus as well as on the train." The shoebox lunch is indeed an African American classic, directly related to all travel. In the community where I grew up in the Florida Panhandle, women would save shoeboxes especially for this purpose. Jackson's family may have used picnic baskets; other families may have used coolers. But the food packed was pervasively similar.

Hearing the many interviewees recall their shoebox lunch experiences triggered strong sensory memories for me: the smell of the shoeboxes full of food and the taste of the food as we kids ate from the boxes on our laps in the car; the sound of my mother's voice, fretting about us messing up our clothes that she'd freshly cleaned and pressed for the trip; the voice of my uncle, humming a hymn or spiritual to himself as he watched his speedometer and the cars around him on the road.

Janée never experienced the shoebox lunch growing up, but she delighted in hearing each person's vividly satisfying childhood recollections. From the beginning of the road trip from Detroit to New Orleans, many people shared with us their fond memories, similar to my own, of the food in the shoebox meals, especially the fried chicken. So it seemed appropriate that at the end of our trip, Janée and I, along with field producer Kemi, treated ourselves to lunch at Dooky Chase's Restaurant in New Orleans. We had talked about this final meal off and on throughout our journey—while eating hot chicken in Nashville, Tennessee; barbecue near the Lorraine Motel in Memphis, Tennessee; and soul food in Jackson, Mississippi, after hearing another story about how delicious the family shoebox meal was. What made Dooky Chase's special is that it remains in the same location as when it began being listed in the 1947 edition of *The Negro Motorist Green Book* as "Dooky—Cor. Orleans & Miro" (corner of Orleans Avenue and Miro Street). (Years later, the listing became "Dooky Restaurant—Cor. Orleans and Miro.") Long before our trip, Janée and I had read many articles in food and travel magazines about the restaurant's legendary, acclaimed owner and chef, Leah Chase. She died shortly before our road trip began. Although we were sad that we would not be able to meet and talk to the legend herself, we found solace in knowing that we would enjoy her enduring legacy—amazing Creole and southern food.

Our gustatory fantasies were full-on when we arrived at 2301 Orleans Avenue. We wondered what the neighborhood had originally looked like. The distinctive New Orleans–style single-family and two-family homes nearby seemed to have been there as long as the restaurant, if not longer. The area was well-cared-for and probably had always been so, given the status of Leah Chase's business. A long line of people with reservations snaked out the door, down the steps of the restaurant's entrance, and onto the street. When we made our way to the front of the line, I discovered that we didn't have a reservation. Something had gone awry. I could tell by the look on the host's face that she had heard this excuse a gazillion times! Thankfully, the good manners and charm that my southern Mama had taught me from the time I was a little boy kicked in. I remembered her words: honey is better than vinegar in most situations. I was apologetic as I kept eye contact with the host. I explained our situation and the twelve-day journey we were concluding. I understood why she had to say no, especially with all the other people waiting; but if we agreed to be out by a certain time, could she find a table where we could enjoy Ms. Chase's delicious food as the penultimate treat for our

Green Book journey? Of course, I had an edition with Dooky Chase's listing, just in case I needed to be a little more persuasive. It wasn't necessary. The host discreetly showed us to a lovely table and quietly reminded me of my promise.

There was a time when Dooky Chase's was the only elegant restaurant in New Orleans where Black people—locals and visitors—could dine. As we walked in, Janée began speculating about how the décor of the place evoked memories of the classy table linen, the plates, the glassware, the art on the walls that people would have seen when walking into the dining room. It would have been a piece of heaven back then. That welcoming spirit is still in the atmosphere today.

Lunch was served buffet style—always too much temptation. Our eyes and our fantasies were definitely bigger than our stomachs, but we wanted to extract every pleasure from this gustatory opportunity. As an homage to the past and what we had learned about the inventive ways Black people adapted to the limitations of traveling during segregation, Janée and I first chose foods that would have been included in the fondly and satisfyingly remembered shoebox lunches. The second round at the buffet was to sample Dooky Chase's Creole classics: gumbo, jambalaya, red beans and rice, fried shrimp, and more. I had sweet, iced tea with my meal, which reminded me of Sunday dinners after church during the hot southern summer.

The fact that this nurturing place is still standing, is still owned by the same family, is still offering its distinct hospitality and food—now to everyone—is a symbol of and a testament to the enduring, knowing, embracing, and quiet determination of Black Americans to become full participants in the American Dream. It also was our way of paying homage to all of the home cooks who fed their families so satisfyingly and memorably well on their road trips.

Interior pages of the 1963–1964 international edition of
The Green Book, explaining civil rights by state.

THE JUST-IN-CASE CARD

Before the appearance of *The Green Book* and other race-focused travel guides, Black people relied on community resources, word of mouth, and social connections when planning and taking trips. Hezekiah Jackson remembered how his and other families' *Green Book*s were shared community resources:

People would borrow [*The Green Books*] in the neighborhoods because a lot of them didn't have [the books]. They would come down [to the house] and say, "Is your Mama here?" And I said,

"No, Mother's not. She's gone to the church," or whatever. Then they would say, "When she gets back here, tell her we need one of those *Green Books*, 'cause somebody just died" in Detroit or New York, or whatever.

While on the road, it helped to have a wide personal network. Many African Americans who traveled on business—salesmen, for example—assembled personal lists of Black professional colleagues, pastors, physicians, teachers, lawyers, mechanics, and even undertakers who would be willing to help them.

Janée and I experienced this wonderful travel hospitality in Nashville that we felt was an evocation of what Black travelers sometimes experienced from their networks. At the end of our interview, we asked Ana Nettles, whose family has deep roots in the city, to recommend a restaurant where we could get a good local meal. Like many of the gracious Black southerners I grew up with in the Florida Panhandle, she immediately invited us to dinner at her mother's house. When Janée and I left our hotel to drive to the address, it was dark and rainy. We had to drive very slowly down an unfamiliar street because we could barely see the addresses on the houses. Eventually we found the correct place. When we pulled into the driveway, Ana and her friend Crystal Churchwell Evans greeted us with umbrellas, towels, and big welcoming smiles and warm hugs. We had wine, delicious food, and a wide-ranging, often funny conversation about our families' histories and our individual life journeys.

Afterward, Janée and I imagined this was the way we would have been welcomed at one of the tourist houses listed in *The Green Book* after a long, perhaps unnerving drive on a stormy night through potentially unfriendly communities. The entire experience felt as if the Fates had enabled us to relive some of the heartwarming history that the travel guide and word of mouth helped make possible.

Of course, people still used their personal connections. This was especially true of people who had been members of fraternities or sororities at one of America's HBCUs. William Williams, an architect who teaches at the University of Cincinnati, told a story that illustrates how members of these fraternities and sororities were ready to provide support and safety to their fellow brothers and sisters, as well as their families. His father was a member of Omega Psi Phi, one of the oldest historically Black college fraternities in the country. Founded in 1911 by three juniors at Howard University, Omega Psi Phi expanded into an international organization that would boast a membership roster that includes Michael Jordan, Martin Luther King Sr., Langston Hughes, Vernon Jordan, Bayard Rustin, Earl Graves, and many other luminaries. For the Williams family, the Omega connection provided invaluable support, as Williams recalled:

My father was an Omega. He didn't use *The Green Book* so much, but he definitely used his fraternity brothers. When we were traveling through Alabama and other places, he always had a list of fraternity brothers' names he could call if something happened. Once our car broke down, and he called a fraternity brother. They came out, got us, took us in, and fed us, no questions asked. That's just what they did.

Other fraternal organizations played a decidedly more complex and subtle role in helping African American travelers receive better treatment. Noelle Trent, director of Interpretation, Collections, and Education at the National Civil Rights Museum in Memphis, once asked her grandmother how her family members knew which places were safe when they traveled from New Jersey back to Virginia and South Carolina, from which the family had migrated. She answered,

"*The Green Book.*" But then her mother explained other, more subtle tactics Trent's grandfather deployed because of his association with a fraternal organization:

My grandfather was a Mason. He would put his ring on whenever they traveled, and he would put his Mason seal on the back of the car. So, every once in a while, my mother remembered, the car would get pulled over. My grandfather would just make sure the ring [on his finger] would be on the steering wheel and make sure that the police officer could see it. If the officer didn't see the seal on the back of the car, my grandfather would rub [the ring] to make sure that he would see it. Somehow, they didn't seem to have any problems. There was this subtle etiquette that helped negotiate these [on-the-road situations].

The leniency that Black Masons received from white Masons was more the rule than the exception, as illustrated by a similar story that Vernetta Sheppard-Pinson related about her uncles:

My uncles were Masons. In those days, the Masonic order was very strong in the South. If you were a Mason, you threw the sign [presented a hand signal] and they would let you go. That helped [my uncles]—it saved their lives. And that has been [the case] through the years. Being a Mason is not as prevalent now. [Back then] if you were a Mason, you had a certain sign that you threw with your hands. If you went to court, if the white judge was a Mason and the white police were from the Masons, they considered you their brother because you were a Mason. So they'd give you more leniency than if you weren't a Mason.

Fraternal organizations like the Masons once had a large and powerful presence in American society. In 1900, between 10 and 15 percent of American men and women were members of such groups.[1] They provided members not just with social connections that might be helpful in business but also benefits like burial insurance. Many of these organizations, including the Masons, the Elks, the Odd Fellows, and the Shriners, had separate Black divisions or lodges. Yet despite the segregation, a modicum of "brotherhood" and empathy existed between Black and white members. I have little doubt, however, that this favorable treatment that the families of Black Masons recalled varied by region.

Other kinds of networks, large and small, existed at every socioeconomic level of African American communities. There were networks of teachers (including teachers of subjects like home economics, science, agriculture, music, and physical education), of school principals, of choir members (Baptist, Methodist, AME), of preachers (especially circuit riders), of high school and university alumni, and of women who worked as maids. Especially important to everyone was experience-based advice and insights, as well as contacts along the route. In essence, each of these many specific communities were helping to keep the larger African American community safe as they traveled near or far from home.

But what if you found yourself in a small town or city where you knew no one and had no network like those described in this section? This happened to Jerome Gray of Montgomery, Alabama. He shares the word-of-mouth advice that helped him find a safe harbor for the night.

So I'm here [in this town], I am thinking, What do I do? I don't know anybody in this town. And I didn't have *The Green Book*. But I had been taught something by my parents about what you do when you are stranded in a place where you don't know anyone. [They said] see if there is a Black funeral home, call it, and see if you can stay at the funeral home. I did that. I asked some Blacks on the street if there was a Black funeral home [in the town] and they said there was. So I called the Black funeral home and the owner told me I could stay. I told him who I was, that I was a teacher. That was the kind of thing our parents taught us about how we needed to be flexible, and the things we could do when we were traveling if we got into a predicament like that.

All of these recollections make one thing clear: especially important to every traveler were contacts along the route as well as experience-based insights and advice.

PROTECTING YOUNG SOULS

African American parents were proactive, in both small and expansive ways, in their efforts to shield their children from the nastiness of racism and its harmful effects. They did this in their communities, when they went shopping, and when they were on the road. This was a loving gift that many people didn't realize until they looked back at their childhood and their parents' behavior. As William Williams explained, the danger came for children as well as parents and grandparents when they left the world they knew: "They might've felt okay in their neighborhood, but that gap between their neighborhood and where they were going was pretty much uncharted territory. You just did not know where it was going to be a safe place to stop, particularly if you had family, if you had kids."

While the "uncharted territory" Williams referred to was the highways of the United States, in truth the same kind of danger might be experienced on the street or inside a drugstore in a local, white downtown area. Because children were unaware of the restrictions on their activities created by Jim Crow and segregation or were too young to understand all the rules, a completely innocent act could put a child in danger from a white person who might see that act as a transgression.

Evelyn Nettles recalled an incident when her grandmother, Essie Nettles, drove to a local drugstore in Mississippi to pick up a prescription. Young Evelyn always accompanied her and would go into the store to get the medication. One day, Evelyn asked her grandmother for a treat:

I asked her, "Can I have some ice cream?" And she said, "Oh, of course," and gave me the money. But it never dawned on her that they had not told me that I was not to sit at the counter. I was just a little girl. I went in and sat at the counter. I noticed I was getting these strange looks. All of a sudden, I saw her [Essie] leap out of the car and come in to get me from that counter, because I was not supposed to sit there. I think she must have said something because it sticks with me to this day. The looks were almost enough to teach me that I really wasn't supposed to be there. She made it out of that car to get me, to keep me from danger. Somehow, I always knew that. She must have said, "You can't sit there," and I must have asked her why and all of that kind of thing. That was my first encounter. I couldn't have been any more than five.

Hank Sanders shared a similar story from his childhood in rural Alabama, when his young, fleeting curiosity provoked a reaction with much more dire overtones:

Sometimes [my mother] would take me with her to the store. Otherwise, we [her children] would have fights while she was gone. So she was in a store and I was sitting out in the car with the door open. This white woman walked past and she had on short shorts. That was strange to have a white woman or anybody in short shorts back at that time. So, I looked up, immediately saw that it was a white woman, and looked down. It was about three seconds or something like that.

Shortly after, a white man came over to me and said, "I saw you looking at that white woman." I said "No, I didn't look. I just looked up and when I saw it was a white woman I looked down." He said, "Well, I'm going to make sure that you don't ever look at a white woman again." I immediately drew my feet in the car because I had the door open and then slammed the door closed. As I was trying to wind the window up, he was trying to reach in, trying to grab me.

My mother came out [of] the store. She said, "Get away from my son!"

He said, "He looked at this white woman and I'm-a teach him a lesson."

My mother said, "I don't give a damn what he looked at. I want you to get away from him." She started really cursing and coming toward him. She was so fierce. He stood there and eventually walked away slowly.

During our road trip, Janée and I took a tour of the 16th Street Baptist Church in Birmingham, Alabama. Our conversation with the tour guide brought back memories of my mother's and grandmother's monthly visits to Tallahassee, Florida. They would never take all seven of us children with them. Usually, only one was invited to go (typically during our birthday month). Quite infrequently they would increase it to two. When we were walking, or sometimes running, along Adams or Monroe Street in Tallahassee, our parent had to make sure we did not inadvertently come too close to or run into a white person. So as we approached that person, our mother or grandmother would point something out in the opposite direction and then strategically move herself on the side approaching the white person so that no accidental contact was possible. Meanwhile, my parent was also carefully monitoring the approaching person's reactions and behavior.

As children, we thought we were being shown the beautiful color of a flowering plant or a building detail similar to one in a picture we had recently looked at in a magazine. Instead, this was a protective dance, thought through and performed so often that it was seamless. It was only as I listened to the recollections shared during our interviews and thought back that I saw the back-and-forth waltz that my mother and grandmother, and so many parents and grandparents, did during walks down streets: distract right, step protectively left; distract left, step protectively right. They all gracefully, gently protected us, because they knew there would come a day or a single dangerous moment when they couldn't.

Children therefore needed to be taught how to avoid risky encounters with white people. Parents had to somehow convey a number of messages to their children that were contradictory. On the one hand, they needed their children to understand the dangers they faced from the largely hostile white society. And on the other hand, Black parents wanted to spare their children the nightmares, insecurities, and feelings of bewilderment that come from living in a world filled with senseless, arbitrary hatred. In the simplest, most basic terms, however, African American parents wanted their children to stay alive. That's at the core of "the drill" that Hezekiah Jackson's mother and father gave their children before they set off on their road trip to Detroit. It was a version of the same conversation that many parents had with their children before a trip:

Daddy would just tell you, matter of fact, that you couldn't do this or you couldn't do that. But mother would give you a drill. If we are stopped or if some white people say anything to us, you are not to talk. We said, "Okay, we're not to talk." And then she said, "And you're not to look at them." I can remember her saying it. We would say, puzzled, "We can't look at them?" I can hear mother saying that we couldn't look at them.

When asked whether he remembered his parents being stopped while traveling with him and his siblings in the car, and what that was like, Jackson responded in a way that's deeply familiar and true for many African American families who were on the road during the time when *The Green Book* was published, as well as years afterward: "It was horrifying. It really introduced us into the real world."

All of these aspects of the trip—checking the condition of the car, preparing all of your food because you might not be able to buy a meal, having a strategy if no bathrooms are available to you, planning for the possibility of not being able to buy gas, making sure you have reliable contacts along the route, knowing how to shield your children from the ugliness of racism—were the additional parts of preparation that Black people had to think through in the hope of lowering the risks of travel. But there was a toll for protective, loving Black parents and grandparents, Bryan Stevenson of the Equal Justice Initiative explained as he reflected on his childhood:

My grandfather would say to me things as a child, like whenever a white person comes up to you don't look them in the eyes; you always say, "yes sir," you always say, "no sir." There were strategies you had to adopt to stay safe. My grandfather was a proud man; he was a smart man. But in the presence of white people, he would become this something else that was deeply painful for him because he wants to model something for me, but at the same time he wants to keep us safe. There is that duality, that burden that I think few people understand.

In a conference room at the National Civil Rights Museum and Lorraine Motel in Memphis, the fifth stop along our road trip, when we asked Noelle Trent what she recalled most vividly about her childhood travels, she spoke about a family tradition that it took her many years to figure out:

I never really understood it, but to this day, when we're taking a road trip, my family insists on getting started by five a.m. "You want to travel during the daylight; nobody travels at night"—that's the message that was drummed into us, especially if we were traveling from North to South. And it was especially important to know the route. I remember very distinctly how our family road trips were mapped out and knowing every stage of the trip: "We're stopping here, here, and here." And this continued twenty, thirty years after the heyday of The Green Book. These are all habits that were taught generationally, ingrained from that generation that was traveling during that time period.

Trent's memories reflect travel patterns and perceptions that were widespread and even today are not uncommon among African Americans: leave in the early morning before sunrise (when the children will fall back to sleep), drive all day, and arrive at your destination before sundown.

"The Magic Hour" was how some people referred to the departure time for the trip. It could be three, four, or five a.m., depending on an individual family's tradition. In any case, travelers wanted to be on the road and well along the way as day broke, before the local police along the route were out setting up traps or capriciously stopping Black travelers with out-of-state license plates. People drove straight through, sometimes more than twenty-four hours, stopping only for gasoline and comfort breaks—usually in wooded areas beside the road. Traveling families would eat in the car, play games in the car, sing songs, tell stories, study Bible lessons—anything to pass the long hours without a pause to rest or relax. They carried with them everything they needed, especially the names of relatives, friends, or acquaintances who lived along or near the route whom they could call in case there was an emergency.

Even short journeys, near to home, required preparation. Eva Baham explained the reason in the context of the social dynamic of that time:

All over the South, the story was the same in every little town. Black people could not show that they were more elevated in any way, especially in socioeconomic status, than the poorest white person. And the poorest white person had the right to do [to Black people] anything they wanted to do without retribution, without punishment or anything. So African Americans learned how to be proactive in avoiding that.

This meant that in some areas it was not just the police who could stop and question a Black person. Any white person could challenge a Black driver for any reason—driving too slowly, driving too fast, overtaking them on a two-lane road, looking at them the "wrong way," having a car that was too nice, having a car that was not nice enough—the possible provocations were unpredictable, often mercurial, and ever-evolving.

The risk was particularly high when African American communities were close to sundown towns, as they often were in the North. Kathryne

Gardette's experience growing up in Cincinnati, Ohio, was commonplace for Black people in the large metropolitan areas to which many migrated:

> I grew up in a community that was right next door to a sundown town, Norwood. If you get on Gilbert [Avenue], it eventually turns into Montgomery Road. When you cross the railroad tracks by Xavier University, you're in Norwood. It was a sundown town. It was only recently that the first Black city council member was elected there.

Often it was just a single road or a set of railroad tracks that separated the segregated Black and white towns, suburbs, or sections of the city. (Years later, the interstate highways were frequently routed by and through cities and town in ways to create more definitive dividing lines and barriers between Blacks and whites.) Just crossing that demarcation line could elicit more than questions and a high-fee ticket for a traffic violation, as Paulette Roby in Birmingham remembered:

> I can remember the time when, as a child, my uncle picked us up at my grandmother's who lived in Cottageville, over where Reverend Fred Shuttlesworth lived. We were in the back seat of the car and we went over those railroad tracks. And as soon as we went across those railroad tracks, the police stopped us. My uncle had a gun, but it wasn't loaded. He [the policeman] took that gun, put it to my uncle's head, and [as he pulled the trigger] the gun went click, click. "N———, if this gun was loaded, you'd be a dead n———." All three of us [girls] were in the back seat just holding one another, afraid.

This was in no way an isolated incident that would have occurred only on the local streets and roads in Dearborn, Norwood, Nashville, or

Birmingham. It was, and remains, the kind of encounter that is a regular occurrence in Black people's lives, as this story from Hezekiah Jackson captured vividly:

I was way out in the suburbs because a fellow who is a friend of mine works for a cleaning service. We were at an affair and he had missed his ride. So, he wanted to know if I would carry him to work. The service that he worked for cleans up a lot of big white churches. This church was way down in the suburbs. So I drove him down there, and there was this huge church with all this property. It was in a cul-de-sac. I dropped him off and I turned around. When I got to the top of this hill, the police surrounded me. I was looking in the rearview mirror. I put my hands on the steering wheel. They seemed to have a drill, like they had practiced it. Two came this way [from the front]. Two came that way [from the side]. Two came that way [from the other side]. And one was at the back of the car.

Because I had been to this affair, I had on a suit, tie, everything. So one of the officers says, "Are you lost, reverend?"

I said, "No, I'm not lost."

He said, "Well, can we help you with something?"

I said, "I just gave someone a ride to work."

He [the police officer] acted like he didn't believe me. He said, "So where do they work?" And I knew the name because I had just happened to look at the big marquee to the church because it's a big nondenominational church. He said, "Oh, okay. We will help you get to the expressway. We will help you."

So they [the police officers] escorted me all the way to the on-ramp. I didn't say anything but "Thank you." I was in this unfamiliar place that was obviously unfriendly and all I wanted to do was get out of there. So he wanted to lead me to the place [the on-ramp]. And I said, "Thank you very much." And then when I got to the on-ramp of the expressway, he said "Well, reverend, you can go on home now."

In his mind, it was not possible that I could live out there. In a lot of their minds in the suburban communities, they do consider them sundown communities. They [the police and the residents] feel like, if we live there, they should already know us. If they don't know us or we're visiting someone, it's problematic.

Jackson's story sounds as if it was from the period during which *The Green Book* was published, when there were many sundown towns and suburbs across the United States. But, in fact, this incident happened in 2017.

DRIVING AS A SURVIVAL TOOL

If even short local trips could be dicey during the period when *The Green Book* was published, imagine how dangerous a longer journey could be. A car driven by a Black person, containing Black passengers and bearing an out-of-state license plate, was a vulnerable target, especially on the two-lane roads that went through the center of many small towns. These factors increased the chances of getting stopped by the ever-vigilant police or someone else simply feeling "authorized" that day.

Keenly aware of these realities, Eva Baham's older sister took what may now seem like extreme measures when she was driving from Michigan back to Louisiana:

The fear of being stopped in the night or the day, especially for a woman with children, [the fear] of being assaulted, perhaps raped, of having your car blown up, stolen, or whatever, or of being stranded was so great that it was best to avoid traveling through some areas. Or if people had to travel through them, they tried to make their travel time as short as they could. My sister, who lived in Michigan, would avoid [going through] Mississippi. She would drive west-southwest, come down through Arkansas, and then come through Shreveport, which is in the upper northern part of the state. Where we're from is at the opposite end of the state, in the southeast. Once she was in Louisiana, she knew where she could go for safe haven.

Yes, the longer route she took forced her to spend more hours on the road and to pay more for gasoline. But it also helped her feel less vulnerable because she knew she was prudently avoiding the predictable dangers that specific communities posed.

The concerns of Baham's sister echo in Joyce Coleman's memories of her mother's long drives with three children to visit relatives in Cincinnati:

We couldn't afford *The Green Book*. My father was killed when I was three years old. My younger brother was one month old the day that we had his funeral. My mother raised three children [by herself]. Our traveling was very fortunate because I had a great-uncle who was a Pullman porter. So, we got to ride the train for free, but we had to sit in the area where the smoke was coming in. We always had our shoebox with fried chicken, some pound cake, some hard-boiled eggs.

We got a car in the 1950s when I was in grade school—'54,

I guess—and after that we traveled in the car. The food in the car was the same food—that was good eating. The rules were: we're going to leave at three a.m.; you be sure you go to the bathroom before we leave; you be sure you have the bottle we carried our water in; we made sure the car had gas, the tires had air, and they were good tires.

My mother was traveling with three of us—a baby and two children. We were three years apart. We stopped along the way in the daytime to get gas if we needed it. If it was dark and the car was getting near empty, we looked for a place where there were [roadside] lights, and my mother would pull the car over and sleep until daylight. And then we would drive just a little bit farther and get gas at a station—Texaco, Esso. A white man would always come out to pump it and say to my mother "What you want, girl?" I got it [the southern drawl] down pretty good.

Coleman laughed as she recalled the particular, peculiar way the white gas station attendant would say "girl"—a memory that she had mimicked many times and that always made her laugh.

Not all on-the-the road stories are disturbing. Many African Americans were able to quell their fears and have an enjoyable time while traveling, especially if no "aggravations" occurred. Many people have wonderful, funny memories of traveling as children with their parents. They remember the logos of the service stations (Esso, Texaco, Phillips 66), the songs they sang, the games they played, the Bible lessons they memorized. They recall the sequential signs carrying rhymed verses advertising Burma-Shave that lined some of the two-lane roads. They also remember wanting to stop at Stuckey's to have pecan rolls, at Howard Johnson's for ice cream, or at a store where they fantasized about shopping—but their parents would simply and firmly say, "No, we brought our food," without any further explanation. And the trip would continue.

When Stuckey's in particular was mentioned by several people (me included), there were always lots of chuckles. Janée shared an insight that has resonated deeply with me: "What I find interesting about the humor [related to recalling Stuckey's] is how at the time the kids didn't know why they couldn't stop; but now they do, and yet they still have a laugh about it. It is a very moving example of setting aside bitterness once the truth is revealed and walking in grace instead."

For Danny Ransom, his trips to New York with his father and uncle were a joy and an inspiration:

[Daddy] bought a new '62 Oldsmobile Starfire. That car was sharp, with the center console. We drove that car to New York—my uncle, my father, and I—'cause Daddy asked me, "Do you want to go with us?" I was eleven years old. That's when I learned how to read a map. I love maps. I always get a new atlas every year.

The trip was just fascinating. Two-lane highways! There were no interstate [highways]. When you got up around New Jersey and New York, they had parkways or whatever they called them then, like the Southern State Parkway on Long Island. We didn't stop really at any eateries and no hotels. I mean, this is in the '60s. Mama had made fried chicken, little sweet snacks like pound cake and stuff. All we stopped for was gasoline.

Those trips really energized me, because I loved a subject that most kids didn't like when I was growing up. What's that? Geography. I can remember even some of the cities we went through back then, like Roanoke, Virginia, and the road along the Blue Ridge Mountains. It was beautiful! I was just a kid. All I had to do was just look. I didn't have to drive then. I loved traveling.

It just built my interest. So, any time Daddy said, "Oh, I'm going to so-and-so," I said quickly, "I want to go." Primarily it was somewhere in Alabama.

But the episodes [of being stopped] that Hezekiah [Jackson] chronicled, I never experienced that. Never, no stops.

While young Danny Ransom was enjoying these trips, there is little doubt that the adults in the car were quite aware of potential problems and were planning ways to avoid them.

Hank Sanders's memories about his feelings during summer drives with friends to New York as a young adult are probably closer to what most Black parents were feeling, while working hard to avoid communicating those emotions to their children:

Any time we drove anywhere, we were always afraid. We didn't know when somebody might stop us or pass by and shoot us. You were just always so afraid. You had to be careful even what service station you stopped at. You could never know if you were stopping at the wrong service station, and even though you weren't doing anything wrong, something might happen to you. You might go inside and look at somebody the wrong way and they would decide, maybe, that's a reason to kill you.

There was a lot of fear here in Alabama. And Alabama wasn't the only state where you were afraid. Whenever in the '60s we would drive back and forth to New York, that was always a terrible experience.

Some drives were inherently endurance tests because of the distances between establishments that would serve African American travelers.

Sydney Cates, retired deputy chief of police for New Orleans, drove to Los Angeles six times, including some trips during the years *The Green Book* was published. Cates remembered fondly, "I had a Chrysler 300. I had three different Cadillacs. And I had a Rambler station wagon. The Cadillac was the most comfortable. We had bucket seats. I had an El Dorado. That was the biggest and the best [for the trip.]" However, Cates had never heard of the travel guide. As he said, "We just got in the car and drove." His knowledge about safe traveling practices came from word of mouth. On those trips, he and his wife traveled with a varying combination of their children, his mother, and his mother-in-law. The cross-country journey was nearly two thousand miles long, and the first half was especially grueling:

I drove from here [New Orleans] to Los Angeles at least six times, and we had a whole lot of difficulty. The only place we could stop was El Paso, Texas, at one motel called La Luz. That was eleven hundred miles from here. We drove it in one trip—straight through. You couldn't stop to buy anything to eat. We had to take sandwiches from here to eat in the car or in roadside parks on the way to the La Luz. It was the place where we knew we could stop. And we could use no bathrooms along the way. Then the other half of the trip was from El Paso to Los Angeles.

La Luz was known by word of mouth to virtually every Black traveler who made the trip from New Orleans to Los Angeles during this time. It was a godsend—the first place in more than a thousand miles where Black people could sleep in a bed, refresh themselves, and sit down for a meal. La Luz (misspelled as La Lug) first appeared in the 1957 edition of the guide, then called *The Negro Travelers' Green Book*. Several early listings highlighted the motel's "Luxury Accommodations, Swimming

Pool, and Coffee Shop on Premises." La Luz was listed in *The Green Book* until the final edition in 1966–1967.

A Black-owned hotel in an unexpected location might be a godsend for weary Black travelers—and some business owners made the most of the fact. Mervin Aubespin's aunt and uncle owned the Syd-Sylvia Motel in Opelousas, Louisiana, one of the few places "between Baton Rouge and the Texas line" where Black travelers were welcome. Better still, it was located in an African American neighborhood, right across the street from "a nice little restaurant" that also had Black owners. To take advantage of their competitive advantage, Aubespin said, "My aunt and uncle were wise enough to have billboards on the road nearby that suggested very strongly that their motel might be the only place you could spend the night"—a message conveyed without words by the picture of Aunt Sylvia that adorned those signs.

Eric Finley of Mobile, Alabama, chuckled ruefully as he recounted stories of the many unwarranted tickets handed out on his family's trips to California. His recollections are familiar to many African Americans:

Going through Texas and them little towns with a Lincoln, we were bound to get stopped. Almost every picture we have on that route was us stopping paying a ticket. You used to get tickets and you would pay them at a constable's office, which would be on the road somewhere. They [the police] were stopping us because, number one, *What are they doing in that car?*, and number two, *We're going to give them a ticket because they've got that car.* So we had an enormous amount of traffic tickets on the way to California.

But the threat of being stopped by the police wasn't the only danger Black travelers faced. Perhaps an even greater one along those long, desolate stretches was being stopped or run off the road by a white traveler. Musician McKinley Jackson, who lives in Detroit and whom we talked with on the first day of our journey, recalled riding on the Motown tour bus with some of the most acclaimed performers of the day—the Temptations, the Four Tops, the Marvelettes, Martha and the Vandellas, Stevie Wonder, and more—along with a band of ten to fifteen pieces. They suffered the usual road trip indignities, like restaurant owners who refused them tables and instead would send out dishes of food laden with "the grit and grime from the grill." But more alarming would be encounters with passing vehicles filled with locals:

A wagon might come by filled with hay and with four or five white guys sitting on it. They'd pick up their rifles and shotguns and point them at us on the bus. But we had a bus filled with Detroit guys! The windows on the bus would quickly go up, and there would be two guns pointing out of every window. As soon as they saw that, the guys on the hay wagon would take off!

Sometimes, the dangers in highway encounters were more subtle but just as threatening. During a road trip to Los Angeles with his (now-late) wife, Sydney Cates was using a once-popular communications device to get information about the conditions ahead:

I remember when CB radios were in use some years back. They were very popular. The truckers used them all the time. We were driving to LA in a brand-new Cadillac with a CB radio in it. I used it mostly to listen to music.

All of a sudden, the program was interrupted when someone came on and said they were driving to Los Angeles. They were talking about the road conditions. I got on the CB radio and said I was driving a brown Cadillac. I was also on the way to Los Angeles, and I wanted to know if the guy saw any trouble with the police up ahead. I asked him to give me a call back and I told him my call sign number.

My wife jumped all over me. She said, "Don't use that radio, because somebody's going to hear it. You've identified the car that you're driving. They're going to give you some trouble."

Well, I didn't worry about that because I was a cop. I had a pistol in my car with me. I figured I could protect us if we had to be protected. So we continued along, and all of a sudden someone interrupted the program again. The guy on the CB radio said, "Listen, when you get up to mile marker number so-and-so, watch out because they've got a Smokey giving out green stamps up here." This was verbiage for a policeman giving out tickets.

After a little while, another guy came on the CB radio and said, "I'm up at that mile marker now that you told me about, and I don't see no Smokies up here. All I see is a bunch of rubber-lip porch monkeys in the school bus." That meant Black kids in the school bus being transported somewhere.

The reaction of Cates's wife was based on her fear. She worried that a racist trucker might recognize their car and terrorize them in some way, maybe by running them off the road and causing them to have an accident. Black travelers tried to be as anonymous as possible on long drives, and Cates's wife felt her husband was breaking their protective cover.

Skin color, or more accurately white people's *perception* of skin color, also had an effect on African Americans' on-the-road experiences—one that most people, Black and white, probably would not think about. Eric Finley talked about a tactic some light-skinned Black travelers could employ:

Back in 1957 or 1958, my dad decided that we would go to California because my mother had a couple of brothers out there. Dad must have been doing pretty well then, 'cause he had a '57 Lincoln Continental, which was brand new. So we packed up the car and headed to California.

Whenever we stopped at a hotel, my dad and I would go in, because he looked white, and I look kind of white-ish or Mexican. My mom, my brother, and my little sister would stay in the car, because they were darker. Dad and I would usually be able to get us a room, and then we would sneak the rest of the family in with us.

I remember at one hotel, the guy behind the counter glanced out the front window and saw our car sitting there. "Listen," he said, "I see the rest of your family out there in the car. I understand what's happening. You can have the room, but I need y'all to stay inside and don't come out, okay?" We did what he asked. And that's how we got to California.

Cates shared his own story about "passing" during one of his trips:

My wife and I were driving back from Los Angeles with her mother when we stopped in Texas at a service station. The two ladies had to use the restroom. So they got out of the car and were walking toward the service station when they saw a big brown dog lying across the entrance.

My mother was a little nervous, so she asked the service station manager, "Is that dog going to worry us?"

"No, no ma'am," he replied, "He don't worry nobody but n———s."

The ladies went in and used the restroom. When they came back out, I said, "Well, now I have to use the restroom."

My mother-in-law started laughing. "You better hurry up and use the restroom before that dog finds out you're a n———," she said. That's the kind of thing that used to happen to us on the road.

During our road trip, we asked each person we interviewed whether they had been stopped by the police while traveling. A few had not. But most didn't answer the question with words; instead, they answered with a sigh of exasperation or by shaking their heads back and forth while looking down. "Too many times," was the answer that didn't need to be said. Others would nod silently in agreement.

LITTLE HARLEMS

BLACK HAVENS IN THE ERA OF *THE GREEN BOOK*

There are stories about these places being beacons in the community. Business people and community leaders were trying to create a social structure for locals and for people who were visiting. The places give you a sense of what Black people aspired to at that time as well as highlight the level of perseverance and resilience we inherited as Black people in America.

— Derrick Adams, multidisciplinary artist based in Brooklyn, New York, and Baltimore, Maryland

Children standing in front of a half-mile concrete wall in Detroit, Michigan, in 1941. This wall was built that August to separate the "colored" section from a white housing development going up on the other side.

I first heard the term "Little Harlem" during an interview with Geno Lee, at his restaurant, the Big Apple Inn, on Farish Street in Jackson, Mississippi. It was 2016. Lee painted me a picture with words of what the street had been like during its heyday in the 1950s and 1960s when it was the center of African American business, culture, and life in the capital city. He said that when the train arrived at the station, Black people would disembark and walk the seven or eight blocks from the station to bustling Farish Street and surrounding streets where businesses happily provided services that Black travelers and locals needed and wanted. "[Black people] built their own buildings, made their own businesses, their own clothing stores, their own fire department, their own restaurants and juke joints. It all happened right here on Farish Street," said Lee.

When I visited in 2016, only four or five business were still open on Farish Street, one of which is the second oldest funeral home in Mississippi. The streets were empty; the buildings were abandoned. It seemed to me that a layer of sand covered everything. When Janée and I arrived on Farish Street in 2019, it looked exactly like it had when I was there before, but maybe a little more neglected.

The Green Book is an evocation of places like Farish Street and a powerful symbol of an often-overlooked aspect of African American life from the 1930s to the 1960s. Its listings of Black-owned, Black-managed, and Black-oriented hotels, motels, tourist homes, restaurants, clubs, cafes, gas stations, beauty parlors, barber shops, and other businesses from coast to coast offer a window into the vibrant world that Black Americans built despite the constraints and restrictions they faced on all aspects of their freedom, including the freedom to move from place to place.

As I said at the beginning of this book, before Janée and I started our road trip, we went to Harlem in New York to meet Maira Liriano, the associate chief librarian of the Schomburg Center for Research in Black Culture. As a student of Black life, Liriano recognizes the value of *The Green Book* as a trove of information about some of our country's most overlooked communities:

The listings in *The Green Book* are really incredibly useful for understanding the local history of towns and cities in the United States. We can learn a lot by seeing which businesses are listed in *The Green Book* as well as by studying the omissions—the businesses that are not listed and the towns that are not included. And then you have to wonder what was happening there. So by digitizing the guides and making them available on our website for free, we're hoping—and I think we've seen some of this play out already—that people will use this information to learn more about their own communities and to learn more about African American business history as well as travel history.

The Black neighborhoods that were the homes of most of the businesses listed in *The Green Book* were havens of safety for travelers of color. But they were more than that. Many also provided livelihoods and sources of social, cultural, and family support for millions of African Americans. Hundreds of relatively successful Black communities embodied and manifested the American spirit, managing to thrive under the radar, despite neglect, disdain, and sometimes outright assaults from whites. Bryan Stevenson, founder of the Equal Justice Initiative, shared with us what older Black people have said to him: "Older people of color come up to me and they say, Mr. Stevenson, I get so angry when I hear somebody on TV talking about how we are dealing with domestic terrorism for the first time in our nation's history after 9/11. They say we grew up with terrorism. We had to worry about being bombed and lynched and menaced every day of our lives."

As we have seen, before and during the years *The Green Book* was published, any white person or group of white people, not just the powerful, could assault a Black person or community with few, if any, legal consequences. This was especially true because of the Jim Crow laws in the South that legally disenfranchised most Black people. This is a side of our national story that Janée and I got a powerful glimpse of while on our road trip exploring the world of *The Green Book*.

We also saw the ingenuity and determination that Black people exhibited. As Jerome Gray, a longtime activist in Montgomery, Alabama, wisely observed, "Where there have been barriers, Blacks have found ways to get around those barriers and really have fun. These places that were listed in *The Green Book* really became wonderful places for Blacks to go to meet, not just for travel. They became social gathering sites."

In places where Black people had access to significant amounts of investment capital—from savings, from Black-owned banks and insurance companies, or from broad-thinking white-owned financial resources—Black communities thrived and became well-known. The streets where the economic, social, and cultural lives of these communities flourished have become legendary. Beale Street in Memphis, State Street in Chicago, Congo Square in New Orleans, and East 125th Street and Lenox Avenue in Central Harlem are among the most famous. But many others are less well-known, including some of those that we visited on our two-thousand-mile drive. As we traveled from Detroit to New Orleans, re-creating the trips "back home" to the South that so many of our forebears took, we visited once-thriving streets and neighborhoods that reflected the richness of a bygone era in African American history—the "Little Harlems."

PARADISE VALLEY, DETROIT: A HUB OF BLACK ENTERTAINMENT

The money flowing through the Black community in Detroit because of jobs in the automotive and related industries made it possible for countless African Americans to accumulate capital and start businesses. Some 350 of those new Black-owned businesses would eventually be located in Paradise Valley, a neighborhood in southeastern Detroit that came to be one of the most prosperous Black communities in the country. Jamon Jordan recalled:

At the time, there were prominent African American musicians like Duke Ellington and Cab Calloway and Count Basie coming to the city of Detroit. They were popular everywhere—they played in the white clubs, they played in the African American clubs. Their music was the pop music of the day, and they were huge stars—the equivalent of Katy Perry and Beyoncé today.

But because of segregation, they couldn't stay everywhere. So where did they stay? They stayed in the upper-class, African American–owned hotels listed in *The Green Book*, places like the Gotham, the Carlton, the Carver, the Mark Twain, many of them right here, in Paradise Valley. And while they stayed here, they also played here, in the Black-owned clubs. And since whites loved their music, too, whites also came to Paradise Valley to hear them. So, Paradise Valley was not just taking in Black dollars; it was taking in a large amount of white dollars, too.

And, by the way, these businesses did not discriminate. Customers at the Black-owned clubs and restaurants and theaters could be of any color. They were fully integrated. That's why they were called "black and tans"—the name used then for a fully integrated club or bar where black people and white people perform onstage together and sit at the same bar or in the same booth with one another. The business owners weren't practitioners of segregation. They didn't perpetuate it.

And as the money, from both white sources and Black sources, flowed through Paradise Valley, the Black community as a whole benefited. Jordan continued:

In the city of Detroit, the African American dollar turned around ten times within the community before it left the community. You spent that dollar at your local chef or baker, candy store or grocer. That Black grocer took the dollar and hired a painter to paint the outside of his building and make signage for him—and that would be an African American painter. And then that painter would take the dollar and invest it in a Black-owned bank. And so you got all of this money transferring from one African American hand to another African American hand, all building wealth for the African American community.

Today the turnover of African American dollars in a Black community tends to be shockingly short. The small Black-owned shops that used to populate these streets are being replaced by stores owned by large corporations. While they often employ local Black residents, the dollars paid by the people who shop at the store quickly flow out of the community. A study by the Selig Center for Economic Growth found that money circulates one time (more precisely for six hours) in the African American community. In white neighborhoods, money circulates nearly an unlimited number of times.[1]

Those early prosperous Black neighborhoods in northern cities, like

Paradise Valley, helped to inspire Black people across the country. When families who were part of the Great Migration traveled back South to visit with families and friends, they talked about their lives up North, sharing the news of what they had achieved. They were proud of their accomplishments and occasionally enjoyed showing them off a little. Janée and I heard so many stories during our road trip about people returning South with their new cars, sporting stylish clothes and the latest hairdos. They embodied the promise of the North, where Black people had a better chance of claiming their share of the American Dream. The message they sent to those still in the South: *You don't have to stay down here, in grinding poverty, getting disrespected, menaced, and even spat on by every white person you meet. Why not join us up North?*

Of course, the North was no racial paradise. Growing up in Detroit in the 1970s, Jordan didn't feel immune to the effects of racial bias:

By the time I got to be ten or eleven years old, we were beginning to take buses to go to the mall with our mom, and then by ourselves. We were told clearly that Jim Crow still existed in the Detroit area—not in law, but in reality. For example, we were warned in no uncertain terms, "You do not go to Fairlane Mall." The reason was simple: Fairlane was in Dearborn, and Dearborn had a long history of segregation that extended even into the 1970s. Orville Hubbard, who was the mayor there for thirty-six years, from 1942 to 1978, was a staunch segregationist until the day he died. He was very proud of his motto: "Keep Dearborn Clean."

Was Dearborn a sundown town? Maybe not officially, but, as Jordan said, "You have unofficial sundown towns around Detroit right now":

There are areas outside of the city of Detroit where, if you're seen driving there and you're African American, and you're not on the main drag, the police will be called. Next thing you know, you'll be pulled over and you'll be getting questioned: "What are you doing over here? Why are you here? What's the purpose?" You'll get the message that you shouldn't be there. No, it's not officially a sundown town, but that's still exactly what it is.

While doing some additional research after our road trip, I came across an article that described the reaction of a Black woman, Delisha Upshaw, who discovered she lives in a former sundown town, Livonia, just two miles west of the Detroit city limits. My conversation with Jordan about the suburbs surrounding Detroit immediately came to mind. When the 2010 census was taken, Livonia was 95 percent white. First, I was surprised that Upshaw, who had lived there for fifteen years, had been able to rent or buy a home in Livonia at all, given the history of steering practiced by white real estate agents in the Detroit metropolitan area. Upshaw had experienced racism in Livonia and become a member of a group called "Livonia Citizens Caring About Black Lives." Part of her motivation was her deep concern for the safety of her thirteen-year-old daughter, who was about to get her driver's license. Upshaw did not want her child to experience the roadside stops, fear, and racism associated with driving while Black. To bring the issue into the open and to encourage conversation about it, the group held a three-day fund-raiser to pay for a billboard it placed on I-96. The billboard read "Driving while Black? Racial profiling just ahead. Welcome to Livonia."

The reaction from the Livonia police chief and probably the many citizens of the former sundown town is one that Black people in the US have heard thousands of times: the police chief said the town's police officers did not target Black drivers. The mayor of Livonia said the board was counterproductive to making Livonia "a welcoming place for all." I wondered: How easy is it for white people in former sundown towns and suburbs to psychologically and emotionally adjust to seeing Black people walking and driving freely in those places? As I read the police chief's and mayor's statements in the article, I recalled another line I had read about how passing the Civil Rights Act of 1964 would not immediately change people's behavior. The article about Delisha Upshaw and Livonia was written in 2020.[2]

One of the realities we glimpsed again and again along our *Green Book* route was the proximity of all-Black and all-white communities and suburbs. They were often right next to each other, even a Black community and a sundown town. Because of the practices and underlying mindset of white supremacy associated with segregation, most white people paid little attention to what was happening in Black communities. There were also barriers. Sometimes they were physical, such as a street, railroad track, or in Detroit, an actual six-foot wall. Jordan explained why the wall was built:

It was built because the federal government was funding and subsidizing housing with low-interest-rate loans during the 1930s, '40s, and '50s. The federal government is helping working-class people get a home. The caveat is working-class white people. The asterisk in this plan is that the neighborhoods have to be racially homogeneous. So, the government has begun subsidizing the construction companies and developers to build these homes, and then it discovers later after they've already begun to fund it that there are African Americans living in close proximity to where these houses [for white people] are being built. The government threatens to stop the funding. They threaten not to offer any of the FHA-backed loans for people who wish to buy these new houses that are being built. So, the developers come up with the concept of building a six-foot, half-mile-long wall, and the federal government accepts the idea.

As we drove to the wall from Jordan's nearby home, he explained that we were actually on what would have been the white side of the wall in the 1940s and most of the 1950s. We would not have been welcome. We might even have encountered hostility. Seeing the actual wall itself, still standing, but now decorated with cheerful images and with a small park beside it, made us think of the Berlin Wall. Janée and I wondered how many Americans even know about this wall in our own country and the racist reason it exists. We suspect few do.

Jordan continued explaining that there is a second wall in Detroit:

The other wall is a psychological wall, a social wall at Eight Mile Road. It is the northern border between Detroit and its northern suburbs, most of which were sundown towns. From the 1920s through the 1960s you had a string of suburbs that were created on the northern side of Eight Mile Road. So the road has served as this kind of symbol of the division between Detroit and its outside suburbs. African Americans in Detroit were surrounded by people and cities that did not allow African Americans to be residents.

Throughout Jordan's conversations, I was reminded of my white friends and neighbors who have said to me that during this period, they assumed that Black people were living lives similar to theirs. However, I suspect they were a small percentage. Most simply bought in to the pervasively negative, white-supremacist-toned points of view that were the prevalent narrative about Black people at that time. Nonetheless, in

Paradise Valley, Detroit's Little Harlem, Black entrepreneurship of all kinds thrived, and the people who went there, both Black and white, had memorable times that those who experienced it still talk about. This was true in Black business areas in cities across the US at that time.

Today, where Paradise Valley once pulsated with ambition and entertainment, there is only a plaque. The area was cleared in the late 1950s and early 1960s during urban renewal in Detroit.

WALNUT STREET, LOUISVILLE: "IT WAS HEAVEN"

In one town after another on our *Green Book* road trip, we heard stories from local citizens about the "glory days" of their own Little Harlems. Carl Westmoreland recalled, in Cincinnati, one of those prosperous Black neighborhoods was in the West End where the Sterling Hotel was located on Mound Street. Another was in the neighborhood known as Walnut Hills, where the Manse Hotel was located. Founded in 1937 by entrepreneur Horace Sudduth, the Manse was a center of cultural and social life for Cincinnati's Black elite. In 1946, the national convention of the NAACP was held at the Manse Hotel, attracting attendees that included attorney Thurgood Marshall, boxer Joe Louis, and members of the Tuskegee Airmen. Today, the Manse Hotel is vacant; in 2019, the development firm that owns the hotel was awarded $1.2 million in tax credits as part of a plan to restore the building and turn it into sixty affordable apartments for seniors and families.

When we visited Louisville, Kentucky, our guide was Kenneth Clay, a lifetime resident, author, and cultural visionary. He told us:

There was an area called Walnut Street. It's now Muhammad Ali Boulevard. But back in the day, Walnut Street ran through downtown Louisville—east and west. It began up on the east side of town and went all the way to the west side. Black people lived in the west side, the West Louisville area. But the strip between Sixth and Thirteenth Street was *the* strip. It was the entertainment strip; it was the Black business strip. It was where the professional doctors and lawyers all had their offices. It was like our Harlem. It was like our Beale Street.

And, you know, for years that was the place that I just loved to be as a youngster. They had three Black-owned movie houses, two Black-owned banks, three Black-owned insurance companies, and a whole assorted grouping of restaurants and eateries and places you could buy clothing and stuff.

Walnut Street, of course, was where there were hotels. There was the Hooks Hotel over on Seventh and Chester, a block away from Walnut Street. There was the Brown Derby Guest House, there was Laird's Hotel.

Walnut Street was the hub of Black social life in Louisville. Every year when the town's signature event—the running of the Kentucky Derby horse race—took place, Walnut Street would be transformed into "Cadillac Alley," as well-heeled Black visitors from nearby towns and cities would park their fine cars there and join the social buzz. The Lyric Theater publicized its twice-daily showings of the latest feature films by having a driver cruise in a car emblazoned with movie posters through the city's Black neighborhoods. The Midnight Ramble presented a nightly variety show featuring Black entertainers known throughout the country.

We asked Clay what it was like to walk around the Walnut Street neighborhood as a young man, seeing the successful Black people in their finery and the thriving life of the community they'd built. His answer was simple: "It was heaven."

The 1932 city directory for Louisville listed 154 Black-owned businesses in the Walnut Street area, and many of those were still thriving in the 1950s. But by 1960, the so-called urban renewal movement sponsored by white-dominated state and local governments had demolished most of them. (No wonder, as Clay reminded us, Black folks in those days referred to "urban renewal" as "Negro removal.") Today, just two notable buildings from the glory days of Walnut Street are still to be seen—the Mammoth Life and Accident Insurance Company building on Sixth Street, and the Church of Our Merciful Saviour on Eleventh Street.[3]

This was another nationwide pattern we saw plainly during our road trip—the impact of post–World War II government policies that were ostensibly intended to revitalize neighborhoods but whose main impact was the destruction of once-thriving Black communities.

NASHVILLE: THE POWER OF BLACK DOLLARS

On our way to Nashville from Louisville, Janée and I talked about how the city became such a point of excellence in the Black community. For as long as I can remember, people I admired had talked about the exceptional education available at Fisk University, Meharry Medical College, Tennessee State University, and the American Baptist College. Each was and remains a top-tier HBCU. Like the Little Harlems we were looking for, these institutions had thrived and produced Black leaders in all fields during segregation and Jim Crow. We met Learotha Williams, who teaches African American history at Tennessee State University, on Nashville's famed Jefferson Street. As Janée, Williams, and I strolled down this famous street on a warm day, he described what the place was like in its heyday:

> This was the place to be seen. If you had an outfit you wanted to show off, you'd come to Jefferson Street. The nightclubs were there. You could go right down the street and see Little Richard perform, and while you're listening to Little Richard, you look around and you might see Jackie Robinson or Joe Louis in the spot.
>
> This street serviced three universities—Tennessee State, Fisk, and Meharry Medical College—and in doing so it created a really intimate relationship between these universities and the community. Not just Jefferson Street but the entire community.

Yet even in cities like Nashville, where Black neighborhoods flourished for a time, free mobility for African Americans was often severely limited. Sometimes the social restrictions were enforced in subtle ways, as suggested by this story from Crystal Churchwell Evans, whom we met in Nashville at the Frist Art Museum:

> Here is a story my dad told me about when he was in college. He went to Vanderbilt [University] and lived in East Nashville. He didn't have a car, so he had to take the bus to Vanderbilt. What was strange was that the bus system picked him up in East Nashville and drove him all around town to take him through Belle Meade to go down west and finally get to Vanderbilt, which is a very roundabout route.
>
> When I heard that, I was like, "Why?" And he said, "Well, because they'd pick up the domestics in East Nashville and drive

them all the way around to get to Belle Meade, to drop them off for their jobs." They'd pick up people along the way, from East Nashville, but by the time the bus arrived in Belle Meade, the only passengers were my dad and all the ladies who were going to work there.

Churchwell stated clearly and with certainty that the bus route her father took was intentionally designed by the city planners. To understand the story and her certainty, it helps to know that Belle Meade is a small independent city that operates as part of the larger city of Nashville. It is named after the Belle Meade Plantation, which John Harding started developing in 1807; he eventually had a magnificent mansion built there by some of the hundreds of people he enslaved. Today, that mansion is a popular tourist site listed on the National Register of Historic Places. As for the town of Belle Meade, according to the 2019 census, its population was 96.5 percent white and 0.79 percent Black.

Facts like these make it obvious that the bus route Churchwell's father had to take was *not* designed with the convenience of Black students at Vanderbilt in mind. Like public transportation systems in cities all over the United States, the convoluted Nashville bus lines were designed to reflect and reinforce patterns of racial discrimination, and help white citizens get the domestic services they wanted. Their Black workers without cars could get to and from work on their own from their segregated Black neighborhoods, although the length of the ride may have been a burden to those, like Churchwell's father, who were not workers in those white neighborhoods.

Still, the experience of commuting every day with the ladies who cleaned and cooked in houses in Belle Meade wasn't all bad. Churchwell continued:

So there was my father, on the bus surrounded by women who were his mother's age or even his grandmother's age. And when they heard he was a student at Vanderbilt, they would say, "Oh baby, we're so proud of you! I hope you do well at Vanderbilt." Some of them even started baking cookies to give him on the bus.

My dad said that by the time he got off the bus at Vanderbilt, he felt the weight of the support from those ladies on his shoulders. He was so struck by the fact that they took pride in him, when he wasn't even a relative of theirs. It reflects how interconnected we are as a Black community.

Like groups of Black citizens across the US, the people in Nashville used their collective economic power to fight back against discrimination. One impressive example can be found in the story of the Nettles family, one of Nashville's leading families. Today, the Nettleses celebrate a multigenerational tradition of oral history that is exemplified by their late, beloved father, Willie M. Nettles, and the many stories he told his children and grandchildren. He possessed an optimistic embrace of the future well into his eighties, as evidenced by the humorous story about his love for his Tesla automobile, which he continued driving to the mailbox and back even as his health declined. His stories also reflect realistically and beautifully how the Nettleses and other proud Black families coped and thrived.

When I interviewed Evelyn Nettles in Nashville, she recalled how her family had been part of a movement to consciously guard and expand the precarious wealth of the Black community. Part of this effort was an organized refusal, back in the 1950s, to spend Black money at businesses that didn't treat Black customers with respect:

When I was little, Black people boycotted all the downtown stores. We used to go to Harveys, Castner-Knotts, and Cain-Sloan—those were the big department stores in Nashville. But even during the Christmas season, even when we knew we wanted something from one of those stores, my daddy wouldn't let us shop there if a boycott was on. So I understand what it means to "walk with your purse," and the power of refusing to give my money to people who don't have my best interests at heart.

The boycott that Nettles described paid off. An account of the "glory days" of Nashville's famous downtown shopping district, Church Street, includes this description of what happened:

Eventually, an Easter boycott of downtown forced merchants to make a choice between integration and eventually bankruptcy. Behind the scenes, the unlikely team of Harvey's [sic] treasurer Greenfield Pitts and Cain-Sloan president John Sloan, two white Nashville businessmen, approached other merchants about the possibility of a quiet desegregation of the lunch counters [in the Church Street department stores]. On May 10, 1960, Harvey's, Cain-Sloan and four other stores permitted blacks to eat at their downtown lunch counters. The struggle for desegregation continued well into the decade, but by 1970, Church Street belonged to everyone.[4]

This made Nashville the first southern segregated city to integrate its lunch counters. The Nashville *Tennessean* published a series of articles (complete with pictures) to commemorate this landmark event's sixtieth anniversary in 2020.[5]

Willie Nettles certainly knew how to use his family's economic power to benefit his community. The same person who made sure his family's hard-earned money would not be spent in white businesses that

The Lorraine Motel in Memphis, circa 1971, where
Martin Luther King Jr. was assassinated. The motel had been
listed in *The Green Book* for years before King's visit.

treated Black people badly also used this money to support civil rights
marches in his city. Evelyn Nettles told us: "I can remember when we
were little, that's when the civil rights marchers came through Nashville.
They were based in Centennial Park and we had to look at all of that
on television, because Daddy wouldn't let us go out to join them. But he
went out and brought food to the marchers over in Centennial Park so
that they would have food as they marched."

It wasn't easy, but over time, community leaders like the Nettleses,
together with many families in Nashville, found ways to use their

economic and social influence to force some US cities to allow Black citizens to participate more fully in civic life—not only in their Little Harlems, but beyond. In cities and towns in other states, Black people opened their homes and provided safe shelter for civil rights protestors, notably the Freedom Riders, who rode interstate buses into the segregated, violent South in 1961.

Perhaps the most memorable and effective economic action of the civil rights movement was the Montgomery Bus Boycott of 1955–1956. For more than a year, Black people, from housekeepers to students to professionals, stopped using the city's segregated bus system. They walked, took cabs, and organized their own volunteer transportation system using private cars. The city indicted the protestors, who proudly and defiantly turned themselves in. The arrests strengthened the resolve of the Black community, and eventually, the Montgomery bus system fell into a financial crisis without Black ridership. It took a ruling of the US Supreme Court to find Alabama's segregation laws for businesses unconstitutional. In reaction, white people violently terrorized Black people in Montgomery. Eventually, however, Black people in that city were able to enjoy the freedom their economic boycott had achieved. Its success inspired other African American communities across the United States.

MEMPHIS: BLACK HISTORY PRESERVED

One high point of our *Green Book* tour was our visit to the Lorraine Motel in Memphis, Tennessee, where Dr. Martin Luther King Jr. was assassinated in 1968. This site is profoundly linked to our nation's history. It's a place where vital symbols of Black America are preserved for the education and inspiration of future generations. You feel the spirit of the place before you even walk through the door. Janée and I both fell silent as soon as we saw it. Nothing needed to be said. For any Black person, the Lorraine Motel is a place of profound reverence.

Today the motel is owned by the Tennessee State Museum and is a Smithsonian Museum affiliate. There we spoke with Noelle Trent, who is its director of interpretation, collections, and education. She reminded us that the Lorraine Motel had already left its mark on African American life and culture even before the rise of the civil rights movement. Purchased by Walter and Loree Bailey in 1945, it was a popular stopping place for people from around the country whenever their travels brought them to Memphis; the motel's guest books include the names of celebrities like Aretha Franklin, Sam Cooke, Jackie Robinson, and Satchel Paige. Mavis Staples and the Staple Singers used to stay there, and two classic songs were written in its rooms: "In the Midnight Hour" by Wilson Pickett and Steve Cropper, and "Knock on Wood" by Cropper and Eddie Floyd.

Trent noted that the Baileys were genuine business partners as well as spouses. They owned and ran the motel as a team and made smart decisions together, such as installing air-conditioning in the early 1960s—an unusual luxury that made the Lorraine Motel especially attractive during the sweltering Tennessee summers—and buying a farm in Shelby County to provide the produce served at the motel's restaurant.

Of course, King's murder is the first thing that comes to mind when the Lorraine Motel is mentioned. Trent set the scene for us:

In 1968, Dr. King was planning his Poor People's Campaign, which called on the country to radically reimagine how we dealt with poverty. He was asking for poor people, all across the country, from all backgrounds, to descend on Washington and camp out there until Congress did something. In March of '68, he brought all of his lieutenants here to the motel to strategize in the conference room.

And here is a piece of the story very few people remember. There was a choir staying in the motel, visiting Memphis from Prairie View A&M, which is an historically Black university in Texas. And sometime in the middle of the night, their choir director found out that Dr. King was on site and working in the conference room with his team. So he ran, woke up all the students, told them to put their clothes on, and gathered them to sing for Dr. King. It's so funny to look at the film footage of that moment: the students are all kind of groggy, and some of the girls still have curlers in their hair. But they sang for Dr. King. And that's the only known film footage we have of Dr. King inside the Lorraine Motel.

On April 4, history made its tragic visit to the Lorraine Motel. Its impact on the Bailey family was particularly profound. Trent explained:

Loree Bailey was actually working the motel switchboard on April 4. So, when Dr. King's associates pick up the phone to call emergency services after the shots were fired, she makes the call. Later, she was handling a lot of the initial calls in the aftermath of the assassination. The next thing we know, she was on the phone with a friend and said, "You know, I'm not feeling well." She went to her room, lay down, went to sleep, and never woke. She suffered a cerebral hemorrhage [at age sixty-eight] and ultimately passed away [five days later] on April 9, 1968—the day of Dr. King's funeral.

After the assassination, Walter Bailey locked off the room where Dr. King stayed, and it was never rented out again.

Mr. Bailey was very particular about honoring that space. He had a deep sense of the moment. But, you know, he and his son-in-law, Dr. Charles Champion, were also the ones who had to clean up the balcony. There are photographs of Mr. Bailey in the middle of the night, after the people from law enforcement had left with all the evidence they'd gathered, having to clean up. There's a gravitas in that moment that I don't think any of us will ever truly understand. There's an intimacy and a sacredness in cleaning up the remains of the dead. There's an honor in that.

Dr. Champion is still alive today, and while he's willing to talk about certain things, there's a depth of emotion there that I don't think we'll ever really see revealed because that space, that moment, is filled with something that is levels below what can be excavated.

So for the Baileys, April 4, 1968, is a doubly tragic day, because Loree Bailey passed away at the same time the national tragedy happened on their property.

Walter Bailey continued to operate the Lorraine Motel for some fifteen years after that, although its business went into a steady decline. It is not hard to imagine why, given how painful it must have been for people to go there, and how deep Walter's grieving must have been for all he had lost on that fateful day.

Today, however, it has been preserved for history. The effort was driven by community passion, as Trent explained to us:

Within hours of Dr. King's assassination, people started leaving flowers on the balcony where he was standing. Room 306 was set aside as a place of honor for years, long before the idea of a museum was created. And then, in the late 1980s, the property was falling apart. Some people were wondering: Should we make it a parking lot? Should we tear down the Lorraine? But the African American community of Memphis said *absolutely not*. And local businesses and citizens began working to save it. People were pooling their pennies and dollars. They were determined to save the Lorraine Motel.

But converting that passion into a practical plan wasn't easy. Jesse Turner Jr., a second-generation banker, talked to us about how the community's vision became a reality:

It started with a citizens' movement. One of the early supporters was Charles Scruggs, who was a longtime radio personality and ultimately manager of WDIA radio. He got together with several people, and they formed a foundation to try to save the Lorraine. They raised a little money, but they couldn't raise very much.

And so, when the owner of the motel decided that he had to put it up to be sold at auction, the community rallied to try to raise enough money to buy it. My father and others connected with the bank worked with this group—my father did the accounting for them.

It was a struggle. The community group raised something like $80,000. That was $50,000 or $60,000 short of what was needed. So they couldn't close the deal. But the bank was willing to step in with a loan to make up the difference, provided the group could get guarantees from local people of substance. And little by little, they did. A civil rights attorney connected with a life insurance company got the company to guarantee part of the loan. Other businesspeople stepped in to guarantee some. And the bank agreed to lend the money on a handshake thanks to the support of these local groups.

Trent is proud of what the people of Memphis and their supporters have been able to accomplish:

> Today, the state owns the museum, and it's on the National Register of Historic Places, which protects the façade of the museum. In 2002, the museum bought the boarding house across the street as well as the park across the street, which protects the view. This sort of preservation is a long-term project. We have a lot of stakeholders involved, people really committed to preserving [the Lorraine Motel] and the area around it, protecting it for generations to come.

Now supporters are working to have the Lorraine Motel assigned World Heritage Site status—a coveted honor, bestowed by the United Nations, which represents the highest level of recognition and protection for a culturally important location.

BIRMINGHAM AND MONTGOMERY: THRIVING AMID THE TERRORISM

Even in the then most provincial regions of the Deep South, Black Americans were able to carve out spaces in which their cultural and social lives could flourish. One of our guides to Birmingham was artist Tony M. Bingham, who is a professor of studio art at Miles College. We were standing together in downtown Birmingham, Alabama, at the intersection of Seventeenth Street North and Fourth Avenue, where some of the most impressive structures from the city's past can be seen.

The Fourth Avenue business district was the heart of Birmingham's Little Harlem. The old Carver Theatre is there, undergoing renovation at the time of our visit. And right across the street is the so-called Colored Masonic Temple, a seven-story building with a cornerstone proclaiming that it was built in 1928. The entire construction cost of $658,000 was financed by contributions, which meant the Masonic fraternal order was able to operate the property debt-free. Designed in Renaissance Revival style, the temple included first-floor spaces for retailers, like a drugstore and a hair salon; offices for Black-owned businesses and professional service firms; a Grand Hall auditorium where concerts were held; and a branch of the public library.[6]

As we gazed up at the still-impressive façade, Bingham remarked: "The fact that the Black community in Birmingham had the where-withal to build such a structure in 1928 is really astounding. Think about all the resources that had to be pulled together—the architects, the contractors, the craftspeople. A project like that would be difficult to pull off today, let alone in 1928."

Birmingham was also the home of a famous Black motel of the Jim Crow era, owned by one of the most successful Black entrepreneurs to venture into the burgeoning hospitality industry during the early twentieth century. Denise Gilmore, director of cultural preservation for the City of Birmingham, shared with us some of the story of A. G. Gaston and the business empire he built.

Born in 1892, the grandson of an enslaved person, Arthur George Gaston started life as a coal miner in Fairfield, Alabama. His entrepreneurial instincts quickly asserted themselves. He started selling lunches to his fellow miners and then began offering them other services, including short-term loans and burial insurance. By the late 1930s, Gaston had expanded into several other businesses. Gilmore explained:

His motto was, "Find a need and fill it." So when he looked throughout the Black community and saw so many things that we deserved and should have a right to—services that the white community would not permit Black people to have access to—he said, "If I see a need, I'm going to fill it." And so he created funeral parlors. He created insurance plans. He opened a penny savings bank. And because there weren't many people doing this, that's how he created his millions.

In 1954, Gaston opened his motel on a site adjacent to Kelly Ingram Park in downtown Birmingham. At the time, Holiday Inns were considered the gold standard for middle-class lodging among American travelers. Believing that Black people had a right to first-class accommodations as they traveled through the segregated South, Gaston vowed to create a motel that would be even more comfortable and attractive than a Holiday Inn. Soon the A. G. Gaston Motel was considered among the top-tier lodgings in the country. It became a popular gathering spot for local people and developed a stellar reputation among entertainers, politicians, vacationers, and everyday people coming through Birmingham. "Anybody who was anybody traveling through the segregated South would have stayed at the Gaston Motel," Gilmore told us. "Old-timers still talk about the parties they enjoyed at the supper club. I had the opportunity to visit with one of A. G. Gaston's granddaughters, and she told me about her grandfather's love for a thick ribeye steak. He made sure that the restaurant in his hotel served steaks better than the best Delmonico steak. People also flocked there for the best lemon pie."

The role of the A. G. Gaston Motel in the civil rights movement is just as important as the safety and luxury it provided. Room 30 on the second floor was known as the War Room. It was where Rev. Fred Shuttlesworth, Dr. Martin Luther King Jr., Ralph Abernathy, and other local pastors and civil rights leaders met to strategize and organize the

1963 campaign in which Black people protested for their civil rights. The hotel was also bombed because of the meetings in Room 30.

Today, Gilmore is overseeing the restoration of the building as a historic landmark.

Some ninety miles south of Birmingham is Montgomery, another stop on our *Green Book* road trip. One of the highlights of our visit there was the historic Ben Moore Hotel. Built in 1951, it is a red-brick structure with twenty-eight rooms that once served a vibrant Black community in the city. It also became a regular meeting site for leaders of the civil rights movement, including Dr. King and Ralph Abernathy. The Majestic Café on the first floor was a popular meeting spot for local citizens and businesspeople who would stop in for breakfast or lunch. The nightclub that occupied the entire fourth floor at the top of the building once featured performers like Tina Turner and B. B. King.

Local folks still speak fondly about the elegance and style that once characterized the hotel and its patrons. Sitting in the offices of the Equal Justice Initiative in Montgomery, I met Jerome Gray, a gracious man with excellent recall about his decades-long, continuing participation in the civil rights movement, including being capriciously and unjustifiably removed in 2013 from the voting rolls in the town where he lives. He vividly recalled his visits to the Ben Moore Hotel: "It was a wonderful place to meet and to fellowship. The other distinction it had was being one of the tallest buildings in Montgomery. So, the Ben Moore Hotel really gave you a bird's-eye view of Montgomery."

The late Gwen Patton, also a groundbreaking civil rights activist who became the first female Student Government Association president at Tuskegee Institute, a legendary HBCU, was a petite lady described as having a "gentle demeanor and a sledgehammer of a mind."[7] She recalled how she always "dressed up sharp" when spending an evening at the Ben Moore's rooftop nightclub, adding with a slightly sly smile, "There was never any contradiction between being a lady and being a freedom fighter!" During my conversation with Patton at the dining table in her memorabilia-filled home, her recollection of her visits to the place made me see how luxurious and alluring the hotel had been:

It was nice, nicely furnished. Downstairs was the Majestic Café. It had opaque, embossed windows. They had an elevator guy. His name was Cat Wiley. You would ride the elevator all the way up to the roof. That was called The Rooftop. You could dance. They had live music. And you could buy your libations. It was grand—absolutely grand! You got into your finest [clothes] when you went to [The Rooftop].

The hotel closed its doors in the 1970s. Today, the empty building, stripped of most of its fixtures and with its doors secured by chains and padlocks, is owned by Edward Davis Jr., whose father purchased it in 1979. For years, Davis has been trying to assemble the funding to renovate the hotel and dedicate it to some new purpose—perhaps offices, a media hub, or a community center. Whatever happens to the building, it will be important to somehow commemorate its historic role as a hub of community life for Black Montgomery in the 1950s and 1960s. Its neglected condition today makes it feel like a decaying remnant of the past. For years only one business continued to operate on the ground floor of the High Street side of the building: Malden Brothers Barber Shop, where Dr. King would get haircuts. The chair King always sat in was still in the shop. Recently the barbershop moved to a new location in Montgomery, so today the Ben Moore Hotel sits totally empty.

JACKSON: "IF YOU DIDN'T GO TO FARISH STREET, THEN YOU HADN'T BEEN TO JACKSON"

For African Americans in Jackson, Mississippi, and in the surrounding areas, Farish Street was the connection to the best in entertainment, fashion, and movies and the latest new products. On Farish Street, people dressed to the nines, they drove shiny cars, and they enjoyed spending their hard-earned money on food, drink, and live entertainment. Shoppers, visitors, and locals would mingle there as they patronized businesses like the Alamo Theatre, the Booker-T Theater, Trumpet Records, Shepherd's Kitchenette, the Davis Salon, the City Barbershop, Paris Cleaners, and the Palace Drug Store.

And although Farish Street was the heart of Jackson's Black community, businesses located on streets nearby were equally famous, like the Summers Hotel and the Edward Lee Hotel, which was patronized by the Black singing groups that came to perform in Jackson, including the Supremes, the Miracles, the Contours, the Marvelettes, Martha and the Vandellas, and others. Nearby was the George Washington Carver Library, which held a weekly book review program featuring a young reader opining on a book he or she had recently read.

Walking along Farish Street looking at the mostly empty buildings, Janée and I met Tony Dennis, standing just inside the doorway of Dennis Brothers Shoe Repair Shop. In his early sixties, Dennis is the third-generation owner of the shop that his grandfather started on Farish Street in 1935. Dennis started shining shoes at the shop when he was ten years old. The wonder of what he saw, of what he experienced, has stayed with him:

You ain't seen nothing like Farish Street. They used to bring people here from the surrounding towns: Philadelphia, Pelahatchie, Canton,

Copiah [County]. They would bring them here by the busload on Fridays and Saturdays and drop them off on the corner [near the Alamo movie theater]. It would be the folks who had work all the fields, chasing chickens. If they made a few dollars, they would come to town to have a good time. There were so many people on the sidewalk, all the way down the sidewalk, and around the corner that you would have to walk in the street. Some people would leave home, thirty miles away, and come to Jackson to take care of grandmama's or mama's bills before heading back home. When you got home, all your friends would ask, "Where were you at yesterday? If you were in Jackson, did you go to Farish Street?" Back then, you wouldn't come to Jackson and not come to Farish Street. If you didn't go to Farish Street, then you hadn't been to Jackson. You [had gone] somewhere else.

Other people Janée and I talked to during our stay in Jackson said they too felt energized just walking along Farish Street, some of whose buildings had been constructed by enslaved people but were now centers of Black entrepreneurship and community life. For the older generation, Farish Street represented the aspirations that had not been possible for themselves but that they had wanted for their children, many who, like me, had been raised on farms. They were inspired by the vision of Black business owners and community leaders—the power of determination, creativity, and collective action, even in the face of institutionalized hatred and isolation.

When we visited Jackson, we were saddened, but not surprised, to see how desolate Farish Street has become. This is often the case with former Black business areas in cities across the US. The location of the once-vibrant Edward Lee Hotel is an empty lot. Where the Summers Hotel stood, a short drive from Farish Street, is now a grassy knoll with a sign that briefly summarizes the hotel's history. Plaques on some of the buildings designate the neighborhood as a historic district. One reads, "This building was erected circa 1900 by Negro masons. This property has been placed on the National Register of Historic Places by its inclusion in the Farish Street Historic District, August 1983." Below that is another plaque that says, "Businesses and family residences 400 to 418 North Farish Street, 1903 to 1983."

Today, Farish Street is home to a few businesses, some of which have been there since the street's heyday: Collins Funeral Home (formerly Frazier and Collins Funeral Home), Big Apple Inn (a restaurant), Dennis Brothers Shoe Repair Shop, and the flower shop (which supplies the funeral home). The legendary Alamo Theatre was renovated and re-opened in 1997 and today is a venue that can be rented for concerts, plays, award ceremonies, meeting, and conferences.

What remains is nothing like the heyday of Black businesses in Jackson, when this area was one of the largest economically independent Black districts in all of Mississippi, occupying some 125 acres.

Frank Figgers, a civil rights activist we met in Jackson, eloquently summarized what this change means for him:

Well, I'm saddened by it. These buildings served a tremendous purpose. And they showed the resourcefulness, the ingenuity, and the determination of a people who lived in a situation that didn't allow for people to live. They offered a place where they could express their humanity inside a system that didn't allow for humanity to develop—a place where they could exercise humanity to the fullest extent possible, no matter how oppressive the greater Mississippi was. So, when I see that the Edward Lee Hotel, and the Summers Hotel, and Parker's Inn, and others are not there anymore, I'm sad.

MOBILE: THE TWO-MILE-LONG AVENUE

When we arrived in Mobile, Alabama, we found more of the same. Janée and I met Eric Finley downtown near the location where the original city had been founded. Finley, who was born and raised in Mobile, took us to Davis Avenue, the African American section of the city. The street was named after Jefferson Davis, the first president of the Confederacy. We strongly suspect that this was not meant to be ironic but to serve as a not-so-subtle reminder. In 1986 the city renamed the thoroughfare Martin Luther King Jr. Avenue. The Avenue, as it was called locally, was two miles long and, as Finley remembers, populated by "nothing but African American business." Finley, who was a teenager when The Avenue was still thriving, remembers that it "was all businesses, back-to-back":

There were no alleys because one building was right next to the other. There were four movie theaters on this street. There were three African American–owned grocery stores. This street was lined with all retail businesses—cleaners, drug stores, clubs, barbershops, beauty salons, medical doctors, dentists, banks, clothing stores, you name it. All of the shopping was done on that street. And because we couldn't go to white restaurants, there was The Grill, which had the best Sunday meal you could get. Going there was like a dream for us.

Near the western end of The Avenue was the remainder of what had been the Le Grand Motel. Like the Lorraine Motel in Memphis and the A. G. Gaston Motel in Birmingham, it was a two-floor structure based on the Holiday Inn model with rooms that opened onto a walkway. Janée asked Finley if the motel lived up to its name, and he answered: "When it first opened it did. It was a very respectable place. The Le Grand was the place where James Brown would stay; also, Smokey Robinson, the Four Tops, the Temptations, and Gorgeous George (Edwyn Collins), who was the MC of the Motown Revue. There was also a nightclub right across the street called the Baby Grand. It was a real nice place for jazz."

The Le Grand Motel is now derelict. Many of the original architectural details can still be seen, but the building is empty and slowly decaying. Where the Baby Grand once stood is an empty lot. Like many Little Harlems, little of The Avenue's glorious past remains. There are a few newly constructed buildings, a technical school, some falling-down houses, and some empty playing fields—and few people are on the sidewalks.

As we drove from Mobile to our final stop, Janée and I reflected on what we had learned, especially from the people we talked with in Cincinnati and Memphis, about what it takes to save these buildings and neighborhoods. Sadly, as Janée pointed out during our conversation with Jesse Turner Jr., we were discovering in city after city that many of the once-popular establishments listed in *The Green Book* no longer exist. And we are losing time and losing opportunities to preserve the ones that do remain. Janée asked Turner about working to preserve the Lorraine Motel: "When you look back at that time, what stands out as the greatest success around that quest for preservation? Was it getting the [Tri-State] bank involved? Was it convincing the community that it was something that needed to happen? Or was it something else?" Turner's answer gave us insight into the type of human capital that is needed:

> You had a group of, quite frankly, Black geniuses who were sup-
> ported by a terrific Black community who had a lot of faith in what
> they were doing. The people who were involved were leaders
> on all kinds of levels. They were leaders in business. They were

leaders in church. They were leaders in politics. They were leaders in voting. So, they were community servants. I think, for the most part, they figured out how to get the support of the people behind things. And from what I gathered, watching them as a teenager and not always understanding what they were doing, they struggled, they made mistakes, they tried things, and some things they had to do over and over again to get them to succeed.

Turner then went straight to the heart of the matter: "Frankly, if we [African Americans] had more wealth, we'd probably save more buildings."

Tony Bingham captured a bit of how I felt as our road trip neared its end and I reflected on the experience of hearing about and seeing the locations of some of the Little Harlems of America:

As you turn the pages of *The Green Book* and find yourself in different cities, you may be fortunate enough to see some of the structures that still exist, or you may find the empty lots where there was once a hotel or a store. You'll be reminded that there was once a vibrant culture where people could just be themselves, feel safe, and invent and carve out what it meant for them as Black people to be part of the American story.

I think of the words of poet Toi Derricotte: "Joy is an act of resistance."[8] The Black neighborhoods we visited, North and South, have changed since their joy-filled heydays in the 1930s, 1940s, 1950s, and even into the 1960s. To quote a phrase we heard from people in cities along our route, each Little Harlem was "the place to be." Creating spaces—streets, hotels, restaurants, clubs, fraternal organizations—was resisting being kept in your place, being denied your freedoms. Walnut Street in Louisville. Jefferson Street in Nashville. Davis Avenue in Mobile. Driving slowly along those vividly remembered, still-talked-about thoroughfares, Janée and I wished that more brick-and-mortar evidence of them, as well as their spirit, remained.

— 8 —

SUMMER RETREATS

AWAY FROM THE WHITE GAZE

Know where you can make a difference. Know where you can make an impact. Know where there can be change. Find out how you can fit in, and then do it.

— Kathryne Gardette, civic leader,
cultural innovator, performer, and
lifelong resident of Cincinnati, Ohio

The wonder of any road trip is arriving at a place that opens the door to a totally new world. That happened during the shortest stopover of our twelve-day trip. On our way from Detroit to Cincinnati, we stopped in Columbus, Ohio, to meet Mary Ellen Tyus at a new residential complex into which she had recently moved. We met her in a

The YWCA summer camp for girls in
Highland Beach, Maryland, in 1930.

comfortable conference room in the management office of the complex. Tyus, who is retired, quickly told us to call her Mary Ellen. Janée and I were excited to talk with her about a place we knew virtually nothing about: Idlewild, in the middle part of western Lower Michigan. It is a Black-only resort where her grandmother, her mother, and now Mary Ellen have vacationed every summer of their lives in a house they own, surrounded by longtime friends. Although she has lived in Columbus most of her life, Mary Ellen says Idlewild is home for her family. Five generations of her family now enjoy summers at Idlewild.

Users of *The Green Book* included many people for whom travel was a necessity: salespeople and others who drove from one town to another for business reasons; musicians, athletes, and other performers for whom road trips were an essential way of generating revenue from their talents; family members who needed to stay in touch with loved ones in distant states. However, a growing number of middle-class and affluent professional Blacks (such as doctors, lawyers, judges, engineers, teachers, and insurance executives) and their families wanted travel to be a source of relaxation, recreation, and cultural enrichment. Because of segregation, they were barred from most of the well-known, high-end resorts across the United States. So Black families with financial resources created their own resorts throughout the country that enabled them to have a respite from the everyday burdens of being Black during the Jim Crow era. As Mary Ellen remembered: "African American families could not go anywhere in the country without being hassled and turned away. Those who came to Idlewild would be affluent families, professional families that could afford to take a vacation. Doctors and teachers and lawyers and social workers and that kind of thing."

Most white Americans and many Black Americans may be unaware of the fact that such resorts existed and how they came into being. I grew up in the rural, agricultural Florida Panhandle totally ignorant of such places. Some of the Black resort communities that were havens during the Jim Crow era include American Beach in Florida; Oak Bluffs on Martha's Vineyard in Massachusetts; Sag Harbor on New York's Long Island; Fox Lake in Angola, Indiana; Bruce's Beach near Los Angeles (which has been returned to the founders' family by the state of California); and Val Verde in Southern California, sometimes called the "Black Palm Springs." The important role these havens played in the lives of Black Americans is reflected in the pages of *The Green Book*, where the lodgings, restaurants, nightclubs, beaches, and other facilities were listed for the convenience of people planning their vacations. Although, word of mouth, more often than not, was the way most professional Black people heard about these places, some did advertise in *The Green Book*.

Some of America's Black resort enclaves have long, interesting histories. For example, Highland Beach in Maryland, some thirty-five miles outside Washington, DC, was founded in 1893 by Charles Douglass (the youngest son of the legendary abolitionist, orator, and writer Frederick Douglass) and his wife, Laura Haley Douglass. The younger Douglass had served as an officer during the Civil War in the famous African American 54th Massachusetts Volunteer Infantry Regiment and then worked for years in the US Treasury Department. He was one of the first African American clerks at the Freedmen's Bureau, established early in Reconstruction to help former slaves.

Despite his personal accomplishments, he was denied service at a restaurant in the nearby resort town of Chesapeake Bay. Incensed, but also determined not to be subject to such treatment again, especially while on vacation, Douglass set about buying beachfront property on the Chesapeake Bay that he resold to family and friends, including leading Black political leaders of the day. His goal was to invest diligently and strategically in real estate to gradually build an oceanfront community where Black Americans could relax in freedom, away from the aggravations of encountering and negotiating racism.

In 1922, after the death of Charles Douglass, his son Haley Douglass worked to make Highland Beach the first African American incorporated municipality in Maryland. Self-governance enabled the Black residents to survive the Jim Crow era without losing control of their properties. By the 1930s, Highland Beach had become a welcoming summer haven for Black citizens from nearby cities like Washington, DC, and Baltimore. Notable visitors included Paul Robeson, W. E. B. Du Bois, and Langston Hughes, and in the decades to come, celebrities with homes in the community would include author Alex Haley and tennis great Arthur Ashe.

By the 1970s, with the worst practices of segregation beginning to ebb, the flow of Black homebuyers and visitors to Highland Beach began to diminish. The annual July Fourth fireworks and the Labor Day celebration were canceled due to lack of attendance. But in recent years, retirees have begun to buy up the historic homes in the community. Many of the purchasers are African Americans who fondly recall their family trips to Highland Beach when they were children. Today, visitors to the community can visit the Frederick Douglass Museum and Cultural Center, housed in Twin Oaks, the original summer cottage that Charles Douglass built in 1895 for his father—but which Frederick Douglass himself did not live long enough to enjoy.[1]

Other Black resorts have had shorter but still notable histories. Atlantic Beach in South Carolina traces its Black heritage to the 1930s, when descendants of enslaved people, most of them of Gullah-Geechee ancestry, began opening motels, restaurants, and nightclubs in the beachfront community. When the Intracoastal Waterway opened to commercial and pleasure boating in 1936, it brought a flow of new tourists to the area, and nearby Myrtle Beach became a vacation and golfing haven for white travelers. African Americans, under local Black Codes, were not permitted to fraternize with white patrons. Black entertainers who performed at the hotels along Myrtle Beach could not stay at those hotels. Instead, they stayed at places in Atlantic Beach. They would also occasionally perform after hours at venues there. As a result, its popularity as a vacation destination grew among African American travelers, including stars. By the 1960s, the town came to be known as "the Black Pearl."

The passage of the Civil Rights Act of 1964 changed the fortunes of Atlantic Beach, as it did many of the high-end Black resorts across the US. Desegregation (or "deseg," as it was colloquially known) opened the doors, so to speak, to hotels and beaches where Blacks had been prohibited from going. Within a few years, the knock-on effect was a declining interest in Atlantic Beach. Black people could now go to Myrtle Beach and North Myrtle Beach for their vacations. (Currently, North Myrtle surrounds Atlantic Beach on three sides.) Also, the local Black-owned businesses did not have the financial resources to compete with white merchants in a more competitive, integrated world. Because it was one of the last all-Black resorts started along the Atlantic coast before the passage of the Civil Rights Act of 1964, Atlantic Beach had one of the shortest lives.

Today, just a few of the hotels from the Jim Crow era remain open. The town is mostly quiet except during the annual Atlantic Beach Bikefest, which draws some 375,000 tourists during Memorial Day weekend.[2] This event, often referred to as Black Bike Week, is bringing new vitality to this once-important vacation safe haven for African Americans.

After hearing about Atlantic Beach, I checked *The Green Book* to see if there were any listings or ads for tourist houses, motels, restaurants, or clubs in the town. There was one: the Theretha Hotel, which was listed for a couple of years. This surprised me, given the popularity of Atlantic Beach. Perhaps this absence was another sign of the limited economic resources and marketing vision of the local Black merchants.

"BLACK EDEN"—MEMORIES OF PERFECT SUMMERS IN IDLEWILD

Idlewild, Michigan, Mary Ellen Tyus's home away from home, is a historic, upper-class Black resort that survived. When Janée and I looked in *The Green Book*, we found that hotels, tourist homes, lodges, restaurants, and taverns in Idlewild advertised there year after year. This certainly sparked our curiosity to know more and also to see the place for ourselves. Unfortunately, it was way north and west of our route south, so we didn't visit it. However, Mary Ellen shared her memories with us.

Idlewild was founded in 1912 by four white families who had teamed up to purchase twenty-seven hundred acres of prime forestland in rural northwestern Michigan. They concocted an unusual plan for realizing the profit from this investment. Recognizing the demand for real estate among Black Americans who were excluded from many communities, they began selling lots to people of color through agents around the country. By 1927, more than sixteen thousand lots had been sold to Black landowners from as far away as Massachusetts and California.

Idlewild was on its way to becoming known as America's "Black Eden." By the 1950s, the town had fourteen motels, six restaurants, nine nightclubs, and hundreds of cottages for rent to vacationers. Because of segregation, Black performers couldn't perform anywhere in the area except Idlewild. Stars from Lionel Hampton and Dizzy Gillespie to Sarah Vaughan and Sammy Davis Jr. performed there during the summers, and during the winter months some of the musicians and comics toured the country with the so-called Idlewild Revue.[3]

Mary Ellen Tyus's grandmother began going there not long after the resort town was founded, and Mary Ellen has been a regular since she was a baby. She described the lasting connection that she and her family forged with Idlewild:

My grandmother was a schoolteacher here in Columbus. She had asthma and hay fever, and one of her friends, I think somebody from Chicago, said to her, "You ought to go up into Michigan. The air is cleaner and cooler, and you might do better with your asthma up there."

She came and she liked it and she took my mom, who was a baby. My grandmother liked it enough that she kept going back. After several years, she built a cottage around 1920 or 1921. Since then, the cottage has not only been expanded but jacked up, put on a flatbed, and moved to the other side of the lake where it is now. The cottage was on the road with the back of the house facing the lake. We call our places cottages, but they are really houses. They are not rustic.

After noting that Mary Ellen is the third generation of one of the first families to settle in Idlewild, Janée said teasingly, "This makes you Idlewild royalty."

Mary Ellen responded, "Yes. So are most of my friends." It is undoubtedly the continuing return of these Black families that has contributed immensely to Idlewild's survival.

Of course, we wanted to know what life was like at an all-Black resort full of professional Black people away from the daily indignities of racism. Mary Ellen shared her memories, smiling throughout:

When I was growing up, that's where people went for vacation. And usually it was the moms and the kids that would go, and the dads who would come on weekends or for a week or so in the summer, because they had to work the rest of the time.

I would spend my summer days in Idlewild hanging out with my friends. We'd have breakfast, and then everybody was turned loose. There was always something going on. Everybody had a rowboat, and some of the boys had a boat with a motor on the back. I couldn't really call them speedboats—they were just boats with motors—but they made the most of that. And so, we always had transportation—some people rode bikes, but mostly we were on the water or in the water. We could go up to an area called The Island where they had concession stands so we could have a hamburger and fries and a milkshake for a dollar and a quarter.

We knew we had to head home for dinner at six o'clock when the fire department siren went off. Then the older kids would get together again in the evening. We'd go down to the beach and do hot dogs and marshmallows or whatever, or just have a dance party at somebody's house. And that was our typical summer.

Mary Ellen also recalled seeing singers Della Reese and Barbara McNair. She especially remembered seeing McNair waterskiing down the lake when she wasn't performing at night.

For high-achieving African American professionals, especially those based in the Midwest, Idlewild represented the fulfillment of their

American Dream—the version of that dream that they had built parallel to the one that whites in the United States were pursuing. In Cincinnati, when we interviewed Joyce Coleman about her family's travels, she spoke about the fun of "escaping" to Idlewild during the summer: "Oh God, you got to go to the [roller] skating rink! That was like going to heaven without dying." And she recalled the pride and pleasure of seeing affluent Black Americans from all over the region—Cincinnati, Cleveland, Chicago, Fort Wayne, Detroit—converging on Idlewild, which was their own special place.

Like the white dream, the Black dream of success had its entry requirements. As Janée had commented, some people were considered "Idlewild royalty," which meant their relatives had been going there for generations. Others had to gain entry to the elevated ranks of Idlewild's summer society through other means—by being invited by someone who lived there, for instance, or by marrying into an Idlewild family. As a result, there was a socially exclusive quality to the leading Black resort communities—somewhat ironically, since these Black enclaves existed in large part as refuges from the racist forms of exclusivity practiced at similar resorts nearby.

When we asked Hezekiah Jackson whether his working-class family had ever visited a Black-oriented resort during his boyhood, his answer was revealing:

We didn't know anything about places like Martha's Vineyard. My uncle had a good friend who was like a lot of other, I would say, upper-middle-class Blacks of that time who knew about those places. So, we got an opportunity to visit Martha's Vineyard, and it was really, almost frightening. We had to go there on the ferry, and I didn't know how to swim. Another time we went to Oak Bluffs, and to me it was just like an out-of-body experience.

Interior page of the 1949 vacation edition of *The Green Book*, advertising the Black resort community of Oak Bluffs, Massachusetts.

Jackson clearly did not feel completely at home in these upscale havens for Black Americans of means. He went on to observe that the existence of Black resorts was *not* a topic that the middle-class Blacks he knew were eager to talk about: "These middle-class families that had their own businesses went to those places and kept it very quiet because they were afraid to let people know that they had those kinds of resources. They didn't want people to know, especially white people."

But despite their exclusivity—or in part because of it—the resorts favored by affluent Black Americans became a treasured part of some families' heritage. Over time, places like Idlewild became havens that people returned to year after year, generation after generation, for the solace and affirmation they offered. And many of them remain so today.

Idlewild is not as vibrant and lively as it was in its heyday from the 1920s to the early 1960s when the town would be jammed with up to twenty-five thousand people during the height of the summer holidays. The biggest stars no longer perform there, since desegregation means that Black singers and comedians have access to stages and studios everywhere. Instead, Idlewild has become a family resort. Second, third, fourth, and in some cases fifth generations of families continue to return. The younger generation is getting the word out about Idlewild. They are determined to create a new-style family resort that builds on their heritage. As a result, new families are buying into the community and, since many of them live in Michigan, they are extending the season into the autumn. The summer population is indeed smaller, around three thousand, but the traditions continue, such as the gala fund-raising dinner hosted every August by the homeowners' association (called the Idlewild Lot Association), complete with a glamorous fashion show, to kick off what's known as Idlewild Week. And over the July 4 holiday and during August, there are many family reunions. Mary Ellen Tyus remains an Idlewild loyalist. She commented:

Some people say, "Well, Idlewild's died." They even had a documentary on TV years ago that said that Idlewild's just a ghost town. That just isn't true. Idlewild still means a lot to many of us.

This is where peace and beauty and friends are. Every year, I feel as though I just have to go there, even if it's just, you know, just to touch base with the people that I care about. Idlewild is home, where most of my lifelong friends have always been. I don't think I've ever missed a summer. And I have this sort of superstitious feeling that, if I don't make it to Idlewild, I'm going to croak!

THE WAY THEY WERE, THE WAY THEY ARE

It's clear that the people who went to Idlewild (in Michigan), Fox Lake (in Angola, Indiana), and Oak Bluffs (in Massachusetts) probably did not need to use *The Green Book*. The important, up-to-date travel information was shared during conversations and other social interactions. Looking at these locations in the 1963–1964 edition of *The Green Book* (published before passage of the Civil Rights Act of 1964), Janée and I found two listings under Fox Lake (a motel and a lodge), eight under Oak Bluffs (all lodgings), and twenty under Idlewild (hotels, tourist homes, restaurants, and taverns). We wondered whether the number of listings was an indication of the popularity or the exclusivity of the places.

Like communities everywhere, Black resort towns are not immune to economic and social forces that make change almost inevitable. Consider, for example, the Black enclaves of Sag Harbor Hills, Azurest, and Ninevah Beach in the Hamptons, the affluent beach region on the eastern end of New York's Long Island. (None of the places have listings in *The Green Book*.) The area's connection to African American history is an old one. It dates back to the late eighteenth and early nineteenth centuries, when Blacks and Native Americans lived in Eastville, just southeast of Sag Harbor, and the AME Church of Eastville was a lively center of worship.

In the years after World War II, when Blacks were excluded from the region's resorts, pools, and beaches, Brooklyn schoolteacher Maude Terry and her sister, an art teacher and architect named Amaza Lee Meredith, came up with the idea of making Sag Harbor Hills a summer retreat for middle-class Black families from the big city. They developed 120 lots and sold them for $1,000 each. Over time, celebrities like singer Lena Horne, restaurateur B. Smith, magazine mogul Earl Graves, basketball star Allan Houston, and novelist Colson Whitehead began spending summers there. In 2019, the cultural importance of the Sag Harbor Hills, Azurest, and Ninevah Beach subdivisions (SANS) was recognized by the inclusion of the SANS Historic District in the National Register of Historic Places.

At the same time, however, the continued growth of real estate values on the Long Island shores has made it difficult for SANS to retain its special character. Developers and investors have been buying houses and parcels of land and seeking town approval to build giant homes far out of scale with the modest residences that date back to the 1950s, 1960s, and 1970s. In 2011 Colson Whitehead observed: "It's already not what it was. The traditions will stay as long as people keep them alive. But real estate in this area [of Long Island] trumps everything else."[4] Black or not, these storied resort towns are caught up in the American capitalist system, in which the dollar ultimately rules.

Yet despite the pressures of economics and other forces of change, a number of the historic Black resorts have managed so far to retain their historic character. One example is Oak Bluffs on Martha's Vineyard, an island four miles off the coastline of Cape Cod in Massachusetts. Blacks began to own land on the island as far back as the eighteenth century, and the town of Oak Bluffs became a vacation destination for middle-class African Americans in the late nineteenth century. The town beach is known as the Inkwell, a name that some say was inspired by the great writers of the Harlem Renaissance who used to visit. Oak Bluffs today remains a favorite summer haunt of African American luminaries from Washington, DC; New York; and Boston. They are attracted to the expansive beach, the beautifully verdant Ocean Park, and the distinctive domestic architecture, especially the colorful, ginger-bread Victorian houses that were once part of a Methodist camp.

Just as Mary Ellen Tyus goes to Idlewild every year, I know families who go to Oak Bluffs every summer. Their return is for them a touchstone, a deeply meaningful connection to a place where they're welcome, where they don't have to negotiate anything about who they are, where they're understood, and where they can be completely comfortable—a place where their world feels knowable and safe.

After we finished our informative and heartwarming conversation with Mary Ellen in Columbus and began our drive to Cincinnati, Janée and I shared some fantasies that Mary Ellen's memories had encouraged. The first was to rent or buy a place in one of these once all-Black resorts for a summer or two. It would be so fascinating to live in the rooms, walk the paths, and feel the spirit of what the place meant to our elders who sought a restorative respite from the indignations and harassments of racism. And what fun it would be to re-create not just Mary Ellen's perfect day in Idlewild, but a perfect two weeks in Idlewild. Our second fantasy was to do another road trip across the US to see and talk to people, like Mary Ellen, who knew these all-Black resorts in their heyday and could capture what it was like to spend time there safe from the gaze and reactions of white people.

Like the many once-thriving Little Harlems, these Black resorts are an essential, though often overlooked, reality of the African American experience. Black Americans have always known it was their right to have equal participation in the American Dream. When denied it, they used their ingenuity, cooperative spirit, hard work, and limited capital to find ways around those cruel barriers and establish places where such barriers didn't exist, if only temporarily. *The Green Book* was one of those workarounds. Like many other Black people with entrepreneurial spirits who saw the growing but then segregated leisure travel industry, the creators of these Black resorts knew their only option was to build a world that was parallel to the white world in America, but also largely out of sight and out of mind of that world's gaze.

— 9 —

WE LIVED IT

For me, storytelling is a way to think about my
past and to give context to my present. It really is
something that I don't like to take for granted.

— Crystal Churchwell Evans, marketing
strategy professional and lifelong
resident of Nashville, Tennessee

There's great power in learning about the story of Black America
through resources like museums, historic sites, and documents
such as the archive of *Green Book* editions preserved at the Schomburg
Center. But as we discovered anew during our road trip, there's no substi-
tute for hearing that story from the people who experienced it firsthand.
The Nashville lawyer Ana Nettles is part of the "millennial" generation

---

Author Alvin Hall in the front yard of his
family's home in Wakulla, Florida, circa 1956–1957.

(those born 1981–1996) and reinforced how important it is to hear and share stories of lived experiences, especially among family members:

[It's] the telling and the retelling. I think we find comfort in each other and consistency in sharing the stories [of what] we've experienced, for example what my mom has experienced. She loves telling me the same stories over and over again. She always starts off by saying, "Now I know I've told you this one before but . . ." I find myself not only telling her stories again but telling her stories back to her. Ultimately the true message really comes through as life lessons. This is such a fundamental part of communication, at least for my family.

Evelyn Nettles, the Tennessee State University administrator we've met before, is Ana's aunt. She reminded us of an undeniable truth about people of her generation and older:

We, in my generation, we lived it. We lived it, even though we didn't let it paralyze us. The statement that you probably heard as you were growing up was, "You've got to be twice as good; you've got to be the best; you cannot be lazy; you need to work, and you need to work hard." And after you study all the language of Jim Crow, you start to understand where some of [these concepts] came from.

Evelyn Nettles's three simple words—*we lived it*—were also said in a more personal way by Kenneth Clay of Louisville, Kentucky—*I lived it*. And it was implied in the tone of voice that many of the older interviewees used when answering certain questions. In many cases, the words were said after a pause, when the person was trying to find the right ones to say that would express and encapsulate their disturbing, astonishing, and diverse experiences in the cities where they grew up—Nashville and Louisville, respectively, for Nettles and Clay—as well as during their visits to their grandparents in small towns in the Deep South. The verb "lived" speaks not only to having seen and survived so much; it is meant to help us—all people—put our contemporary experiences, our points of view, our reactions in context. And it denotes continuing to survive—with resilience, with imagination, with hope. It says quietly, determinedly, "I have been strong. I remain strong. And I want my people to be strong."

The question that came to mind repeatedly while hearing stories from our interviewees' lives was, "Where does this strength come from?" This question brought forth stories of other generations—the elders—who also "lived it." From each story, there was much to be gleaned, much to be absorbed and used, much to be passed on about continuing to live better and freer as an individual, as a family, and as a community—just as Victor Hugo Green wanted in all areas of African American life, on the roadways of the United States and beyond.

Sitting in his office at an apartment building he owns in downtown Selma, Alabama, Hank Sanders, an Alabama state senator from 1983 to 2018, told a story about a drive he made one night in Alabama during the height of the civil rights movement. His story sounded and felt like a scene from a psychological horror film:

I went down to southeast Alabama [where] I was attending this [civil rights] meeting. There was a white woman who worked with Black people at the meeting. When I got ready to leave, some Black people at the meeting asked me if I would drop her off in a town twenty miles up north. The very first thing that crossed my mind was [that driving at night with a white woman in my car was] enough to get me killed. But I thought about it, and I said [to myself], okay, otherwise they [the organizers] have to drive forty miles—twenty miles up and twenty miles back. And against my better judgment, I decided to go ahead and take her. We hadn't got far out of town when this truck, the kind that you automatically know has guns in a rack on the back [window], came up behind me. It was dusk dark. I made sure that I didn't drive too fast or too slow. The truck kept following me. It would get right up on [the rear of my car]. When I would speed up, the truck would speed up. When I would slow down, it would slow down. Finally, when I slowed down enough, the truck pulled up beside my car. I just knew that we were going to get shot. But then the truck pushed on and drove on off. Then I became concerned about even going further down the road. As I kept driving, I wondered to myself, should I turn around or should I just keep driving? It ran against the grain for me to not want to take [the woman home], but it ran against the grain for me to want to take her home. That fear was so great because so much had happened [on those back roads at night.]

Sanders's vivid recollection shows the deep well of courage and determination Black people had to have in order to overcome fear and keep moving forward. I asked Sanders whether he thought the people in that truck were committing an act of terror against him. His answer was unequivocal:

It was definitely terrorism, in my mind. There are all kinds of forms of terrorism, but many people would not understand that was terrorism because they don't understand the background. You've spent all of your life being told that even looking at a white woman is enough to cause a problem. So, the drivers might say, "Oh, we were just in our truck." But following us the way they did was certainly an act of terrorism.

"There are all kinds of forms of terrorism." Sanders's words unexpectedly opened my eyes to a different perspective on some scenes from my childhood. Acts of terrorism can be large or small. I thought about my mother working as a day maid (now called a domestic) for people in Tallahassee, Florida. I thought of the times she would come home steaming with anger at the way one of the white people she worked for had treated her. She would never talk about it. There was no use asking what happened because the anger might turn toward you. Instead, she would go into her room or sit silently in a chair on the front porch and "pray on it." Only after my interview with Sanders did I realize that one of the purposes of those weekly Wednesday prayer meetings held at the Baptist church near our home was to help the people in my community get in touch with "God's divine grace" so they could get through the week of working with or in a world of white people who may have been terrorizing them in small, deliberate ways.

Crystal Churchwell Evans, who lives and works in Nashville, shared a story about her grandmother that shows how such antagonisms can have a lasting effect:

My grandmother lives in East Nashville, which was half white and half Black with a definite, clear divide during segregation. Her world was mostly all Black, and there was this fear of being in spaces that were predominantly white. We used to pick her up and do Sunday drives. My dad, my mom, my brother, and I would go pick her up. We used to drive in this area called Belle Meade on the west side of town. It's beautiful. We would look at the homes with their beautiful, manicured lawns. As we were driving my grandmother was starting to get a little antsy in her seat. I ask my grandma, "What going on?" She responded, "Why are we over here?" I explained that we are just going on a Sunday drive. Again she asked, "But why are we over here?" She was increasingly uncomfortable. Then she kept repeating with more and more anxiety each time, "We need to leave. We need to leave. We need to leave." My dad explained to me that she was not comfortable, so we took a different route. Later in a similar situation, my dad explained that my grandmother was uncomfortable because [Belle Meade] was the area that you could not go to unless you were working there. You had to leave at night. You got on the [city] bus when you finished your shift if you weren't working in Belle Meade [after sundown].

In the Nettles family, as we have seen, one source of strength was Evelyn's late father, Willie. He imparted strength through his actions and his storytelling. Evelyn describes him as a "storyteller extraordinaire." Evelyn's niece, Ana Nettles, says that storytelling was Willie's purposeful way of showing his caring and love for them. He wanted to impart to his family, through words and actions, the wisdom he had accumulated that could help them in their journeys through life as Black people in America.

But there was also another, even more deeply personal intent, as Evelyn explained:

I think he told some of those stories so my brother [Michael] would be careful. He was in the middle, and he was our only boy. Daddy wanted to make sure that he [my brother] did not do anything that would put him in any danger. So I think that's why he told us many of those stories. I think some of the other stories he told us were because if something happened politically—and you just don't know what can happen—he wanted us to be aware of where it came from and where we came from.

Willie told his stories during the family's times together, at social gatherings in the community, and when people just dropped by to visit with him. His children—Evelyn, Michael, and Francine—remember that Willie had lived many of the stories he told, as Evelyn said:

He talked about when he would drive through the South. Even in his [military] uniform, when he was coming from the base to go to Moss Point [Mississippi], sometimes he would be stopped. He wore his uniform just because of that. But he said that sometimes even that didn't make a difference to some people. They would take you off the road and you'd have to pay your fine. Of course, if you didn't have the money, that was a very fearful time.

He also talked about going from Piney Woods [Mississippi] down to Moss Point, even taking the bus. And one time, he was put off the bus in the middle of nowhere. He figured this was a really bad situation. He waited for the next bus to come through. It picked him up and then he got where he was going. I really wish Willie were here so he could tell you what his feelings were about that.

Willie also shared stories about other generations of the Nettles family, like his mother, Essie, an entrepreneur who owned a restaurant (Essie's Place), and his father, who owned a barbershop in Moss Point. Following an incident in the town between a white man and a Black man, Essie bravely and determinedly used her influence to communicate the concerns of the Black community and to get an answer to take back to them to allay their fears. Evelyn shared her recollection of Willie's story about that incident:

One story that we found amusing. We had to ask our mother if Daddy was lying, [because] he could exaggerate a little. She said, "Oh no, that one's okay." It's about a sheriff in Mississippi. His son had sent away and bought a sheriff's uniform. And even though he wasn't a sheriff, he would [use that uniform to] antagonize the Black people on Sunday. He would go and pick up his girlfriend in a car. Then while he was in his sheriff's uniform, he would stop Black people—men—and make them dance for her. It was like a minstrel show.

One Sunday, he stopped the wrong fellow. That fellow beat him good and made him take his uniform off. Of course, that fellow had to get out of town. The Black people were really scared. People came to my grandmother and said, "Miss Essie, we're really concerned because of what has happened here. They may start lynching people."

She went to the mayor because she had worked for him in his kitchen. He said, "It'll be okay, Essie. You don't have to worry about anything."

She said, "Oh no, the people are really fearful of possible lynchings."

He said, "No, don't worry." They must have talked to the white community, because nothing happened. But the [Black] fellow did have to leave town.

This story about Essie demonstrates that she was willing to step forward, to use her connections to local authorities to express her community's anxiety about a potentially violent reaction, a terrorist action to be frank, by local white people against Black people. She knew from experience that using her connections and her respectability with the white mayor could get information and, at the same time, perhaps mitigate the situation. Based on my experiences growing up in the segregated South, I suspect the white community knew something about the behavior of the sheriff's son that caused them to look the other way. Using today's language, Essie's intervention could be read as her feeling that "we are all in this together" and "I will do my part for the safety of all of our people."

Living through urban renewal and experiencing its effects on Black-owned businesses and homes, as well as the overall community, is another story we heard in city after city. The phrase "urban renewal" was invariably accompanied by a chuckle and the mention of the deeply ironic phrase "Negro removal" that was widely used in the Black community. The events in Nashville are a case study. In 1968, local white politicians deliberately routed the interstate highway system in a way that cut off and cut through the areas around Jefferson Street, often using the legal doctrine of eminent domain to seize land and destroy properties on land along the path. This effectively caused an economic decline in that thriving Black community. Professor Learotha Williams Jr. and his students at Tennessee State University researched the routing of I-40. He told us:

[I-40] intersects Jefferson Street up there at Tenth Avenue and further down at Twenty-eighth Avenue. [The routing] displaced more than a thousand homes. Eight hundred businesses [were] removed. Since they [city government officials] were talking about urban renewal, we wanted to see [in our research] if they were talking about removing poor folk. So, what my students and

I did, we looked at homeownership along that strip. The majority of those folk, at least along the first couple of blocks, were home-owners. We found the same thing down there at Twenty-eighth Avenue.

Before a city decides where a route is going to go, the federal government required the city or the people planning it to hold community meetings to inform the citizens about what was being contemplated. The city held meetings in places where Black folks did not go, could not go, or it was difficult to go. On one occa-sion they put announcements about [the meeting] in a post office that did not serve this community. Later, [another] meeting was changed at the last minute. Folks [in the affected neighborhoods] rallied and filed a lawsuit. They lost the first round. Then the suit went on appeal, and the judge during the appeal conceded that things were not done properly, but he couldn't really say that it was because of race, which for me is an incredible statement because about 95 percent of all of the people who lived [in that community] were Black.

Williams noted that this is a common story, one we would see again if we examined the routing of many of the interstate highways in US cities, including I-65 to Birmingham, Alabama, which was one of the stops on our journey.

The day before we arrived in Nashville, we had met Kenneth Clay on a street in downtown Louisville, Kentucky. He lived it, too. For him, Walnut Street and Chestnut Street were where he "wanted to be." Clay brought a stack of old black-and-white photographs from a local archive that he had included in his book (written with Mervin Aubespin and J. Blaine Hudson) *Two Centuries of Black Louisville: A Photographic History*. Going through the stack and seeing pictures of local celebrations and the stars who came to them gave us a sense of how vibrant life was on Walnut and Chestnut Streets in the 1950s and 1960s. In addition to writing books, Clay has mounted cultural events—plays, concerts, readings, celebrations—to make people, especially young people, aware of often-overlooked parts of history and to connect that knowledge to the present. In his work, he honors the rich history that existed even during segregation, emphasizing the inspiring people and the strong communities that motivated him to achieve.

Clay's work in the public arena is important because it informs Black people whose family members have not chosen to share their personal stories with their children or others of the next generation. Not everyone wants to tell stories about the past. The reasons are many. Some, like my own family, want to keep the next generation focused on the future—the part of their story that they can influence. While growing up during segregation, I often heard family members who had probably seen, experienced, or heard about some racial horror say, "It's my past, not yours." Many relatives, including my beloved grandmother, would say to me, "You need to focus on what's ahead of *you*, not what's behind *me*." People often ask me whether I feel this was wrong of my relatives. They ask whether I wanted or want to know who "my people" are, referring to my ancestors. I feel my parents and relatives gave me an amazing gift: to be unencumbered by the emotional resonances of their past. They raised me to have an open heart, an open mind, and at the same time, they imparted enough common sense and wisdom to me so that I could, in my life away from them, connect to other people who would become part of the family I would build for myself. They knew a time would come when I would be ready to find out about their lives as well as my ancestors.

In truth, the podcast *Driving the Green Book* became unexpectedly part of that personal journey. Hearing other people's lived stories and their reflections about them has led to my connecting to and understanding, sometimes suddenly, many of my relatives' recollections, mostly stated in passing, of their experiences. Now when I ask questions, clearly ready to talk about the past, they are also ready to talk about the past too.

THE POWER OF EXPERIENCES SHARED

T. Marie King, a community organizer, facilitator, and trainer, grew up in a family that avoided talking about the worst aspects of their past. Her one-word answer to the question, "Did your mom ever talk to you about Jim Crow or segregation?" confirms this point of view. She simply said, "Never." When asked why, she explained: "I think because of the traumatic nature of it. I would hear stories from my grandmother, who's from Lowndes County [Alabama], which is a part of Montgomery. I had a great-uncle who was killed. He was a part of a terror killing in Lowndes County. So, I remember him through bits and stories about that, but nobody ever really focuses on that time. Nobody really talks about that."

Upon hearing about the silence in King's family today, many might see that silence as being withholding, secretive, selfish, or ungenerous. But when we reflect on the emotional cost involved even in thinking about horrific past events, the silence is understandable and forgivable.

This practice of silence raises the question of how our past history can be preserved. If King's family never talked about the terror killing, then how did she find out about it, other than from the "bits and stories" she infrequently heard from family members? Some of her education came from her visit to the National Memorial for Peace and Justice (more commonly referred to as the national lynching memorial) created in Montgomery by the Equal Justice Initiative. While viewing the collection of jars of soil gathered from sites of racist terror killings, King was brought up short by an unexpected family connection:

I'm walking through and I'm like, "Whoa. Hold up! I know that name!" It was mind-blowing! There's actually a jar with his [her great-uncle's] name on it. That blew my mind, because I wasn't expecting to see Ed Bracy. He was killed in 1935. I thought the memorial is focused only on lynchings. Instead, they are focused on all terror killings that were documented. So my uncle's name is also on the Corten Steel monument for Lowndes County. That was a shock to me. I had heard the story in bits and pieces; but to actually see his name there, it was like, Wow!

Ed Bracy had been working to unionize sharecroppers in Lowndes County—and he wasn't willing to back down to the threats of the KKK. King said, "It's kind of a bittersweet moment, in the sense that I hate that my uncle lost his life that way, but I'm proud that he stood up for what he believed in." One wonders how remaining silent about the terror killing affected her family. "I would say it impacted the older ones who were around at that time," King told us. "They were young kids, and that was major for them. But for us [the younger generation], it just wasn't brought up. So, there is no impact because we don't know that was there. And those of us who did hear about it, we never got the full details."

Sometimes this silence was intended as a protective gift—to free the next generation from the ghosts and emotional weight of hurt, skepticism, mistrust, and anger and the desire for vengeance. Black families want to give the young—their children, grandchildren, nieces, nephews, cousins, and others—freedom, a sense of an open future. They don't want to see the new generation burdened, especially at an early age, with the restrictions, hardships, and acrimonies that they endured themselves. However, the silence can be protective in a different way, as King explained: "I think because of the trauma the terror killing caused them, they didn't want to revisit it. They just couldn't. It's like, that's gone, that has happened, we've moved past it. What's the reason to bring it back up?"

Inspired by what she learned at the National Memorial for Peace and Justice, King has joined a group known as the Jefferson County Memorial Project that's now working to bring to her home county the extra Corten Steel monument created by the Equal Justice Initiative that lists and honors the victims of racist violence. (The EJI made two copies for each county: one to remain installed at the memorial in Montgomery and the other to be erected in the county named, given the political will.) King has clearly inherited her uncle's strength—his activism and his belief in doing what's right and fair for his fellow citizens. Finding out more about Ed Bracy's terror killing has no doubt increased her fighting spirit and her resolve to stand up for the causes on which she works.

This work has also made King more aware of the sensitivities and emotional nuances related to the terror killing within her family. When asked if she thought the inclusion of her uncle's name in the memorial would help or inspire her family to talk more about what happened, her answer was full of empathy and generosity:

I would hope it would, but I'm not sure. I think that the older generation has their feelings about it. I don't really see that generation kind of jumping back in [to the discussion], but I would hope it would. For me, I'm all for it. I'm ready to have the conversation anytime. But I'm also sensitive that other people may not be where I am. So if I talk to people, and they say, "I ain't ready for that conversation," or "I don't know how I feel about that," it's cool with me. We don't have to go any further. So, I'm open for where people are.

Many African Americans cite the lives of their fathers and mothers—specific incidents they witnessed or heard that their parents handled—

as the sources of their understanding of the world beyond their homes and communities. These stories also gave them insights into their parents. Over time, these insights evolved to become sources of inner strength and eventually wisdom. Hank Sanders, who grew up in poverty, without even an outhouse, in rural Baldwin County, Alabama, talked about what he had learned from his parents, Sam and Ola Mae Sanders:

My father was a very quiet man, a very strong man, but very quiet, who worked all the time. I work fourteen- to sixteen-hour days just like my father did, even today.

My mother had a peculiar confidence in her children. Sometimes in that three-room house, when things got real bad, my mother would make us all come to the front room. . . . She sat in the only chair. We only had one chair. She would sit in that chair and she would make us sit on the floor in front of her. And she would say, "Children, things are always kinda bad with this big, poor family. But they are real bad now." And then she'd just go silent for a moment, making us focus in on her. And then she'd say, "But don't y'all worry. I'm at my best when things get bad."

It was such a powerful moment. Even thinking about it makes me cry. And she was at her best, and I'd like to think that I have a little of that, and that her other children have a little of that. And so, when things get bad, we try to be at our best.

My mother was a fighter—she really was. She was an extraordinary woman. My father was extraordinary, too. But my mother had the gift of words; my father had the gift of example.

Sanders took these gifts, along with the memorable incidents in his young life, and transformed them into an inner fire that tempered his mind, spirit, and resolve. Growing up poor in the rural South, he began

A civil rights march in Washington, DC, in 1963.

dreaming of becoming a lawyer after reading an article about Thurgood Marshall in a newspaper given to the family to use as toilet paper. His schoolmates laughed at him when he told them about his ambition to be a lawyer. In their small, remote part of Alabama, they had never seen a Black lawyer and could not even imagine one. Sanders's dream seemed hilarious to them.

Although their laughter hurt him deeply and made him cry, he transformed that painful memory into three simple words: "Yes, I will!" And Sanders did. He earned his undergraduate degree from Talladega College and attained his law degree from Harvard University, attending the university on the Felix Frankfurter Scholarship that is awarded to "poor young men who show great promise."

We asked Sanders to reflect on the changes he'd seen in his lifetime. His response was sobering:

In 1966, when I was working to help people vote in Lowndes County, I thought that five years would be enough. By then, I thought the Voting Rights Act would be fully implemented. Dr. King asked, "How long?" If I could speak to him today, I would tell him, "I didn't know you were talking about time measured in biblical terms."

I really didn't understand the depth of white supremacy. When Obama was elected president, I thought that was going to make race relationships better. But it made it worse. It really intensified. That's some of the power of white supremacy.

So I am deeply disappointed about the impact of white supremacy, but probably even more disappointed that many of the Black people we have put in office have not protected our rights, have not implemented justice. I would also say to Dr. King, "You fought until your life was taken—so I'm going to keep fighting."

PROGRESS IN TRAVEL AND LIFE

The words "great promise," which Harvard saw in the young Hank Sanders, were certainly part of what motivated Victor and Alma Green to create and publish *The Green Book* for three decades. In promoting the freedom to travel without aggravation, the Greens also envisioned a country that would open opportunities for social and economic growth for African Americans. Victor's words in the 1949 *Green Book*, "There will be a day sometime in the near future when this guide will not have to be published," reflect the motivating optimism that simmers in the lived stories our interviewees shared about themselves and their ancestors.

That's one reason Black people continue to tell these stories to the next generation and the generation after that. But there's another reason:

to prepare them for situations where the past is also the present. Or, to paraphrase what Evelyn Nettles said about her father's stories, if something happens—and you just don't know what can happen—our elders want us to be aware of where *it* came from and where *we* came from.

Carl Westmoreland, a Cincinnati resident, recalled for us an incident that happened in the 1990s that connected viscerally to past experiences:

Traveling in the 1940s, '50s, and '60s was insane. You were reminded constantly that you were less than, in the perception of the white community, a human being. At the same time, if you look back, it was miraculous to watch our parents and the elders make adjustments and develop networks of contact so they could move around, so they could balance the ugly we saw en route with decent places to sleep, warm places to eat and to be received with courtesy. There were [gas stations] where they didn't want you to go to the bathroom, even if they were willing to sell you gas. You had to hold your water.

This disappeared, but it didn't really disappear. In the 1990s my youngest son was going to Morehouse [College in Atlanta]. On [Interstate] 275 or 285 going around Atlanta, I needed to buy gas at a service station and I needed to go to the bathroom. The man [at the station] didn't want to let me go to the bathroom after he had already put gas in [my car]. We got into it. I'm in my late fifties, and I'm about to go to war with a guy in his late twenties, and I didn't care. This is in the 1990s and the dude got in my face. My son, who is a wide receiver, figured out what was going on, walked in, and suddenly had me behind him. He said to the attendant, "He will try you, but I'll knock you out. Daddy go to the bathroom."

I didn't need to take a moment to think about the decades of memories of being denied access to a bathroom or having to "hold your water" that boiled up at that service station in the 1990s. Reflecting on those memories—and on the many similar incidents they represent, from his life and the lives of people he knows—Westmoreland added, "I think we've made a mistake by not sharing stories like these with our young people, so they can understand how tenuous our status is in this country."

THE CONVERSATION

Today, young Black people sometimes grow up in communities where this kind of information is not a part of their lives. They have to be proactive in seeking it out, typically through courses, books, movies, and other media. As Hezekiah Jackson in Birmingham, Alabama, said about his nephew: "He was like most other young people today. He thought what we told him about, warned him about, was some kind of fairy tale, until the police stopped him," and he didn't know what to do:

> He called us on his cell phone and said, "The police have stopped me right here before you get on the freeway." And we said, "We are on the way." He then said, "I don't know what to do." So, I said to him, "Put your hands on the steering wheel and don't move. I don't care what they tell you to do, don't move. Don't move." It was always our biggest fear that he would be trying to get his license or something, and [a police officer] would say he was trying to get a gun. We were just five minutes away from where he was. He had just left home.

After this incident, Jackson and his sister had "The Conversation" with the young man repeatedly about how to act when being stopped by the police. These stops by police, in particular, have so much deep negative, threatening resonances for Black people in America. After recalling this incident about his nephew, Jackson seamlessly began connecting it to his own encounters: "I've been stopped myself too many times. They [the police] will stop you because your car is not good enough or because it is too good, you have a broken taillight, or your brake lights are not working—all kinds of things."

Tiffany Shawn, standing in a small mall across the street from the Ferguson Police Department headquarters in 2016, recalled the day she heard "The Conversation" in her own family:

> My brother was maybe eighteen or nineteen. He's in his early twenties right now, so it wasn't that many years ago. Our dad was having a conversation with him, saying, "Never leave your house without your ID. If you come across a police officer, just be honest about what you are doing. Show him your ID right away even if he doesn't ask. Tell him what you're doing before you pull it out of your pocket."
>
> I was in awe and asked, "Do you all have these kinds of conversations all the time?" As his Black daughter, he wasn't having that conversation with me, but he knew he had to have it with a Black son because of how things are in St. Louis.

Reverend Starsky Wilson, who cochaired the Ferguson Commission, formed after the death of Michael Brown, confirmed the necessity of the talk Shawn's father had and then reflected on his own need to have The Conversation in his own family:

Yes, this is a pervasive issue for African American families in this country, that we have to talk with our young people about how to survive. I have three boys and I shudder to think. But I know the day will come when I'll need to have that conversation with each of them. And quite frankly, soon, very soon, for my eleven-year-old.

For other young people like Jackson's nephew, the moment of understanding comes when they encounter a problem at a hotel—or are completely ignored while waiting for service in a shop or restaurant. For one of Jackson's nieces it happened when one of the white boys in her school said to her that if he raped her, nothing would be done about it because he was white. For Kemi Aladesuyi, the producer of our 2019 road trip, such a moment occurred at one of our stops: "When we stopped at a gas station on our way to Louisiana, there were two cashiers checking people out, but one line. I went to the cashier who was next available, but she completely ignored me, scowled, and looked off in the distance. She was white. The other cashier sighed and called me over to check me out. She was Black."

The stories that interviewees shared with us in every town and city from Detroit to New Orleans made us feel as if we were being welcomed into the trusting camaraderie of their extended family. With their generosity, they enriched our perspective and increased our wisdom by sharing with us lived experiences—their own and that of others. Within the words of each story was so much to be gleaned about courage, inner strength, negotiation, survival, resilience, and hope. Indeed, they lived it. But thinking about that history, their experiences, as well as Carl Westmoreland's and Kemi's experience at the service stations, leads us to only one possible conclusion: We are *still* living it.

— 10 —

THE GREEN BOOK'S LEGACY

DOING WHAT I CAN, WHERE I AM

My father had a lot of faith in the future. Sometimes I'm sure he had down moments about where things would go. But I think his feeling ultimately was that, if you could release the human potential that's in the Black community—and also in women, in low-income whites, in other ethnics—there's so much we could achieve. There's so much talent that doesn't get promoted and developed.

> — Jesse J. Turner Jr., former president of the Tri-State Bank of Memphis, Tennessee

Derrick Adams's left panel of *Kings on Vacation* (Martin), 2021, archival inkjet print on Hahnemuhle German etching 310 gsm paper; 22.5 x 17 inches each.

Janée and I talked during the drives between the cities on our journey about what we learned from the people we had just met and what this steady accumulation of information and insights, especially the new perspectives, made us feel. Our emotions undoubtedly caused us to look differently at the landscapes and roads between the cities. When we started out, we were like any traveler today: we put our destination into a GPS navigation app and focused on how long it would take us to get from one location to the next. Along the way, we figured out where to stop, often spontaneously. However, by the time we left Cincinnati, we started talking about how the forests beside the secondary roads would have been viewed by travelers during the days of *The Green Book*. As African Americans approached certain cities, were they more or less worried about being pulled over? Was driving through those cities to get to a relative's house or through the city's "Little Harlem" a greater or lesser anxiety than being on the road?

We asked ourselves these questions, and they could be asked of us all:

- What have you learned about African American history that you never knew before?
- What do you think was the source of strength and resilience in the Black people we talked with?
- What did you get from the people we interviewed and what did you learn about yourself in the process?
- What story or experience today do you most identify with? Why?
- What did you hear that made you think of a current event? What about it surprised or shocked you?

- Why do you think this part of American history has been so pervasively ignored?
- Are you surprised by how many white Americans went along with the racist-motivated policies for the privileges they were given?
- What do you think of the movement today to continue white-washing history?

Every question seemed to take us back to the inner strength, optimism, and other capacities that stopped African Americans from being crushed—on the streets of their hometowns, on the highways across the country, anywhere they were moving from one place to the next—under the weighty inconveniences, aggravations, embarrassments, and harassment innate in the white supremacist ideas that were so widely accepted, whether actively or passively, by so much of America. We kept remembering and quoting Maya Angelou's poem about history, "Still I Rise," in which she says we rise again like dust, like air, like hope. Lies cannot keep us down.

After our visit to Jackson, Mississippi, the phrase "like dust" reminded me of the way Farish Street looks today—like there is a cover of sandy dust over the sidewalks and the buildings. How does one capture the importance that these destinations once had, the inspiration that once emanated from them?

The Green Book, through its various name changes and evolutions, remains a North Star of that period of African Americans' movement toward greater freedom and humanity in the United States. I say *a* North Star rather than *the* North Star because there were other travel guides offering similar information, but *The Green Book* is the one that had the longest life. Perhaps most important, it's the one that has been rediscovered and that now guides us to the truth about Black people's travels and their lives during that time—from its first edition, in 1936, to its last, in 1967. It has become more than an artifact; it has become a symbol for the spirit of resilience, as captured in the words of activist and lifelong resident of Jackson, Mississippi, Frank Figgers: "Do what you can, with what you have, where you are, in order to make a better life and a fair deal."

The Green Book has also become, quite unintentionally, an archive of local and national cultural history, an inspiration for creativity, and a model for other types of guides. In being all of these things, *The Green Book* helps us to better understand the publication itself, to recognize the legacies from its time as they echo in current events, and to propose practical, workable solutions that might benefit all Americans today.

It must also be remembered that there was among Black Americans another perspective on the travel guide, as William T. Williams at the University of Cincinnati pointed out: "When I talk to people, they all remember *The Green Book* and now they kind of remember it fondly. I think at the time they probably thought of it as more of a necessary evil. It wasn't something that they were proud of. It was just something that they had to have."

The phrase "necessary evil" denotes something unpleasant—a love-hate feeling about it. Clearly, *The Green Book* was not "evil." But the guide did embody "necessary": it was something "that must be accepted in order to achieve a particular result."

The Green Book, its purpose, and the results it enabled in people's lives are key topics for four contemporary visual artists I met. One accompanied me on the first road trip from my past in segregated Tallahassee, Florida, to then contemporary events in Ferguson, Missouri. The others joined me at different points during the second road trip with Janée. Their creative responses to *The Green Book* embody many histories and truths, obvious and not-so-obvious, that African American artists of all types are mining, interpreting, and sharing with wider audiences. I hope their works inspire people to investigate and find out more about *The Green Book*, the America that made it necessary, and the many yet-to-be-told lived experiences of African Americans from that time.

JONATHAN CALM: DRIVING HIS *GREEN BOOK*

Jonathan Calm, an artist and assistant professor of photography at Stanford University, accompanied producer Jeremy Grange and me on our 2016 road trip from Tallahassee, Florida, to Ferguson, Missouri. Calm took more than two thousand photographs that captured all aspects of the trip—the people, the places, the atmosphere.

Importantly, Calm brought a fresh perspective to the trip. He was born in the early 1970s and grew up in New York City. This was his first trip to the American South, a place he'd previously merely read about in high school and college classes. On the trip, he quickly became aware of the specific manifestations and details of the history of the South and its relationship to *The Green Book*. As Calm put it, the trip took him "back in time, to a lot of emptiness, to cities and towns that were hollowed out."

This road trip and the travel guide inspired Calm to create a performative, on-the-road art project. Using the guide's listings for the West Coast—California, Oregon, and Washington—Calm has since traveled to as many of *The Green Book* sites as he possibly can, to get "a sense of what are these locations today." What he's looking for is "the classic, quintessential 'What is America.'"

Calm, in essence, reenacts road trips that African American travelers might have taken during the era of *The Green Book*, and along the way he photographs locations and buildings—or what's left of them. The spot he captures is often a decaying building, a pile of rubble, or an empty lot. If the original building listed in *The Green Book* still stands, it rarely offers the same services or houses the original business. Most have been repurposed—for example, as an Airbnb property, as a halfway house, or as a gift shop. Calm's black-and-white photographs do more than document these locations; they capture each one's emotionality. They make you think about what was there and wonder why is it no longer there. This body of work by Calm is about both the nostalgia surrounding the American myth of road travel and the loss of places that were vital and essential in African American lives, but not included in the widely accepted version of the myth.

As a Black man behind the wheel of a nice car in America today, Calm has some of the same on-the-road worries and fears that African Americans who drove the highways during *The Green Book* years had. This emotional continuum with past travelers is important to his artwork. He's feeling, thinking about, and examining the past as a way of understanding where America is today, especially as it relates to the freedom that was Victor Hugo Green's goal when he created his publication. Calm observes:

I don't think the hotels or the buildings I'm photographing are the destinations, actually. It's having the experiences between each site—the actual driving and stopping and eating, my connection to being on that landscape and on the highways. There aren't Black photographers doing that. And so, I see part of this work as a performative act. I want to be free. My drive is investigating that level of freedom today.

Every time Calm drives to search for and reach one or more of the safe havens listed in *The Green Book* that offered welcoming services to African Americans, he is accumulating insights and wisdom from both the past and the present. Although many of the buildings and locations have been sorely neglected or demolished, Calm thinks about the determination, the resourcefulness, and the ingenuity that each site represented—African Americans creating, constructing, carving out spaces where they could express their culture and humanity freely and safely. By producing works that "walk in their footsteps" in real and metaphorical ways, Calm's performance and the resulting photographs remind us of the ways Black Americans persevered, often through their own apprehensions and other people's fears, to attain the broad freedoms that Victor Hugo Green believed were possible for his people in the United States.

Calm's performances also remind us of another truth that, like *The Green Book*, has been forgotten or ignored by Americans. In his book *The Color of Law: A Forgotten History of How Our Government Segregated America*, Richard Rothstein shows how ongoing restrictive housing and lending policies combined with routing "White Men's Roads Through Black Men's Homes" resulted in huge socioeconomic setbacks for African Americans at all income levels. (The phrase is the title of an article by Deborah Archer about the building of the interstate highway system.)[1] Along our road trip, we saw the consequences of this, felt the benign neglect, imagined each place in its prime as we drove around what's left of Black Bottom in Detroit, along Jefferson Street in Nashville, along Walnut Street (now Muhammad Ali Boulevard) in Louisville, along Davis Avenue (now Martin Luther King Jr. Avenue) in Mobile, along streets in one urban community after another.

TONY BINGHAM: *THE GREEN BOOK* FOUND HIM

Artist Tony M. Bingham, professor of studio art at Miles College in Birmingham, Alabama, recalls how he came across *The Green Book*—or, as he likes to say, how *The Green Book* found him:

I'm from Atlanta and was in school at Georgia State University in the sculpture graduate program. The studio happened to be just around the corner from Auburn Avenue. There was a building that was being torn down. I decided to investigate what was inside and found all kinds of documents and papers, old *Jet* magazines—things that were going to be tossed into some dumpster. I came across this book. It said *Negro Traveler's Guide*. I thought, when you find something and it has the word "negro" on it, even if you're not quite sure what it is, go for it.

Until this chance discovery in 2001 or 2002, neither Bingham nor his parents had used or even heard of the travel guide. Like many people who first discover *The Green Book*, Bingham wondered whether any of the places listed in the publication still existed, and whether any of those addresses still could be found.

Bingham's artistic ideas started with his thinking about the safe places for travelers in the state-by-state listings. His curiosity-heightened creative energy began to spark when he started investigating the places travelers had to navigate around to get to safety:

When I use vintage photographs in my collages, which also contain earth, found letters, and various markings that I make, I'm thinking about the kinds of white folks who might be obstacles if I were traveling using *The Green Book*. Would the family in the vintage photo, for example, be welcoming? Who might I encounter that might make my journey difficult? How might I have to carefully navigate that situation? Because if I don't make it to safety, it could be fatal, or troublesome at the least.

The found materials that Bingham selects and assembles into his collages are intended to evoke, symbolically and emotionally, an essential historical and cultural truth he knows about African American individuals and communities. He sees this unalterable fact existing quietly among the listings in *The Green Book*: the legacy of survival, the foundation that enabled African Americans to get *to* and *through* today, and every today to come:

In any time or era in which we have found ourselves, we utilize the tools and resources that we had to express ourselves. When there were constraints imposed by policies and laws, we found a way around them. That's a foundation that has enabled us to be where we are today. So, in the works that I make and exhibit, I don't want us to forget that. I want us to consider the materials, externally and internally, that people had to work with [in the past]. What messages are in those materials? I want to use the materials in creative ways to tell stories that their users perhaps could not have told. I sometimes think of a statement I heard from older Black folk: "Making a way out of no way." That's what we often had to do.

In thinking about *The Green Book* today, Bingham reflects on the different ways that people learn history. He sees the arts as enlivening the past and therefore animating history in people's imaginations:

I think the arts make history so much more colorful and insightful. It can cover the full range of emotions—happy things, sad things, hard things. Artists can do it through dance, through song, through film, through sculpture, through drawing, through conversations. So I think that the arts are a powerful way—one of the many powerful ways—to bring our young people and older people into their proud legacy.

DERRICK ADAMS: *THE GREEN BOOK* AS "SANCTUARY"

In 2018 when I walked off the elevator and walked into the exhibition *Sanctuary* at the Museum of Art and Design in New York, I immediately encountered a wooden roadway that multidisciplinary artist Derrick Adams had constructed. I had to walk through or around the roadway to enter the exhibition. In effect, I and other visitors to the exhibition were walking through an opening into the time when *The Negro Motorist Green Book* was an essential travel tool for African Americans. *Sanctuary* connotes the many ways—practical, emotional, and psychological—the travel guide served African Americans. Using artistically interpreted symbols of travel from that time, such as suitcases, flat caps, car doors, and two-lane roadways, Adams created fifty mixed-media collages on wood panels as well as sculptures inspired by *The Green Book*.

During a conversation in 2019 at his studio in Brooklyn before the start of the road trip, Adams and I talked about the insights he gained from doing research about *The Green Book*:

What was really striking to me was not only that *The Green Book* was a tool for African Americans to navigate the US while traveling, but the fact that the individual, Victor Hugo Green, a postal worker in Harlem, decided to do the publication out of his own desire to assist in a certain level of progress for his people.

I thought, as a citizen, this was amazing. When people think

Derrick Adams, *Kings on Vacation* (Coretta, right panel), 2021, archival inkjet print on Hahnemuhle German etching 310 gsm paper; 22.5 x 17 inches each.

about activism, most times in contemporary culture today, they think of activism as being very outspoken and visible. But the fact that Green did this in his time off, without the idea of activism as a motivation, made him kind of revolutionary. I thought this is what activism can be in contemporary culture. You may not be able to change the world, but you can do things in your neighborhood. You can do small things, like the small publication Green did on his own by compiling information.

Adams reminds us of a meaning of the word "sanctuary" that's perhaps closer to Green's original intent: a refuge. It is traveling for vacation and leisure—motoring safely to places where Black people could relax and have a good time, free, if only temporarily, of the restrictions of that time and the white gaze. This aspect is often overshadowed by the difficulties and traumas that the guide helped people avoid. Adams's deeper exploration of the guide provides an interesting parallel between his own artistic practice and a less obvious aspect of Green's publication, although the guide included articles related to the pleasures that traveling, especially with *The Green Book* by your side, made possible. Adams notes:

It was always interesting to look at the year of the listing of places and services offered in *The Green Book*, and then look at what was happening politically around that same year. *The Green Book* didn't acknowledge any political unrest at all. I thought that was really interesting about Mr. Green, because I know that as a Black man he was dealing with those things himself. During my exhibition, some people even asked me why I didn't put some of the traumatic things that were happening in America [back then] in my work. I think it's more of a challenge to live through those things, to pull out aspects that will make you stronger. Trauma rarely makes people stronger. I was really thinking about that. So the pieces I created for my exhibition represented all those different parts of leisure as well as personal care and development.

Adams's works convey an upbeat feeling. Through the colors (for example, the sky blue), the vintage-feeling patterns of the fabrics, the shapes of the luggage, and the front-door-like opening, viewers enter the exhibition. On the one hand, Adams's show about relaxed motoring to beautiful settings for good times is about participating in a part of the American Dream that African Americans of all socioeconomic levels wanted and hoped for and that *The Green Book* was designed to help them make a reality. On the other hand, Adams also sees a second implication in the pursuit and enjoyment of leisure. It is a political act, embracing the same resistance and refusal implicit in Green's creation of the travel guide.

All three artists—Jonathan Calm, Tony Bingham, and Derrick Adams—see an increased interest in *The Green Book* as a source of creative inspiration among artists in various media. Certainly, part of this is spurred by the fact that many people had never previously heard of the travel guide. Because of integration and various federal laws intended to eliminate legal segregation, the guide was no longer needed for travel after the late 1960s and therefore faded from memory. However, with its rediscovery, people are particularly curious about the listings in or near the places where they grew up or currently live.

Most white people had never heard of the publication until the 2018 movie bearing its name premiered and won multiple awards, including the Academy Award for Best Picture. Perhaps closer to the truth, many white people during the time it was published could not have imagined that Black people could be resourceful enough to create and distribute such a directory. They had given little, if any, thought to what it was like for African Americans to drive the roadways; to buy gasoline; to stop to eat food, drink water, or use a bathroom. This oppressive, trouble-laden reality of travel from the days of *The Green Book* was one of the factors that prompted Adams to focus on capturing the opposite feelings in his exhibition and other artwork:

I was trying to use the idea of how the highway became an obstacle for us in a lot of ways. But we figured out how to get through it, to build around it—not by building architecturally, but by building communities. We were, and are, able to still be here, driving and moving forward. I think that is something that we should celebrate more than some of the other things that were put in our path. I thought it was important for people to understand the movement *The Green Book* helped make possible more than the individuals who used the guide. I felt it was important in my exhibition *Sanctuary* for people to feel *The Green Book* is alive, stimulating viewers' imaginations to see the guide in a way that was positive.

One thing I think about a lot with my work is how do we present a level of optimism through visual art that is not necessarily romantic? I think artists can respond to the oppressive parts of society by using their imagination to present positive stories and histories that are not highlighted. We, as African Americans, have so many. We can never run out of, not just positive stories, but accurate stories depicting Black people doing things that will surprise even contemporary culture to learn about—histories that most people don't know.

The Green Book is getting a second life in people's consciousness, both within the more diverse Black community in the United States today (many of whose members have little in-depth awareness of this history) and in American society overall. Through the media of painting, sculpture, plays, films, memoirs, and storytelling, artists have begun important contemporary conversations about what individuals, groups, and institutions can do at a time when mobility and safety remain issues for people of color—Black, Latino, Asian, Indigenous—moving throughout the United States. In Adams's words: "*The Green Book* has become a reference to revisit, to think about how can we create something—for example, a database—that empowers people to feel safe and to feel free. I think the idea of *The Green Book* can exist in contemporary culture in a way that can probably be more impactful than even previously."

Adams's words are prophetic. Artists and entrepreneurs in African American communities across the country are reimagining how the idea of *The Green Book* can be applied to today's world. In addition to websites, like TravelNoire, Noirbnb, and JourneyBlackHome, which help travelers find Black-owned accommodations on Airbnb, and Black Twitter, many young people are creating online enterprises, often incorporating the name "Green Book," whose primary purpose is marketing Black-owned businesses or providing networking opportunities for Black talent. An example in Birmingham, Alabama, one of the cities on our road trip, is the website the Modern Green Book (www.moderngreenbook.net). Its tagline is "A Legacy Reimagined." The website explains that the reason Theo Edwards-Butler established it in 2020 was because she saw "a need for a community that supports, celebrates, and uplifts Black Owned Businesses and Organizations." With *The Green Book* as a foundation, the database accessed through the website, along with quarterly and annual publications, "wants to ground its community in history, while building a legacy for future generations."

A similar database is "(For)bes The Culture's Green Book Guide," founded by Rashaad Lambert, who also works at *Forbes* magazine. Like

Edwards-Butler's enterprise, this website's focus is on marketing, giving visibility to Black businesses in a variety of sectors: healthcare and beauty, fashion, media and communications, food and beverages, as well as lifestyle. Updated quarterly, Lambert's goal is to provide "a definitive and current road map for buying Black every day."[2]

Another enterprise is the Photographer's Green Book Directory.[3] Founded by Jay Simple, this website and traditional directory honors its indebtedness to the original publication through the explanation of its services on its website:

> Between 1936 and 1966 the Negro Motorist Green Book was a list of safe places for Black people during their travels throughout the segregated USA. Founded in 2020, the Photographer's Green Book, in that tradition, started as a list of resources to navigate the photographic community, which has historically denied the voices of those other than predominantly white cis male artists. Our work expands on the original Green Book's target audience to include other individuals whose voices have been under-supported or underrepresented in academic and arts institutions.

JAN MILES: ANOTHER KIND OF *GREEN BOOK*

Jan Miles, a writer and publisher Janée and I met in New Orleans on the final day of our road trip, shows how Bingham's and Adams's thoughts about the future influence of *The Green Book* are being realized in a different medium. Partly inspired by the original travel guide, Miles created and published *The Post-Racial Negro Green Book* in 2017. In the introduction, she writes that her book is a state-by-state "collection of occurrences, information and dates that document a pattern of racial bias against Black people in the 21st century. The events included took place between the years 2013 and 2016. There is no commentary included in this book—just factual information. The format of the book, however, is commentary: it is based on the 20th-century *Negro Motorist Green Book*."

Victor Hugo Green started compiling his list after the on-the-road "inconveniences" and "embarrassments" he and Alma had driving to Virginia to visit her relatives. Miles told us she started compiling her list after experiences she was seeing, hearing, and reading about in the news cycle:

I actually started compiling incidents of racism around 2015, because somewhere around 2012 or 2013 I started seeing an uptick. There were more and more incidents, and they were coming through the news cycles so quickly that at some point it occurred to me, this is actual contemporary history. These are important incidents, and someone should be preserving this, and I didn't see anyone else doing it. So I started doing it.

At first, I was recording these events on a little website, and then I realized, because my background actually is book publishing, it would make a lot of sense if I put it in a book. I happened to have a facsimile copy of *The Negro Motorist Green Book*, and I had been working with another book called *100 Years of Lynchings*, which is a collection of stories of lynchings. I realized that if I put those concepts together, it would be really impactful. So that's how it happened.

Miles takes care to let readers know the qualifications she used to sort through and select the events included in her book. As a result of her process, two features of the book stand out. The first are the types of incidents documented, which are listed on the cover:

SYSTEMIC RACISM

POLICE BRUTALITY

MASS INCARCERATION

OVERPOLICING

SENTENCING DISPARITY

RACIAL PROFILING

IMPLICIT BIAS

WHITE PRIVILEGE

MICROAGGRESSIONS

This list reflects how the underlying, widely accepted societal and political practices that prompted Victor Green to create his original publication still exist but have morphed into broader, often more pernicious forms. An adage immediately comes to mind with two important additional words: "The more things change, the more they stay *more subtly* the same."

In talking about the context of her publication, Miles delivered a reality check that can't be denied or dismissed:

When the laws changed, what do you suppose happened to the vehement and the violent? Do you believe their opinions of Black people changed? Do you think they decided they had been wrong and adjusted their ideologies and beliefs? Of course not. They had to comply with new societal standards and public laws, but their feelings remained the same. And . . . these people had children. And their children had children.

In memories often shaded by optimism, people want to think the years the original *Green Book* were published, 1936 to 1967, and the period of US history that made it necessary were a long time ago—not quite ancient times, but several generations ago. Miles delivered another reality check, however, that removed optimism's gossamer. She equated this period with the lifespan of a beloved relative: "My grandmother would have been a teenager when publication of the book began, and she's still alive. That is to say, we're talking less than the span of a human lifetime from when Black people had to sit in separate areas until today. My grandmother is still alive, and so are the people who supported racial segregation."

Any person interested in history, facts, and truth can't help relating Miles's statement about her grandmother to their own family timeline. For example, my mother was born shortly after *The Green Book* was first published. I was born right in the middle of its thirty-year run. I remember the media coverage of the time—shocking film footage of brutality; horrific photographs accompanying newspaper and magazine articles; people spewing vicious language, even spitting on Black people, without embarrassment or guilt, but full of entitlement. Miles's comparing the timeline to her grandmother's life has a relatability that should make each of us stop and think the next time we are about to use the phrase "so long ago" when talking about segregation, Jim Crow, and their legacy.

The timeline makes me think about the European immigrants who came to the United States before and during the years of *The Green Book*'s publication who were not considered "white" by American standards. It seems that part of becoming American and an accepted member of white society was embracing the racism and ideas of white supremacy at that time. Was this part of the immigrants' misinterpretation of what it means to be "American," or was it, in fact, a necessary transformation for them to gain access to the social and economic benefits of the American Dream?

It is difficult for people to see, much less admit, that some part of their economic success may have been built on an uneven socioeconomic playing field. Their unspoken fear is that acknowledging this fact will lead to something being taken from them, thereby diminishing what they have achieved. I hope that hearing the truth about the widespread discriminatory practices from the period *The Green Book* was published and necessary will create greater understanding, insight, and empathy, which in turn will spark people across all demographic groups to work together toward ensuring the benefits of full citizenship for all Americans, not just white Americans.

Tony Bingham's statement about the power of all types of art to evoke a wide range of feelings was swirling though my mind as I paged through Miles's book before and after our interview. Also on my mind was Derrick Adams's focus on the positive, uplifting truths that were always present in African American communities but denied, ignored, or stereotyped by much of white America.

Miles's book is a difficult read. It is a list of unjust acts. It is a list of ever-accumulating atrocities. It is a list of haunting traumas—small and big. It shares elements of what we heard during our road trip, especially the stories people told of their own and their families' histories of encounters with racial discrimination, exclusion, and hostility on the road and in their local communities. When reading Miles's book, it was difficult not to be dismayed, depressed, even angry. Most difficult was reading its accounts after having heard people recount incidents in the twenty-first century that were almost identical to stories from what one person called "the *Green Book* days."

With the turn of each page, a question welled up again and again:

How did reading, culling through, and selecting all of this negative, distressing information affect Miles? Here's her answer:

> It was a very long process, and at times it was emotionally draining. But as the process went on, it became cathartic. Normally, we're receiving this information all the time, we're seeing it in our newsfeeds or hearing about it, and we don't have anything to do but internalize it. I actually created a place to put it, and it was healing for me to be able to say, "All right, this thing happened, and now I've put it down in this book and now I move on."

After a respite, Jan Miles is updating her book. There were a few years when Victor Green did not publish his annual travel guide. These gaps were mostly due to World War II, but from the beginning, he and Alma imagined and hoped for a time when publishing their guide would no longer be necessary. Miles too hopes for a time when publishing *The Post-Racial Negro Green Book* will no longer be necessary. But given her qualitative research and what she has learned about America from it, can she imagine a time when she will stop cataloging such events? "Not in my lifetime," she said.

> I don't see it. I don't foresee an end to it now. Maybe in someone else's lifetime. If I had a child, probably not in that person's lifetime either.
>
> I don't know how we fix this. But let me tell you something that is a positive. In addition to seeing this increase in coverage of racial incidents, I'm also now seeing an increase in others who are not people of color advocating around changing things. I'm seeing more white people being vocal. I'm seeing people forming groups. There are so many that are springing up, like anti-racism organizations.

So, on a positive note, I am seeing people attempting to address the issues. I'm seeing people using their voices, which is what I was trying to do [when I published *The Post-Racial Negro Green Book*]. The thing that I'm comfortable with is publishing. So that's what I did in hope of contributing something useful. I am seeing an uptick in those kinds of contributions from people, and that is positive.

The difference between Miles's and Green's listings and updates is stark. Green's was a chronicle of the expansion of freedom as more people in towns and cities across the United States created new businesses, deploying their financial and emotional capital to help make life better for locals and for people traveling through their areas. By contrast, Miles's ongoing listings feel like a narrowing of or regression from the freedoms achieved. Or is it an unveiling of a truth, via technology and social media, that never went away during the years of perceived openness, of racial progress?

These comparisons, reflections, and thoughts invariably lead to the question: Is a travel guide like *The Green Book* needed in the United States today?

We asked this question of many of our interviewees during the trip, and it seems that the end of the journey is the right place to think about an answer to it, given all we've seen, been told, experienced, and learned. In Nashville, Evelyn Nettles's quick, emphatic answer was unequivocal and reflects the opinion of many of the people who lived and traveled during the period *The Green Book* was published: "We will not accept *The Green Book* today. Not doing that. I pay taxes in this country. My father served this country. We will not accept just being able to go to one location. I need to be able to go where I want."

Nonetheless, Nettles does see one aspect of the guide she would find beneficial today: "I think it would be nice to know where Black-owned businesses are. I really would like that. But more than likely, they're not going to be on the interstate. You would have to go into a given town to patronize them. I would like to know the information, but I want to be able to go where I want to go and feel welcomed and comfortable."

Some young African Americans haven't fully grasped the enduring power of racism and its impact on their lives. As Learotha Williams put it, "You're dealing with a generation that has been taught that there are no limits to what they can do, that there's no space that they are excluded from. I know better because I was born in a segregated hospital."

Williams's observation has some truth; nonetheless, many members of the younger generation agree that there is a need for a guide, either in print or online, that would enable them to patronize Black-owned businesses, especially while traveling. Derrick Adams explained the additional, more nuanced reasons why such a guide would be useful from his generation's point of view:

I think it's normal to go to a city and scout around for places that you would want to go to. The fact that you have something on hand that you can just flip through and look at and know exactly that this place is going to welcome you cuts down on the time of searching. Also, who wants to go to a place where they're not welcome? I want to go to a place that caters to my type of customer and has my type of vibe.

Adams also sees a bigger goal beyond helping a younger generation of African Americans find their own vibe when traveling. He sees a *Green Book*–like guide as a motivation for activism:

I did the exhibition at the Museum of Art and Design thinking this is a way of talking to the younger generation at a time when some people feel helpless because of the political space that we're in. *The Green Book* is something a postal worker did. By extension, my exhibition asks: Now what are you going to do? I know you don't like what's going on, but what can you do to change, to move forward on things that will make you, collectively, have some type of power?

The collection of the twenty-one editions of *The Green Book* at the New York Public Library has become and will remain creative inspiration for historians, moviemakers, podcasters, artists, playwrights, zine producers, and digital database compilers, as well as everyday people who want to know a more truthful history of the United States. In the same way, driving from Detroit to New Orleans using *The Green Book* as our guide enabled and inspired us, through the voices and stories of every person we interviewed, to create a living history. The truth will set minds free to imagine, to create paths to new knowledge and understanding.

Fifty years from now, I want the story of *The Green Book* and people's real-life experiences of traveling in the United States during that time included in history books used in every school across the country. I often think about how many of my white, Hispanic, and Asian friends have said that they never knew about any of this part of American history. They assumed everyone was participating in the American Dream the way they and their families were, and anyone not achieving the same benefits was not working hard enough. The podcast *Driving the Green Book* was at times a disturbing revelation for them. Yet I could tell that part of them didn't want to believe that the incidents recounted in the podcasts had really happened. Kemi, herself a first-generation immigrant, said, "I hope that stories of the hardships Black Americans faced will be a part of the greater collective responsibility of listening to, learning from, and passing on. When people listen, I hope they won't be surprised."

Even more difficult for these friends was the realization that they were unknowing participants in the structural racism that government policies and societal restrictions created across the United States. Policies enacted by elected government officials—local, state, and federal—had given their parents, and consequently them, cover. In fifty years, I want to see the cover of the myth pulled back and the fuller truth about the African American experience in the United States told from the point of view of the people who lived it. Janée speaks directly to why this is important:

> One of the many reasons why we wanted to collect and share these stories is because our current education system doesn't highlight or celebrate these stories. American history is told from the perspective that primarily white people shaped our country from the time the *Mayflower* landed on Plymouth Rock. Preserving the stories we recorded as living history is our contribution to correcting that narrative to include the struggles and triumphs of African Americans during the *Green Book* era, in the actual voices of the Black people who lived these experiences.

Also, fifty years from today, Black people in the United States will be more diverse, many having little or no knowledge of the period of African American history covered here, as well as other "hidden" episodes of this country's history related to racial issues. The same will probably be true for many people of color. I hope this book, along with other books, articles, and podcasts, will help dispel the long-promulgated stereotypes about Black people in the United States and provide all Americans with a greater ability to know and understand the true story, and to see the humanity in everyone. I hope the resulting greater empathy and understanding in turn lead people to become more proactive in helping to dismantle the long-held, long-standing, always morphing structural racism in the United States. I want people to be activists in their everyday lives, waking up with the words of Frank Figgers of Jackson, Mississippi, in their minds, consciously or unconsciously: "Do what you can, with what you have, where you are, in order to make a better life and a fair deal."

On my *Green Book* journeys I have had the privilege of meeting many social activists who are in their early twenties or thirties and have never heard of *The Green Book*. They come to my talks and often make comments or ask questions from a perspective that makes me pause and ponder. One of them, who appeared in a film I was making, said she thought the creators chose the color green to echo what it means on a traffic light—that it is okay to go to the places listed. This interpretation had never crossed my mind. Each time I explain the period of history that necessitated the creation of *The Green Book* as a life-saving tool for Black travelers, many young African Americans, and recent Black immigrants, are at first amazed that such a guide was ever needed in the United States. This too surprises me and tells me that they have probably not explored or have been protected from the harsh events of this history. As I look at their faces, I can see that it takes only a short time for them to begin connecting various points in their own lives—current racial incidents in the news, travel practices among their family members, a personal story their grandparents alluded to, and sometimes even the neighborhoods in which they grew up. Paging through the various editions of *The Green Book* on the New York Public Library's website becomes a quiet autobiographical journey. They look up the names of streets in cities and towns where they have or had relatives. Fascination turns to curiosity. Each of them wants to know more of the history, more truth, and how it affected their family.

Each time I observe this, I always think about the future, let's say two generations from now, when even fewer people will have heard of *The Green Book*. If history is any judge, I doubt the current resurrection of information about the travel guide will result in its being included in textbooks approved by largely conservative white state and local education committees in the US. Therefore, *The Green Book*'s contribution to the lives of African Americans and the history of the United States will fade again, until a horrifying national racial event needs to be understood, needs context. Then a new generation of Black, Brown, Asian, and white people will discover, for the first time again, along with incidents like the Red Summer of 1919 and the fate of Negro Wall Street in Tulsa in 1921, *The Negro Motorist Green Book*.

ACKNOWLEDGMENTS

My journeys with *The Negro Motorist Green Book*—two road trips, a BBC Radio 4 program, a ten-episode podcast series, a short film documentary, many interviews, and this book—were made possible by many people.

Jeremy Grange, BBC Wales, who produced the BBC Radio 4 program *The Green Book*.

Jonathan Calm, assistant professor at Stanford University, who accompanied us, documenting the five-day road trip to produce the Radio 4 program.

Oluwakemi Aladesuyi, who diligently and persuasively researched and organized the second road trip to create the podcast and then, as field producer, recorded all of the interviews and asked questions that helped clarify points along the way.

Janée Woods Weber, associate producer of the podcasts, who was always the right friend with whom to explore this overlooked part of American history. Her deep experience in social justice and her talking to different groups of people across the United States helped to bring greater empathy to our interviews about this history and to connect it to current events.

Juleyka Lantigua of LWC Studios, the singularly brilliant editor of the podcast, who is extraordinary. From the first day we met, it was joyfully clear that she understood my idea intellectually and emotionally as we sorted through all the interviews to find the stories, voices, themes, and narrative arc for the series. Juleyka and I not only wanted to tell the story of *The Green Book*, but also to capture the real-life experiences and feelings of the people who lived through and survived that time with their clear-eyed, generous hearts and souls still amazingly, wonderfully focused on making living in America more equitable and just for everyone.

Cedric Wilson, the young composer who wrote a beautifully haunting score for the podcast that evokes the past but sounds and feels contemporary. His expert soundscaping gave the series a subtle aural atmosphere that made the stories and voices more powerful, more emotionally penetrating. Wilson's melodies helped listeners hear and feel.

Alyssa Martino truly understood why the podcast was important and championed it at Macmillan Podcasts every step of the way until she left the company.

Kathy Doyle, who had unwavering belief in the podcast and who worked with Macmillan's marketing team, which set up with Apple podcasts in a first-of-its-kind partnership that included information about *The Green Book* and the podcast on Apple Maps, Apple Music, and Apple Books.

Morgan Ratner, Michelle Margulis, Jasmine Faustino, Becky Celestino, all part of Kathy Doyle's team, who love the *Driving the Green Book* podcast as much as I do. They were dedicated, diligent, enthusiastic, and supportive during every phase of production and marketing.

Karl Weber, my longtime friend, whose insights and writing expertise were essential in helping me capture and preserve the stories as well as the individual voices of the Black Americans who shared their lived experiences in interviews and conversations during both road trips.

Judith Curr, president and publisher of the HarperOne Group, whose long-standing belief in me and my writing has opened the door to new opportunities in my life.

Elizabeth "Biz" Mitchell, who truly embraced and believed in my book, seeing its importance from moment one, and who shared her experience and wisdom to help me think about and revise the content to make it informative, captivating, affecting, and inspiring in all of the ways it needs to be today, and in the future.

Ghjulia Romiti, who asked insightful questions and offered comments that refined my thinking through the revision process and who kept me and the book on track.

And finally, J. Stephen Sheppard, of Cowan, DeBaets, Abrahams & Sheppard, who as my lawyer and my agent was unwavering in his belief in the importance of the podcast and the book. He worked hard to make the deal for both the podcast and the book happen and to make them fair. Steve is also my dear friend, whose experienced, wise words and well-honed sense of humor buoyed my spirits, keeping me focused on why the stories in the BBC Radio 4 program, on the podcast series, and in this book had to be captured, preserved, and shared.

The following individuals graciously shared their experiences and insights in interviews during our podcast road trip:

In New York City: Derrick Adams (multidisciplinary contemporary artist).

In Detroit, Michigan: Jamon Jordan (historian and tour leader for Black Scroll Network History and Tours), McKinley Jackson (musician, arranger, orchestrator, producer), Kefentse Chike (community activist, African cultural musician, professor of African American studies), and Vernetta Sheppard-Pinson (community activist, minister, Realtor, and retired social worker).

In Columbus, Ohio: Mary Ellen Tyus (lifelong resident of Columbus, Ohio, and Idlewild, Michigan)

In Cincinnati, Ohio: Joyce Coleman (resident of Cincinnati and amateur historian), Carl Westmoreland (senior historian at the National Underground Railroad Freedom Center), William Williams (professor of architecture, University of Cincinnati), and Kathryne Gardette (lifelong resident of Cincinnati).

In Louisville, Kentucky: Kenneth Clay (historian, events promoter, entertainment producer of Louisville's WorldFest, and coauthor of *Two Centuries of Black Louisville: A Photographic History*) and Mervin Aubespin (retired associate editor of the *Courier-Journal*, coauthor of *Two Centuries of Black Louisville: A Photographic History*, and artist).

In Nashville, Tennessee: Evelyn Nettles (associate vice president of academic affairs at Tennessee State University), Ana Nettles (commercial litigator), Crystal Churchwell Evans (director of development, Frist Art Museum), and Learotha Williams Jr. (associate professor of African American and Public History at Tennessee State University and coordinator for the North Nashville Heritage Project).

In Memphis, Tennessee: Noelle Trent (director of interpretation, collections, and education at the National Civil Rights Museum) and Jesse H. Turner Jr. (owner of Jesse H. Turner Jr. Certified Public

Accountant, retired president of Tri-State Bank of Memphis, treasurer of the NAACP's national Board of Directors).

In Jackson, Mississippi: Tony Dennis (a.k.a. Dr. Shoemaker, third-generation owner of Dennis Brothers Shoe Repair Shop, founded by brothers Cleophis [the oldest], Frank [Tony's father], and Percy [the youngest]) and Frank Figgers (civil rights activist).

In Birmingham, Alabama: Denise E. Gilmore (senior director of the Office of Social Justice and Racial Equity for the City of Birmingham), James Poindexter (construction site supervisor and former resident of the Gaston Motel), Paulette Roby (chairperson of the Civil Rights Activist Committee), Hezekiah Jackson (member of the Civil Rights Activist Committee), Tony Ramsey, and T. Marie King (community organizer, facilitator, and trainer).

In Selma, Alabama: Senator Hank Sanders (lawyer, civil rights activist).

In Mobile, Alabama: Eric Franklin Finley (tour coordinator for the Dora Franklin Finley African-American Heritage Trail).

In New Orleans, Louisiana: Eva Baham (assistant professor of history, Dillard University), Jan Miles (publisher, editor of *The Post-Racial Negro Motorist Green Book*), and Odile Clark Washington (owner of the Starlight Café).

For the BBC Radio 4 program: Carolyn Bailey Champion, Charles Champion, Leah Dickerman, Jerome Gray, Allyson Hobbs, Ryan Jones, Maira Liriano, Nelson Malden, Ron McCoy, Robert Moman, Gwendolyn Patton, Calvin Ramsey, Tiffany Shawn, Rev. Henry Steel, and Rev. Starsky Wilson.

I also extend my thanks to Bryan Stevenson (founder of the Equal Justice Initiative), whom I interviewed in Montgomery, Alabama, in connection with the BBC Radio 4 program about *The Green Book*.

To everyone who agreed to be interviewed and share a part of their lives with us during the road trip, I thank you for giving me your words and your feelings to use in realizing this living history. I will think of each of you when I hear this lyric from one of my favorite songs: "Your grace will lead us home." Home to truth. Home to a broader, more empathetic understanding and acceptance of what we endured, yet survived. Home to freedom, without aggravation.

Alvin Hall
New York City

NOTES

Chapter 1

1. Ted Fox, *Showtime at the Apollo* (New York: Holt, Rinehart and Winston, 1983), 77.
2. "Same Work, Different Unions: Carriers Contend with Legacy of Segregation," *Postal Record*, June 2011, https://www.nalc.org/news/the -postal-record/2011/june-2011/document/06–2011_segregation.pdf.

Chapter 2

1. Quoted in Kathleen Franz, "African-Americans Take to the Open Road," in *Major Problems in American Popular Culture*, edited by Kathleen Franz and Susan Smulyan (Boston: Wadsworth Cengage Learning, 2011), 242.
2. Quoted in Mark S. Foster, "In the Face of 'Jim Crow': Prosperous Blacks and Vacations, Travel and Outdoor Leisure, 1890–1945," *Journal of Negro History* 84, no. 2 (1999): 130–49, quotation at 141.
3. "Democracy Defined at Moscow," *The Crisis*, April 1947, 105.
4. In Gretchen Sorin, *Driving While Black: African American Travel and the Road to Civil Rights* (New York: Liveright, 2020), 181.
5. Gretchen Sorin, "Driving While Black: Chronicling a Chapter in America's History on the Road," Motortrend, June 19, 2020, https://www .motortrend.com/news/driving-while-black-history/.
6. Erin Blakemore, "Jim Crow Laws Created 'Slavery by Another Name,'" *National Geographic*, February 5, 2020, https://www.nationalgeographic .com/history/article/jim-crow-laws-created-slavery-another-name.

7. "Motels Along Highway 66 Ban Negroes, NAACP Aide Says," newspaper clipping available at "Was There a Ban of Black Customers at Route 66 Motels in Eastern New Mexico?," Route 66 News, https://www .route66news.com/2018/09/16/was-there-a-ban-of-black-customers-along -route-66-motels-in-eastern-new-mexico/.

Chapter 3

1. *The Social and Economic Status of the Black Population of the United States, 1971*, US Bureau of the Census, July 1972, page 1, https://www2.census .gov/library/publications/1972/demographics/p23-042.pdf.
2. Henry Louis Taylor Jr., D. Gavin Luter, and Camden Miller, "The University, Neighborhood Revitalization, and Civic Engagement: Toward Civic Engagement 3.0," *Societies* 8, no. 4 (2018): 10, https://doi .org/10.3390/soc8040106.
3. James W. Loewen, *Sundown Towns: A Hidden Dimension of American Racism* (New York: New Press, 2018), 56–57.
4. Loewen, *Sundown Towns*, 4.
5. Loewen, *Sundown Towns*, 173.
6. Loewen, *Sundown Towns*, 98.

Chapter 4

1. Equal Justice Initiative, *Lynching in America: Confronting the Legacy of Racial Terror*, 3rd ed., 2015, https://lynchinginamerica.eji.org/report/.
2. Allan Nevins, *Hamilton Fish: The Inner History of the Grant Administration* (New York: Dodd, Mead, 1936), 2:853–54; quoted in Douglas A. Blackmon, *Slavery by Another Name: The Re-Enslavement of Black Americans from the Civil War to World War II* (New York: Random House, 2008), 87.
3. Matt Ford, "The Racist Roots of Virginia's Felon Disenfranchisement," *Atlantic*, April 27, 2016, https://www.theatlantic.com/politics /archive/2016/04/virginia-felon-disenfranchisement/480072/.
4. Michael Perman, *Struggle for Mastery: Disfranchisement in the South, 1888–1908* (Chapel Hill: Univ. of North Carolina Press, 2001), 195–224, quotation at 221.

5. See, for example, James Q. Whitman, *Hitler's American Model: The United States and the Making of Nazi Race Law* (Princeton, NJ: Princeton Univ. Press, 2017).

6. Glenda Elizabeth Gilmore, "'Somewhere' in the Nadir of African American History, 1890–1920," Freedom's Story: Teaching African American Literature and History, TeacherServe, National Humanities Center, http://nationalhumanitiescenter.org/tserve/freedom/1865–1917/essays/nadir.htm.

7. Alana Semuels, "The Destruction of a Black Suburb," *Atlantic*, July 13, 2015, https://www.theatlantic.com/business/archive/2015/07/lincoln-heights-black-suburb/398303/.

8. See Ta-Nehisi Coates, "The Case for Reparations," *Atlantic*, June 15, 2014; and John R. Logan, "Separate and Unequal in Suburbia," Census Brief prepared for Project US2010, December 1, 2014, https://s4.ad.brown.edu/Projects/Diversity/data/report/report12012014.pdf.

9. National Association of Real Estate Boards, Code of Ethics, 1950.

10. Ann Choi, Keith Herbert, Olivia Winslow, and Arthur Browne, "Long Island Divided," *Newsday*, November 17, 2019, https://projects.newsday.com/long-island/real-estate-agents-investigation/.

Chapter 5

1. Quoted in Gretchen Sorin, *Driving While Black: African American Travel and the Road to Civil Rights* (New York: Liveright, 2020), 163.

2. Cynthia Tucker, "Traveling While Negro," *Bitter Southerner*, https://bittersoutherner.com/traveling-while-negro-green-book-cynthia-tucker.

3. Lee Howard, "New London Woman Penned Precursor to Green Book," *The Day*, January 10, 2020, https://www.theday.com/local-news/20200111/new-london-woman-penned-precursor-to-green-book/.

4. "The Green Book: The Forgotten Story of One Carrier's Legacy Helping Others Navigate Jim Crow's Highways," *Postal Record*, September 2013, http://nalc.bytrilogy.com/news/the-postal-record/2013/september-2013/document/09-2013_green-book.pdf.

5. Debra Yeo, "The Real Book Behind Green Book: A Means to Keep Black Americans Safe but Also a Guide to Having Fun," *Toronto Star*, February 19, 2019, last updated February 21, 2019, https://www.thestar.com/entertainment

/television/2019/02/19/the-real-book-behind-green-book-a-means-to-keep
-black-americans-safe-but-also-a-guide-to-having-fun.html.

6. James A. Jackson, "Big Business Wants Negro Dollars," *The Crisis*, February
1935, 46.

7. Victor H. Green, "'Green Book' in 26th Year," *Pittsburgh Courier*, June
1962, 19.

8. Celia McGee, "The Open Road Wasn't Quite Open to All," *New York
Times*, August 22, 2010, https://www.nytimes.com/2010/08/23
/books/23green.html.

Chapter 6

1. Burke Gray, "Fraternalism in America (1860–1920)," Phoenix Masonry,
http://www.phoenixmasonry.org/masonicmuseum/fraternalism
/fraternalism_in_america.htm.

Chapter 7

1. Clay Williams, "The *Guide for Colored Travelers*: A Reflection of the
Urban League," *Journal of American and Comparative Cultures* 24, no. 3/4
(Fall 2001): 71–79.

2. Bryce Huffman, "Detroit Suburbs Grapple with the History of Being
Anti-Black 'Sundown Towns,'" *Detroit Bridge*, July 9, 2020, https://www
.bridgedetroit.com/detroit-suburbs-grapple-with-the-history-of-being-anti
-black-sundown-towns/.

3. Mervin Aubespin, Kenneth Clay, and J. Blaine Hudson, *Two Centuries
of Black Louisville: A Photographic History* (Louisville, KY: Butler Books,
2011), 15–16.

4. Jim Ridley, "The Street Where We Lived: Recalling Church Street's Glory
Days," *Nashville Scene*, February 8, 1996, https://web.archive
.org/web/20190104215240/https://www.nashvillescene.com/news
/article/13000360/the-street-where-we-lived.

5. Jessica Bliss, "60 Years Ago, They Sat Down at Nashville Lunch Counters—
and Sparked a Movement Against Segregation," *Nashville Tennessean*,
February 13, 2020, https://www.tennessean.com/story/news/local/2020
/02/13/nashville-lunch-counter-sit-ins-60th-anniversary/4729614002/.

6. Leland Kent, "Colored Masonic Temple," *Abandoned Southeast: Preserving the Past*, https://abandonedsoutheast.com/2016/08/11/masonic-temple/.

7. "Dr. Gwendolyn M. Patton, 1943–2017," obituary, Veterans of the Civil Rights Movement website, https://www.crmvet.org/vet/patton.htm.

8. Toi Dericotte, "Joy Is an Act of Resistance, and: Special Ears, and: Another Poem of a Small Grieving for My Fish Telly, and: On the Reasons I Loved Telly the Fish," *Prairie Schooner* 82, no. 3 (2008): 22.

Chapter 8

1. Annys Shin, "Highland Beach: A Historic Refuge from Racism Finds Itself at a Crossroads," *Washington Post*, August 25, 2012.

2. Ronald J. Stephens, "Atlantic Beach, South Carolina (1966–)," BlackPast .org, April 14, 2012, https://www.blackpast.org/african-american-history /atlantic-beach-south-carolina-1966/.

3. Rick Coates, "The Rise and Fall of Idlewild," *Northern Express*, June 6, 2002.

4. Trymaine Lee, "Black Hamptons Enclaves Caught Between Change and Tradition," *Huffington Post*, August 9, 2011, last updated October 9, 2011, https://www.huffpost.com/entry/black-hamptons-enclaves-c_n_922196.

Chapter 10

1. Deborah N. Archer, "'White Men's Roads Through Black Men's Homes': Advancing Racial Equity Through Highway Reconstruction," *Vanderbilt Law Review*, October 2020, https://cdn.vanderbilt.edu/vu-wp0/wp -content/uploads/sites/278/2020/10/19130728/White-Mens -Roads-Through-Black-Mens-Homes-Advancing-Racial-Equity-Through -Highway-Reconstruction.pdf.

2. Rashaad Lambert, "For(bes) The Culture Green Book Guide," *Forbes*, November 23, 2021, https://www.forbes.com/sites/rashaadlambert/2021 /11/23/forbes-the-culture-presents-green-book-guide/?sh=7ee97101667e.

3. "The Photographer's Green Book Directory," www.photogreenbook.com.

CREDITS AND PERMISSIONS

p. x Schomburg Center for Research in Black Culture, Manuscripts, Archives and Rare Books Division, The New York Public Library. *The Negro Travelers' Green Book: Fall 1956*, The New York Public Library Digital Collections, 1956.

p. x Schomburg Center for Research in Black Culture, Manuscripts, Archives and Rare Books Division, The New York Public Library. *The Travelers' Green Book: 1960*, The New York Public Library Digital Collections, 1960.

p. x Schomburg Center for Research in Black Culture, Manuscripts, Archives and Rare Books Division, The New York Public Library. *The Travelers' Green Book: 1961*, The New York Public Library Digital Collections, 1961.

p. 10 Schomburg Center for Research in Black Culture, Manuscripts, Archives and Rare Books Division, The New York Public Library. *The Travelers' Green Book: 1961*, The New York Public Library Digital Collections, 1961.

p. 21 Schomburg Center for Research in Black Culture, Photographs and Prints Division, The New York Public Library. "Shoeshiners, 135th St. and Lenox Ave.," The New York Public Library Digital Collections, 1939.

p. 24 Freeman, R. L., photographer, 1969. Retrieved from the Library of Congress.

p. 36 Delano, Jack, June 1940, Washington DC, Library of Congress.

p. 50 Russell, Lee/AP/Library of Congress/Farm Security Administration.

p. 62 Schomburg Center for Research in Black Culture, Jean Blackwell Hutson Research and Reference Division, The New York Public Library. "A Negro Family Just Arrived in Chicago from the Rural South," The New York Public Library Digital Collections, 1922.

p. 68 Wolcott, Marion Post, 1939.

p. 88 Lee, Russell. Retrieved from Library of Congress,https://www.loc.gov/pictures/item/2017740552/.

p. 94 Retrieved from the Library of Congress, https://www.loc.gov/item/2020655500/.

p. 108 Schomburg Center for Research in Black Culture, Manuscripts, Archives and Rare Books Division, The New York Public Library. *The Travelers' Green Book: 1960*, The New York Public Library Digital Collections, 1960.

p. 122 Schomburg Center for Research in Black Culture, Jean Blackwell Hutson Research and Reference Division, The New York Public

Library. *The Green Book Vacation Guide: 1949,* The New York Public Library Digital Collections, 1949, https://digitalcollections.nypl.org/items/92f52390-84cb-0133-7a6d-00505686d14e.

p. 129 Wolcott, M. P. Retrieved from the Library of Congress.

p. 135 Schomburg Center for Research in Black Culture, Manuscripts, Archives and Rare Books Division, The New York Public Library. *Travelers' Green Book: 1963–64 International Edition,* The New York Public Library Digital Collections, 1963.

p. 135 Schomburg Center for Research in Black Culture, Manuscripts, Archives and Rare Books Division, The New York Public Library. *Travelers' Green Book: 1963–64 International Edition,* The New York Public Library Digital Collections, 1963.

p. 160 Vachon, John, photographer, 1941 Aug., Library of Congress Digital Collections.

p. 178 Trikosko, M. S., photographer. Retrieved from the Library of Congress, https://www.loc.gov/item/2017646278/.

p. 196 Scurlock Studio Records, Archives Center, National Museum of American History, Smithsonian Institution.

p. 206 Schomburg Center for Research in Black Culture, Jean Blackwell Hutson Research and Reference Division, The New York Public Library. *The Green Book Vacation Guide: 1949,* The New York Public Library Digital Collections, 1949, https://digitalcollections.nypl.org/items/93789060-84cb-0133-8cf5-00505686d14e.

p. 212 Courtesy of Alvin Hall.

p. 228 Leffler, W. K., photographer. Retrieved from the Library of Congress Digital Archives.

p. 234 Courtesy of Derrick Adams Studio © 2021.

p. 245 Courtesy of Derrick Adams Studio © 2021.